National Gallery in Prague European Old Masters

Šternberk Palace

National Gallery in Prague

European Old Masters

Šternberk Palace

NG

Réunion des Musées Nationaux

Contributors:

Ladislav Daniel	L.D.
Jan Chlíbec	J.Ch.
Olga Kotková	O.K.
Pavel Preiss	P.P.
Olga Pujmanová	O.P.
Hana Seifertová	H.S.
Lubomír Slavíček	L.S.

This work has been published
with the support of TOTAL.

ISBN 2 7118 2674 0
GA 20 2674
(ISBN 2 7118 2672 4 French edition)
(ISBN 2 7118 2673 2 Czech edition)

Contents

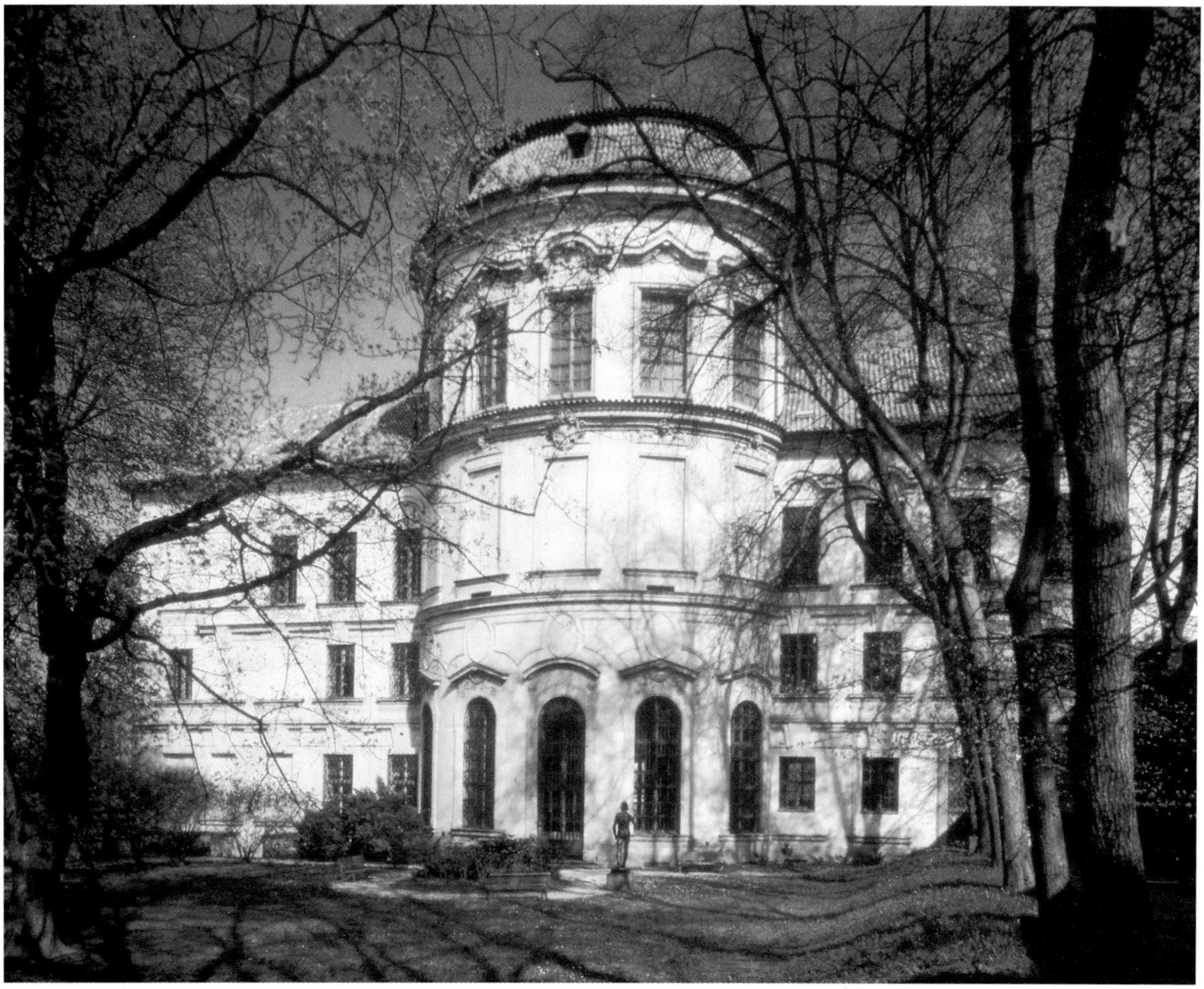

Introduction

"When love for my native land impelled me to dispose, while there was yet time, of those possessions to which I have devoted almost forty years of unceasing care and made not little sacrifice, it was my intention that in becoming the people's common property they should render a service to the nation to which I am proud to belong."

Dr Josef Hoser, Prague, 1843

In Prague art-collecting has a tradition reaching back over several centuries. Indeed, the town became internationally famous at the turn of the sixteenth and seventeenth centuries, when the emperor Rudolph II established his remarkable collection and gathered round him the most important artists of his day. This collection, and Rudolphian art, were thenceforward linked with Prague despite the fact that so soon after the death of the imperial collector his artistic treasures were to be dispersed throughout Europe. Since Prague ceased to be the capital of the Empire, part of the collection was transferred to Vienna, another part was sold, and yet another was carried off as war booty in 1648. Very little now remains of the treasures that were the glory, once so famous, of the royal residence of Prague, and the town which had been until that time the cultural heart of the Kingdom of Bohemia went into a decline, outshone by imperial Vienna. At the end of the eighteenth century, when the ideas of the Enlightenment spread across Europe, the urge was felt in Bohemia to make good this loss of status. Whereas Vienna, and Dresden and Munich too, could boast each their own magnificent Pinakothek, Prague, once so renowned for the splendour of its collections, began to feel the lack of such an institution. A *Society of Patriot Friends of the Arts in Bohemia* was founded in 1796 on the initiative of a Bohemian nobleman, F.A. Sternberg. The society's aim was to create a public Art Gallery together with an institute for the education of young art-lovers. The support of the society's members, who mostly belonged to the Bohemian nobility and could contribute works from their private collections, enabled both aims to be achieved before long, and despite financial and organizational problems the society's collection continued to be built up. The nineteenth century brought further enlargement and enrichment through important bequests, in particular the entire collection of paintings from the Netherlands and Central Europe which were the gift of the Czech patriot and personal physician to the Emperor, Josef Hoser. Initially titled the *Picture Gallery of the Patriot Friends of the Arts in Bohemia*, this collection became the property of the Czechoslovak State in 1937 and was renamed *National Gallery* in Prague in 1945.

A collection which is made up from gifts contributed by members of the artistocracy and the enlightened middle class will naturally reflect its origins. In this case the majority of the works included show where the interests of the collectors of Central Europe lay: painting of the Netherlands, Flemish and especially Dutch 16th and 17th century painters. It follows that smaller-scale work is well represented: landscapes, moralizing genre painting and still life. But there are also a number of fine works from earlier periods: altar pieces, such as *The Adoration of the Magi* by Haarlem Geertgen tot Sint Jans or the triptpych on the same theme by Joos van Cleve from Antwerp, or again a large panel representing *Saint Luke painting the Virgin* by Jan Gossaert, also called Mabuse, in whose work the medieval tradition links up with Renaissance ideas which Mabuse came to know in Italy. The major work in this section of the collection is undoubtedly Pieter Bruegels's *Haymaking* which is on loan to the National Gallery from the Lobkowicz collection at Roudnice on the Elbe. It is one of the series called *The Months* which Bruegel painted for the Antwerp humanist Nicolaes Jongelinck.

The golden age of Dutch painting is represented by the works of minor masters, which include an admirable set of landscapes of exceptional quality that continue in the tradition set by those of Herri met de Bles and Lucas Gassel in the 16th century and are a perfect illustration of the way this genre evolved in the 17th century: Esaias van de Velde, Pieter Molyn, Salomon van Ruysdael, Jan van Goyen, Jacob van Ruisdael. The dominant position in this collection of Dutch painting is reserved for moralizing genre painting and still life. Of the portraits which originated in major cities such as Amsterdam, The Hague and Deventer, the most impressive is Frans Hals' *Portrait of Jasper Schade*. Large scale compositions on historical themes are less numerous. The National Gallery did not come into possession of an important work by Rembrandt van Rijn until 1946, when his *Scholar in his study*, painted in 1634, was acquired. Rembrandt's conception of art is clearly recognizable in the fragment of an *Annunciation* and in the works of his disciples Gerbrand van den Eeckhout and Aert de Gelder.

The collection's Flemish component is more modest but includes work by the greatest masters of the period: Petrus Paulus Rubens, Anthoon van Dyck, Jacob Jordaens. For visitors Rubens is the main attraction, he is presented in three different skills: the portrait, the mythological and the religious painting; also in preparatory studies for a fresco and an altarpiece, and for graphic works! His monumental *Martyrdom of Saint Thomas* was painted in 1637-1638 for the church of the Augustinians in Prague. Among the Flemish works there are also landscapes, genre paintings and still life, and above all masterpieces by Jan Bruegel the Elder and his brother Pieter.

Schools of painting which developed north of the Alps included a flourishing German school, of which the Gallery was able to acquire representative works from its foundation. Hans Baldung Grien's *Beheading of Saint Dorothea* is among these, as well as two panels from the Hohenburg altarpiece by Hans Holbein the Elder. It was the Emperor Rudolph II, a great admirer of Dürer, who acquired the famous *Feast of the Rosary* which was commissioned in 1505 by the German merchant community in Venice for their San Bartolomeo church. This *Feast of the Rosary* is one of the few works which have come down to us from the famous Rudolph collection.

In its early years, when the gallery was still known as the Pinakothek, it had very few works of the Italian, Spanish and French schools. Time has now made good this lack and the collection gives adequate coverage of the period stretching from the 14th to the 18th century. The acquisition in the 1940's of one of the oldest collections of trecento and quattrocento paintings to be brought together north of the Alps enriched it with a large number. These include some fine polyptychs, such as the *Adoration of the Child* triptych by Antonio Vivarini and Giovanni d'Allemagna, and a set of small portable altarpieces designed for private prayer which contains the remarkable triptych by Bernardo Daddi and a panel from a dramatic *Lamentation* by Lorenzo Monaco. The beginnings of the Italian Renaissance are represented by Venetian artists. Among their works are two bearing the same title, Holy Conversation, by Pasqualino Veneto and Vincenza Catena, both showing the influence of Giovanni Bellini. Agnolo Bronzino's *Portrait of Cosimo I de Medici* has recently taken its place alongside the same artist's *Portrait of Eleonor of Toledo*. Together they mark the apogee of the Florentine Renaissance. The 17th and 18th century period is well represented by many Venetian works: Sebastiano Ricci, Giambattista Piazetta or Giovanni Battista Tiepolo, but the one which is best appreciated by the public is Canaletto's *View of London with the Thames*, which was loaned to the National Gallery from the Lobkowicz collection in 1946.

The representation of the other schools of painting is more limited in scope but includes some masterpieces: Greco's *Christ in Prayer*, Goya's *Portrait of Don Miguel de Lardizábal*, and works by Simon Vouet, Sebastian Bourdon, Charles Le Brun, Pierre Mignard, François Boucher. Notable recent additions to the National Gallery in Prague are several remarkable works from Antiquity, a series of Byzantine icons, works by masters of the Creto-Venetian school and a series of Russian icons.

The gallery's collection of the older European art, though not extensive, gives a well-balanced panorama of European painting and its evolution through the centuries, together with a sufficient number of masterpieces to attract a large public, from both home and abroad, well aware that it constitutes the finest art collection in the country.

H.S.

The Šternberk Palace

The initial project for the building of the Šternberk Palace underwent several modifications and was never completely realized. Remarkable as it is, this baroque palace is a mere fragment of what was intended. Its creator, the cultured and ambitious aristocrat Wenceslaus Adalbert Sternberg, commissioned the plans while his castle of Troja in the vicinity of Prague was in the final stages of construction. Troja was a summer residence, conceived in the manner of Roman villas by Jean-Baptiste Mathey, called Mattheus Burgundus and originating from Burgundy. One of Prague's mostly highly regarded architects, Mathey was among those responsible for introducing the Roman baroque style into Bohemia. He was in fact residing in Rome when he was summoned to Bohemia in 1675 by Count J.F. Valdštejn, archbishop resident in Prague. In 1695 Mathey left Prague for Paris, where he died that same year.

By the end of 1672 Count Sternberg had negotiated an agreement with the architect Domenico Martinelli (1650-1718) from Lucca for the conception of his Prague residence. Martinelli had also been trained in Rome but had been active primarily in central Europe, where he was one of the creators of the baroque style. This project is the subject of a message found in the Count's correspondence, together with three plans which correspond to the plot which then belonged to Sternberg and was to be enlarged in 1697 with the acquisition of a neighbouring building and some existing Renaissance constructions. According to the plans, the north-east façade was be realigned, (though this change was not carried out), and extended in the direction of the Deer Moat, where Sternberg intended to buy further plots of land.

In Count Sternberg's correspondence with his cousin Dominic Andrew Kaunitz, who lived in The Hague, there are two references to the architect Martinelli, who also lived in The Hague, both relating to the building of the palace. It seems that Martinelli was unwilling to leave for Vienna or Prague, and intended rather to journey to London. However, after passing through Rome, Martinelli reluctantly traveled to Vienna and eventually Prague, where he made a short stay during the winter of 1702-1703. In Prague, his services were sought for a different project, the reconstruction of the palace of Norbert Leopold Libštejnský of Kolowrat (1655-1716), which stood between the New Castle Steps and Ostruhova (presently Nerudova) Street. This extremely ambitious project was never realized because the Kolowrat finances proved inadequate.

Martinelli's design for the groundplan of the Šternberk palace dates from after 1697 and involved extending it as far as Hradčany Square by a narrow wing. However it evidently underwent fundamental alterations, as can be seen from the structure and features of the architecture. At the end of the 17th century, constuction was entrusted to Christoph Dientzenhofer's firm, though we have no proof that he himself had any hand in the design. In the final stages of the project we come across the name of another great architect active in Prague, Giovanni Battista Alliprandi (c.1655-1720), who is mentioned in a statement of accounts dated 6 March 1706 for one hundred florins, which corresponds to the fee for an entire project. There is an undeniable affinity between the Šternberk palace and other palaces and châteaux created by Alliprandi in Bohemia. Their architectural conception is identical, especially in respect to the garden façade, where an oval projection is carried up the entire height of building.

Within the count's lifetime (he died in 1708) the walls of the inner courtyard were covered with stucco by Giuseppe Donato Frisoni (1683-1735), while two ceilings representing the tragic victims of Love, Artemisia and Dido, were executed by Michael Wenceslas Halbax (1661-1711). The Swiss painter John Rudolf Bys (1662-1738) carried out *trompe-l'œil* frescos in two cabinets, and the Chinese Cabinet was decorated by John Adalbert Kratochvíl in the *chinoiserie* style.

As the plans of the Rome architect Carlo Fontana demonstrate, the Count never gave up the idea of enlarging his place as far as Hradčany Square, as a counterpart to that of another branch of the Sternbergs. But those plans were never realized, and the existing, unfinished palace has no ceremonial rooms and even lacks a Great Hall.

P.P.

Art of Antiquity and the Icons

Painter from Fayum

active probably in the second half of the second century A.D.

1 Portrait of a young lady

Wood. 40.5 × 20.5 cm
Acquired in 1925 from the Theodore Graf Collection, Vienna.
Inv. n° O 1420

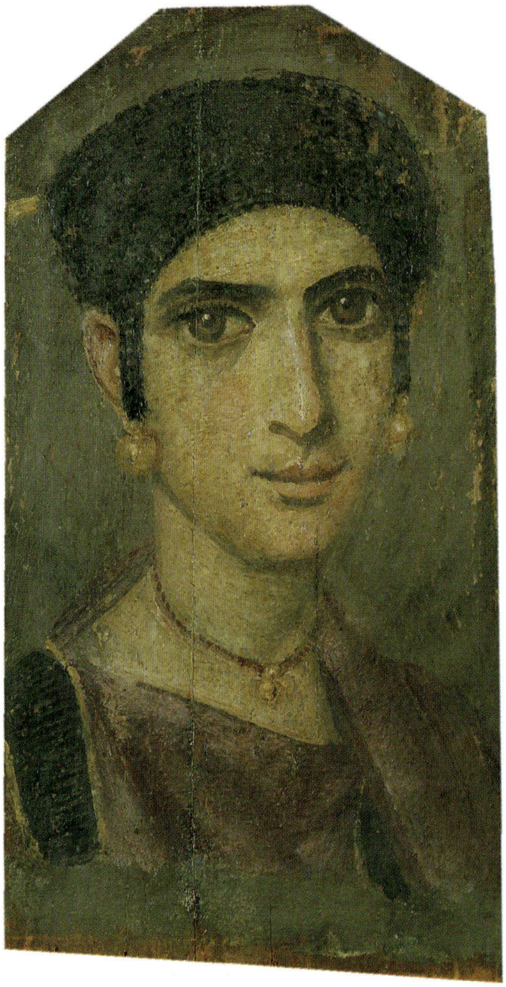

The young woman is shown full-face, turned slightly to the left. Her eyes are enlarged, gazing intently at the onlooker. The encaustic technique has been applied to a wooden panel (with natural colours mixed with bees wax), giving the picture its characteristic discreet colouring: the ochre tint of the flesh, the mauve of the dress and the grey of the background are heightened simply by the black of the hair and the brilliant gold of the necklace and ear-rings. Though looking distant, the woman seems to be exercising her fascination on the spectator. Portraits of this type, known as Fayum portraits, were fixed to the mummy above the face of the deceased. They are a synthesis of the classical culture of antiquity and those oriental cultures which flourished from the 1st to the 4th century when Rome ruled over Egypt. By their function they link up with the funeral cult of ancient Egypt. However the technique used by the artist is that of the Roman portrait. The Fayum portraits are among the finest examples of painted portraits to have come down to us from antiquity. They prefigure not only the art of Byzantine icons but also that of many modern portraits.

These Fayum portraits were practically unknown until their discovery towards the end of the 19th century in Egypt, particularly in the Fayum oasis. A large number of the paintings discovered at that time were bought by Theodore Graf, who brought them to the attention of the international public through a travelling exhibition which came to Prague in 1892. The National Gallery holds another Fayum portrait deriving from the Graf collection, *Portrait of a Young Girl* (Inv. n° O 1781), executed in tempera towards the middle of the 4th century.

O.P.

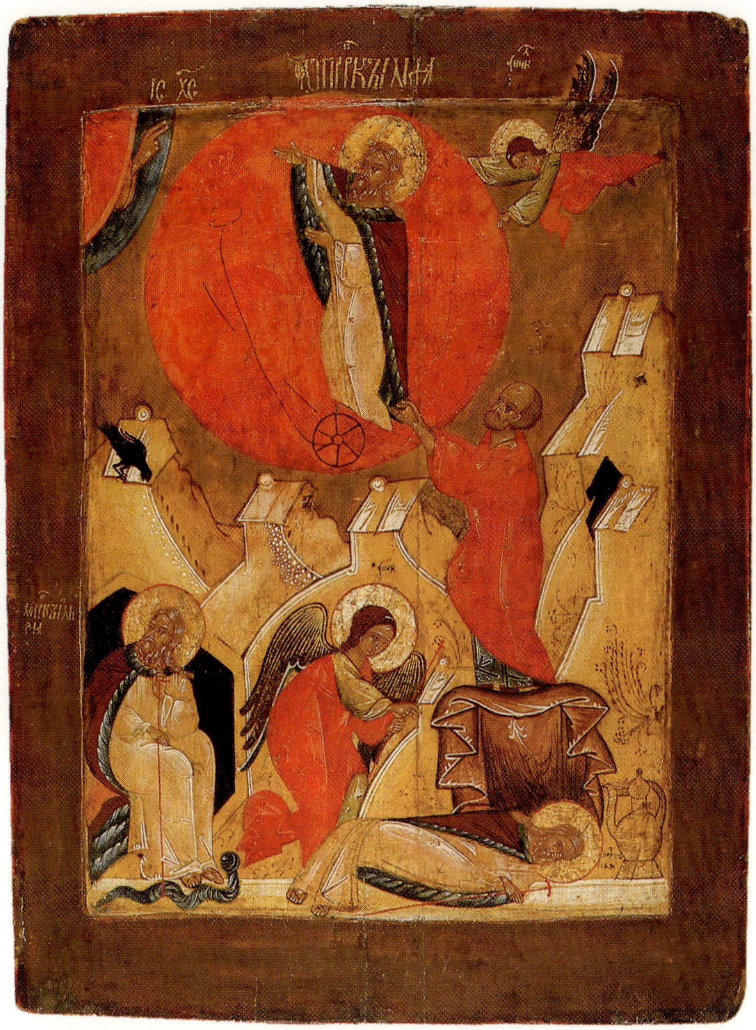

Painter from Northern Russia
late fifteenth century

2 The Prophet Elijah taken up into heaven

Wood. 51.5 × 40 cm.
A.V. Soldatenko collection, Kondakov Institute in Prague.
On loan from the Czechoslovak Academy of Sciences since 1974.
Inv. n° VO 292

Russia was fertile ground for the expansion of Byzantine culture and has a history of icon painting going back to the late tenth century. Prince Vladimir received Christianity from Constantinople and so Byzantine culture became the official culture of the Principality of Kiev. From the 12th century other towns join Kiev as centres of culture: Greater Novgorod, Iaroslavl, Vladimir, Souzdal and Moscow. This last town grew in prestige especially after the fall of Constantinople (1453), to which Moscow claimed to be heir and successor. Although Russian icons preserve their character as cult objects they soon come into closer relation to the believer and reveal that typical Russian tendency whereby the holy image becomes an intimate one. This is the feature we meet with in the icon of Elijah, who was venerated as the protector against fire. The icon shows three scenes from his life: Elijah taken up into heaven in the presence of the prophet Elisha; Elijah hiding in the valley of the Kerith torrent where the Lord ordered him to be fed by crows (Kings I, 17, 1-7); Elijah asleep by a juniper tree and awoken by an angel offering him "loaves baked on coals and a cup of water" (Kings I, 12, 2-8). And the picture does in fact show a water-jug near the prophet, giving the composition as a whole an intimist note.

O.P.

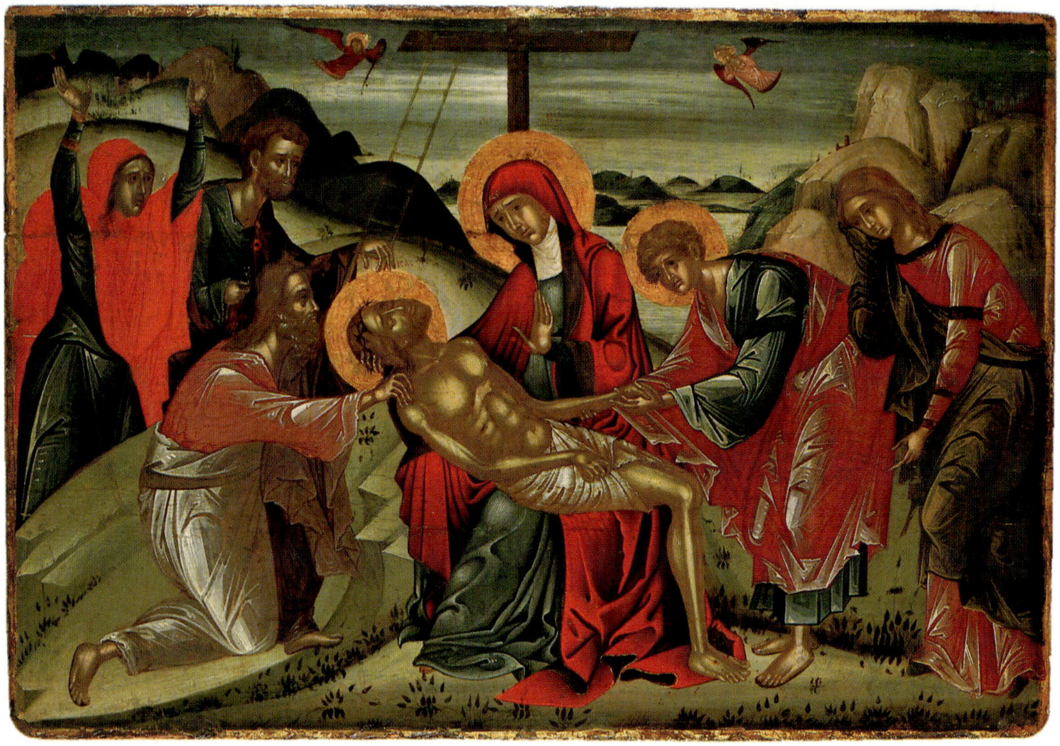

Creto-Venetian painter
Sixteenth century

3 The Lamentation

Wood. 57.5 × 84 cm
D'Este collection, Konopiště Castle. Acquired in 1939.
Inv. n° O 11938

The Lamentation is a brief episode intervening between the Descent from the Cross and the Entombement. Although rarely mentioned in the Gospels this episode became a well-known theme of Christian iconography in Central Europe from the time of its first appearance in Byzantine art in the 11th century. The traditional Byzantine schema has Christ's body lying on the ground or on a rock. The Virgin represented as bearing Christ's body on her knees belongs to the western tradition of the Pietà, whereas the incarnadine of the persons surrounding her is effected in the Byzantine style. What characterizes the picture's colouring is the contrast between greens and reds. The simultaneous use of Byzantine and Italian elements entails some lack of unity in the means of expression of the picture, visible also in the treatment of the draperies. Whereas the Virgin is dressed in a supply shaped robe, the other characters in the scene are wearing clothes falling in austere, geometric folds. This work is a typical example of the abundant output of the Creto-Venetian painters, called *Madonneri*, who worked on the Island of Crete when it was a Venetian dominion. In quality however, this painting surpasses the standard of general production, which is better regarded as artisan work. What is particularly striking here is the representation in the background of a landscape by the sea, probably inspired by Quattrocento Venetian painting of the circle of Bellini.

O.P.

Italian painting
from the 14th to the end of the 16th century

Jacopo del Casentino

Active around 1339 in Florence - died in 1349 or 1358.
In collaboration with a disciple

4 Triptych with "The Virgin and Child in Majesty", surrounded by two angels, Saint John the Baptist and an unidentified saint

Wood. Central panel 31 × 19.5 cm
Wings 30 × 9 cm
Before 1805 in the collection of Tommaso degli Obizzi, Catajo, region of Padua. D'Este collection, Konopiště castle. Acquired in 1939.
Inv. n° O 11956, O 11957, O 11958

Most of the Gothic and Renaissance paintings of the Prague National Gallery derive from the collection of Archduke François Ferdinand d'Este in Konopiště castle. The nucleus of this collection was that of Tommaso degli Obizzi in Catajo, in the region of Padua, which was brought together at the end of 18th century and is one of Europe's oldest collections of Italian Primitives. It was made up of two sets of works, and their positioning in the museum respects this distinction. On the one hand there are Venetian and North Italian paintings which came together by chance in the vicinity of Catajo; and on the other, Siennese and Florentine works which were probably collected owing to the growing interest of the time for the Tuscan Renaissance. The triptych belongs to this second set.

Jacopo del Casentino was not a member of the avant-garde of Florentine painting. His archaic and eclectic style is probably a reflection of his rural origins. The way this Prague altar-piece distributes its themes is reminiscent of another work attributed to the same artist, the so-called *Cagnola Triptych* (Florence, Uffizi). In both cases the left panel shows Saint Francis receiving the Stigmata. The Prague work is characteristic of Jacopo with its elongated figures but is distinct by its brushwork, which has the lightness of a watercolour. There is an unusual freshness of interpretation which was probably contributed by one of the artist's collaborators. Jacopo del Casentino was an ambitious painter owning a large studio which produced numerous small-scale paintings for the local market and also for export. These were sold not only in distant parts of Italy but also in Avignon and other foreign markets, notably in Champagne.

O.P.

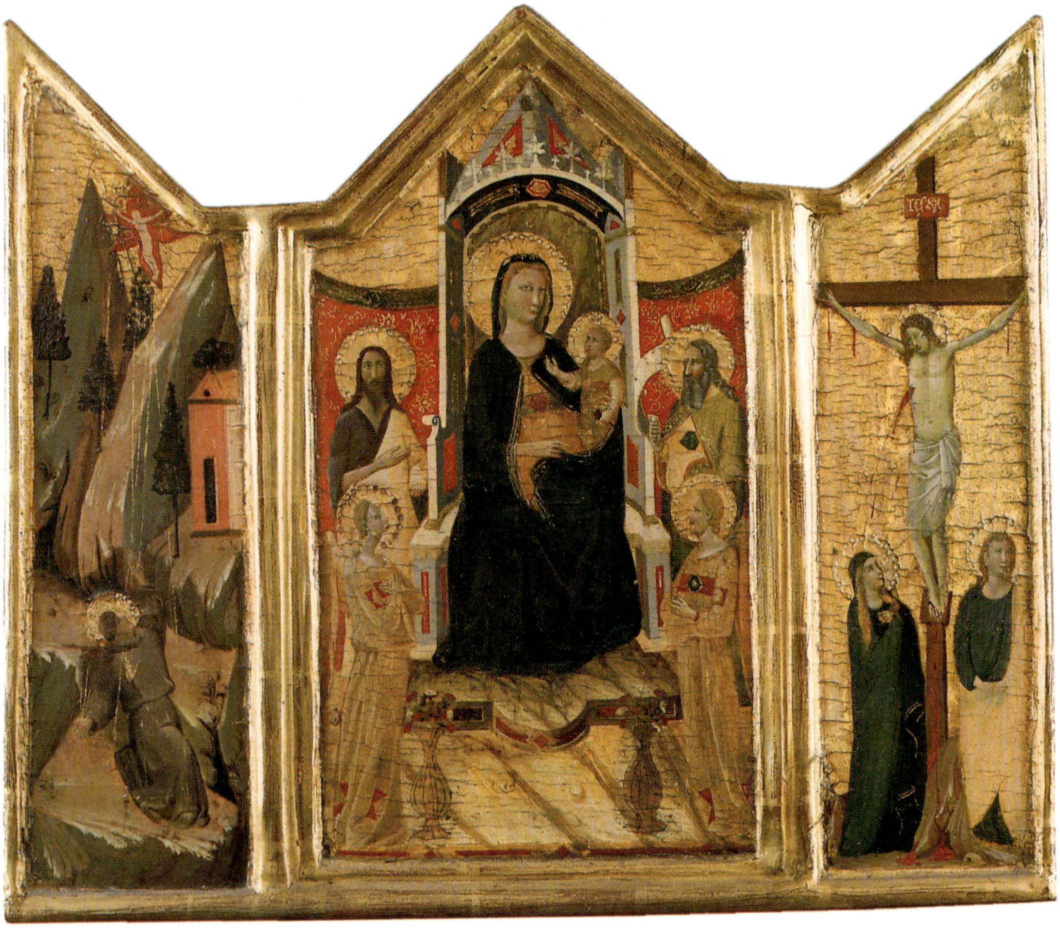

Bernardo Daddi

active from 1327, died in 1348 in Florence. Bernardo Daddi - workshop

5 Triptych with "The Mystic Marriage of Saint Catherine, Saint Bartholomew and Saint Benedict"

Wood. Central panel 33 × 18 cm. Wings 38 × 11 cm
Before 1805 in the collection of Tommaso degli Obizzi, Catajo, D'Este collection, Konopiště castle. Acquired in 1939.
Inv. n° O 11967, O 11968, O 11969

Bernardo Daddi belongs to the generation immediately following Giotto and was his disciple and most faithful companion. Unlike Giotto he devoted himself more to painting on wood panels than to fresco painting. He created a whole series of large altarpieces as well as small ones used for private devotions at home or on a journey: single panels, diptychs or triptychs. He was especially responsible for the introduction of the small triptych into the houses of Florence, where he became very popular. His studio was very active and produced them in large numbers. The National Gallery holds two other paintings of this style, and all three bear marks typical of Daddi's style: a clear and well-ordered composition, a unified scale for the figures and their environment, and an attempt at spatial construction — features inherited directly from Giotto, to which Daddi adds a personal note of subtle charm. The dramatic pathos of Giotto being foreign to his nature, Daddi painted the Christian mysteries with tenderness, in an intimist and moving manner. Siennese painting was the source of his inspiration, in particular the work of Ambrogio Lorenzetti (post 1330). An especially Siennese feature of this triptych is the Jesus Child standing on his mother's knees and holding on to her dress with his right hand. This manner of presentation was probably first realized by Simone Martini in his *Maestà*, executed for the Palazzo Publico of Siena in 1305.

O.P.

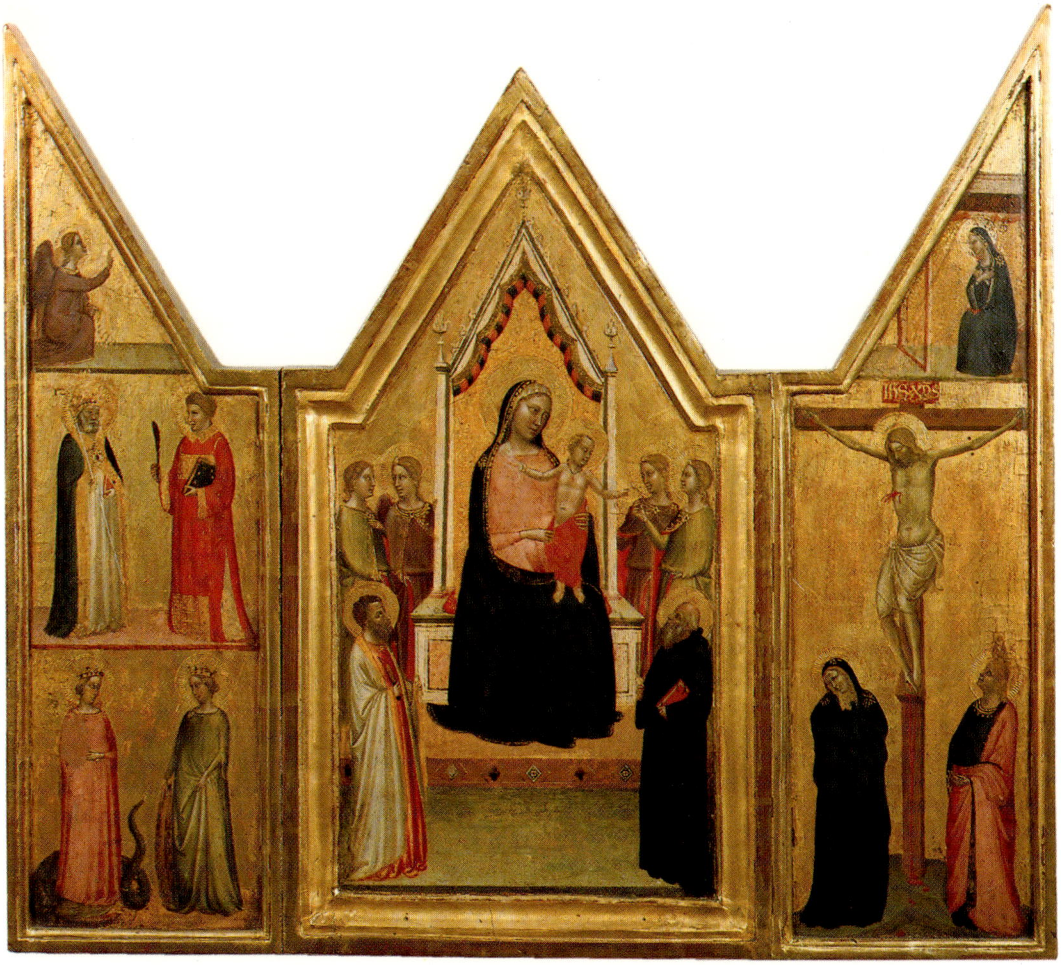

Pietro Lorenzetti
1280 or 1290 - 1348 Siena

6 Holy Martyr Saint Anthony Abbot

Wood. 45 × 38 cm.
Acquired in 1946
Inv. DO 5014, DO 5015

The triangular format is evidence that these two Prague panels were originally the pinnacles of a complex altarpiece. They belonged to a work referred to as the Loeser Polyptych, whose central panel represents the Virgin and Child (Florence, Palazzo Vecchio, Loeser donation). Four panels with bust-length saints flanked the central painting. Three of them are now known to us: Saint Catherine of Alexandria, now in New York (Metropolitan Museum), Saint Margaret in Assisi (San Francesco) and Saint James in La Spezia (private collection). Originally these panels bore inscriptions relating to the paintings of the upper register of the polyptych, witness the inscription "Saint Agnes" preserved on the New York panel. The Loeser Polyptych was therefore similar to that of the Duccio studio, which is now in Siena (Pinacoteca Nazionale). Opinions diverge as to the identity of the artist, whether Pietro Lorenzetti or one of his collaborators. We believe it to be the work of Pietro himself. The modelling of the two figures of the saints is achieved by subtle shadowing: the plasticity of the figures is accentuated by contrasts of light and shade, just as we see in works whose attribution to Pietro Lorenzetti is undoubted. This *Holy Martyr*, as well as the *Saint Anthony Abbot*, clearly show the influence of Giotto's painting and Giovanni Pisano's sculpture. We meet with both these influences in most of Pietro's works, which have as their point of departure the traditional painting of Duccio.

Pietro Lorenzetti is one of the four most highly regarded painters of the Siennese Trecento, although less well known than Duccio di Buoninsegna, Simone Martini or Ambrogio Lorenzetti, whose fame rests above all on the frescos representing *The Allegories of Good and Bad Government* at the Palazzo Publico in Siena. Nowadays none of Pietro's works can equal this degree of fame. Yet in his own time he was held in equal esteem with his brother Ambrogio, and rightly so, and like him too, fell victim to the plague of 1348.

O.P.

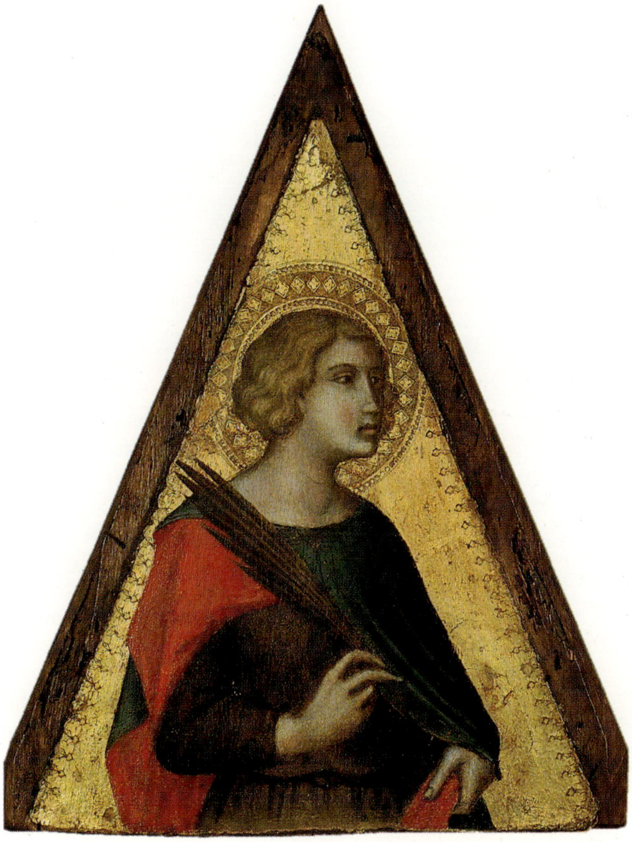

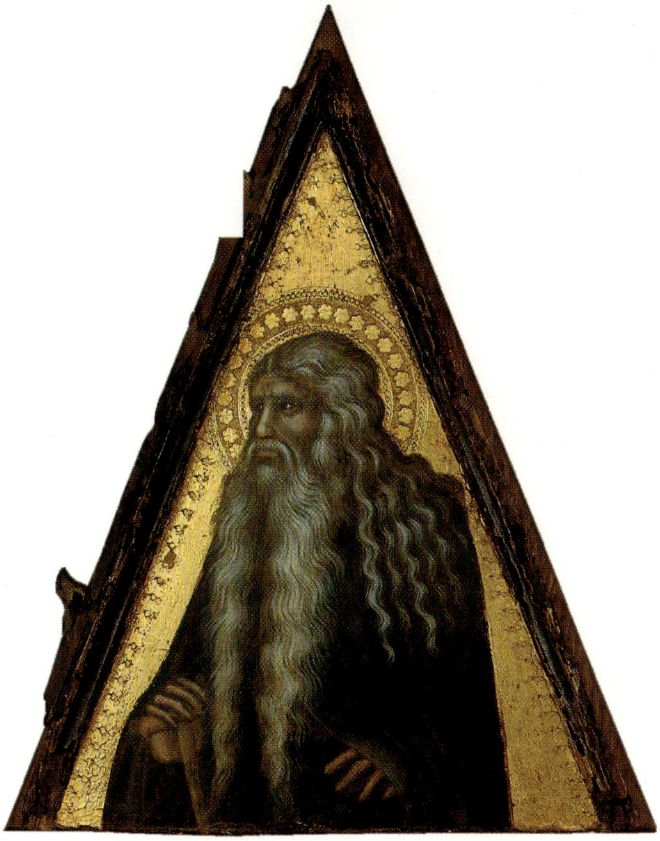

Jacopo di Cione

Active in Florence around 1360-1398

7 Virgin and Child in Majesty

Wood. 71.5 × 43.5 cm
Before 1805 in the collection of Tommaso degli Obizzi, Catajo.
D'Este collection, Konopiště castle. Acquired in 1939.
Inv. nº O 11887

The Virgin seated on a throne surrounded by angels and saints is referred to in Italy as *Maestà*. Unlike the monumental *Maestà* which began in the thirteenth century to adorn the altars of Tuscan churches, this painting was intended for private devotions. It is in fact one of those numerous intimist paintings which were an indispensable feature of patrician houses in Florence in the second half of the Trecento.

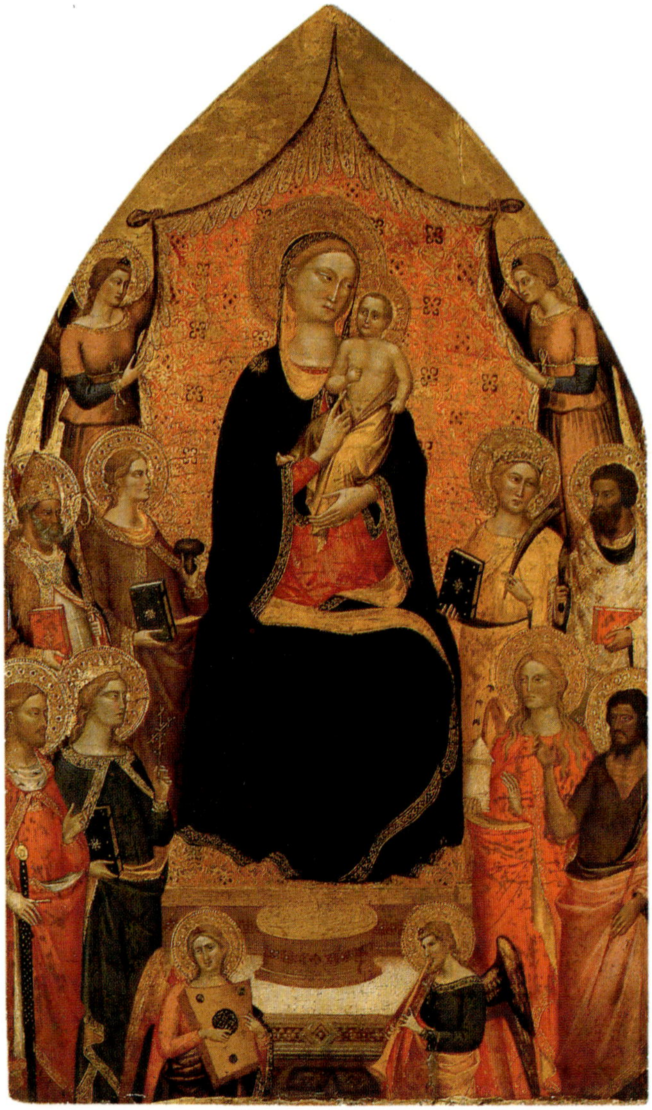

Jacopo di Cione never attained the artistic heights of his famous brothers Nardo di Cione and Andrea called Orcagna, whose studio he directed after their deaths. He lacked both the creative power of d'Orcagna and the nobility which marks the works of Nardo. The Virgin and Child of the Prague collection comes close to the formal perfection of Orcagna's works but it is more schematic in conception. The figures have more sharply drawn features but the colouring, so far from having the delicacy of Nardo, is loud and even violent in tone. The hanging which two angels are holding up behind the Virgin emphasizes the artist's taste for those richly patterned cloths which were at that time one of Florence's sources of wealth. It was a time when the Republic of Florence flourished thanks to its growing banking and textile industries. The Florentines dyed cloth imported from France and Flanders, wove the wool they bought mostly in England and created brocades with gold and silver thread which were the admiration of all Italy as well as foreign parts.

O.P.

Niccolo di Tommaso

Active in Florence between 1343 and 1376

8 The Coronation of the Virgin

Wood. 71 × 37 cm
Before 1805 in the collection of Tommaso degli Obizzi, Catajo.
D'Este collection, Konopiště castle. Acquired in 1939.
Inv. O 11889

The format of this work and the symmetrical composition of the scene suggest that it is probably the central panel of a triptych intended for private devotions. The wings have been cut away, thereby removing the figures which must have been shown beside the saints witnessing at the central scene. In the lower left hand corner there are remnants of Saint Catherine: her left hand, holding a book, and a wheel, the instrument of torture which became her attribute.

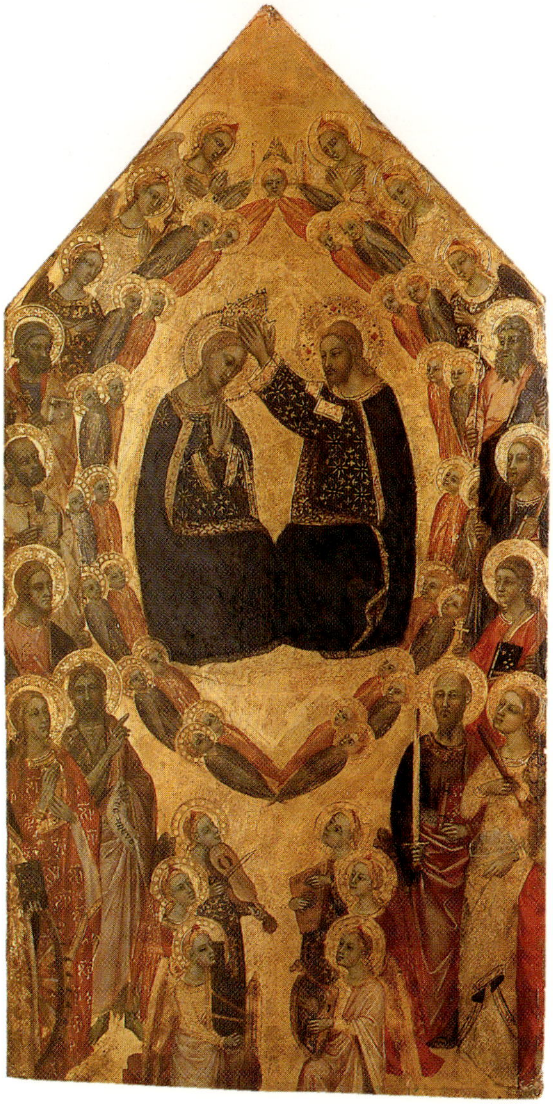

The Coronation of the Virgin is a comparatively recent theme, known only to the art of western Europe. In the 12th century the Virgin was shown seated on a throne and crowned by angels; from the 13th the artists show Christ himself placing the crown on the Virgin's head. In early Trecento art the scene takes place on earth; the throne with Christ and the Virgin is on slightly higher ground, the angels and saints are grouped nearby. In this painting the lay-out is different: Christ and the Virgin are seated, though their seat is not visible; they are separated from the angels and saints by a mandorla of cherubim, whereby the artist creates the impression that the scene is taking place in heaven, and is not subject to the laws of gravity. The work is therefore more reminiscent of 13th century representations. This taste for archaism, and the preponderance of hieratic elements, is characteristic of Florentine painting between 1350 and 1370. In his style, Tommaso is successor to Nardo di Cione, though he worked for less demanding clients, such as the Antoniani order of Pistoia. Most of his painting is of static figures, such as those of the panels in the Prague collection. Apart from the Coronation there is another smaller painting by Niccolo di Tomasso in the National Gallery, the *Virgin and Child* (Inv. n° 0 1365).

O.P.

Nardo di Cione

Existence in 1343 assured, died in 1365/66 in Florence

9 # Polyptych with the "Virgin and Child between Saint James Major, Saint Jerome, Saint John the Baptist and Saint Ranieri" referred to as the "Bojnice Altarpiece"

Wood. Main register (Centre) 117 × 59 cm
(Wings) 103 × 44 cm
Predella (Centre) 38 × 44 cm
(Wings) 38 × 44 cm
Acquired from the collection of J. Palffy of Bojnice in 1942
Inv. n° O 2376 - O 2385

The *Bojnice Altarpiece* is the only one of Nardo's compositions to have been preserved entire. It is probably a youthful work, painted towards the middle of the Trecento and showing the influence of the preceding period. There is a certain spatial depth to be seen in the representation of the saints of the main register. The intimate gesture of the Infant Jesus holding the Madonna by the chin is taken up by Bernardo Daddi (see n° 5). The Virgin's cloak, lined with ermine and ostentatiously spread out, and the demanding technique of decoration by scraping against the gold background (see the dress of the saints of the lower register) indicate the importance of this commission. It is a work of exceptional quality and was probably commissioned from Pisa, whose patron saint, Ranieri, is shown in the main register on the right, next to John the Baptist.

Nardo di Cione came from a family of artists (see Jacopo di Cione). His elder brother, Andrea, called Orcagna, also known as sculptor and architect, was the most distinguished member and somewhat overshadowed Nardo, who for several centuries was mentioned only as Orcagna's collaborator. This is why the frescos of the Strozzi chapel in Santa Maria Novella in Florence were for so long considered to be the work of Orcagna despite the fact that they had long ago been attributed to Nardo by Ghiberti (1378-1455). The Bojnice Altarpiece was likewise attributed to Orcagna until recently, when a finer differentiation between the works of the Cione brothers became possible, proving that this refined altarpiece, so fascinating by its majesty and elegance and its meticulous execution, is properly the work of Nardo (H. Gronau). However Orcagna may have contributed to its execution. Saint John the Baptist gives a more robust impression than the other, slighter, figures which are Nardo's, and reminds one of Orcagna's figures. The two brothers had a studio in common. The parrot motif of the hanging in the central panel is a feature of Nardo's work as well as that of Orcagna. Nardo di Cione and Orcagna were the most important and the most typical representatives of Florentine painting after the plague of 1348, and their influence is visible in the work of most of the Tuscan painters of the second half of the Trecento.

O.P.

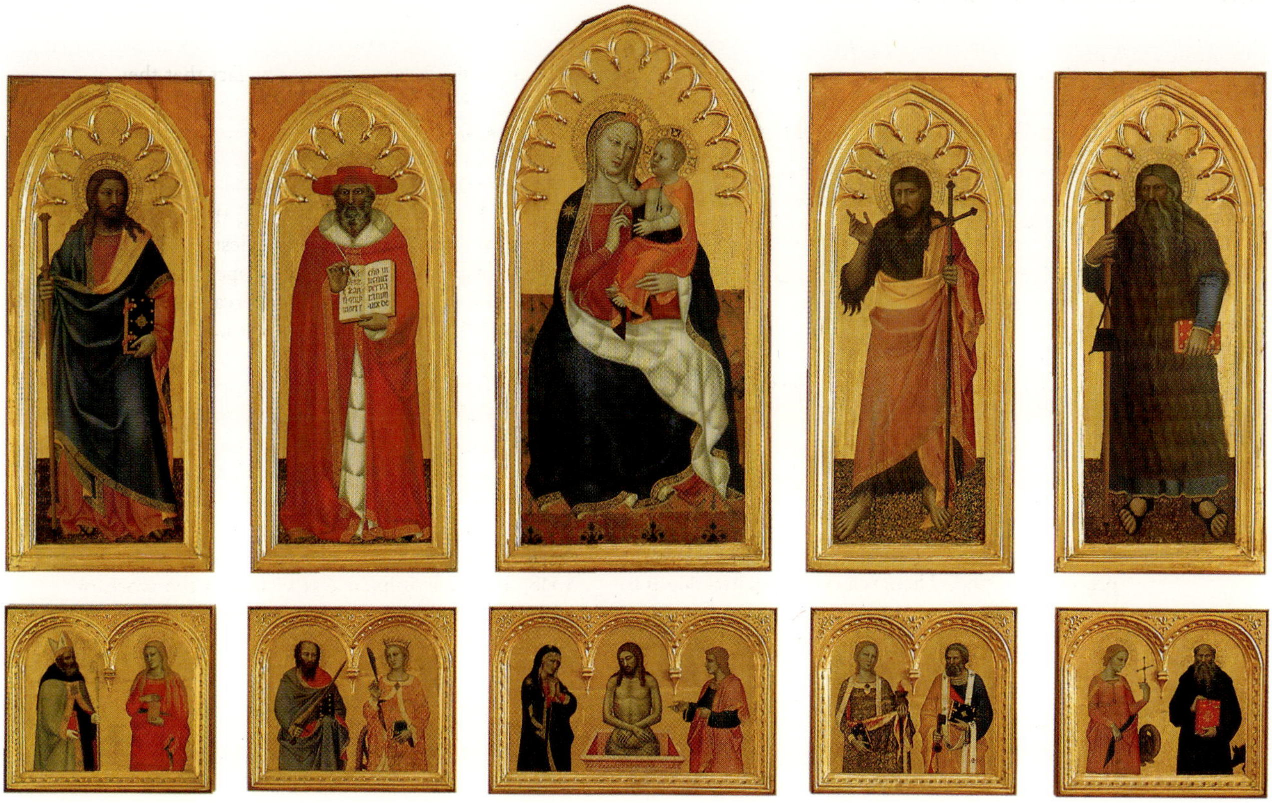

Master of the Pietà
active in Siena between 1350 and 1375

10 Diptych with "The Virgin and Child in Majesty" and "Crucifixion" ("Annunciation" on the pinnacles)

Wood. 63.5 × 29 mm (each panel)
Collection of Tommaso degli Obizzi, Catajo. D'Este collection, Konopiště castle.
Acquired in 1939.
Inv. n° O 11923, O 11915

The diptych was much in favour during the Middle Ages for the performance of private devotions, often representing the Crucifixion, and scenes from the life of Christ or that of the Virgin. In Italian art of the Trecento the counterpart of the Crucifixion was usually the Virgin in Majesty. This is what we have in the Prague diptych by an anonymous artist known as the Master of the Pietà, who is held to be one of the finest painters of the mid-Trecento, bringing together the elegance of Simone Martini and the plastic sensitivity of the Lorenzetti brothers. This artist painted mostly small altarpieces, and the Prague diptych is no exception. We know of a similar one, now divided between Milan (formerly Foretti collection) and Kisters in Switzerland (Heinz collection).

A curious feature of the iconography here is that the Infant Jesus is holding a cross. The cross is of course treated in Christian art in countless ways but to see it in the hands of the Infant Jesus is unusual. Comparison with several other Siennese paintings of this period shows that underlying this representation is the phrase from Saint Matthew's Gospel (16/24): "If anyone wants to be a follower of mine, let him renounce himself and take up his cross and follow me!" This call to a life of piety expresses the deeper and more fervent faith provoked at the time by the recent epidemic of plague and social strife, and by the revelations of Saint Catherine of Siena.

O.P.

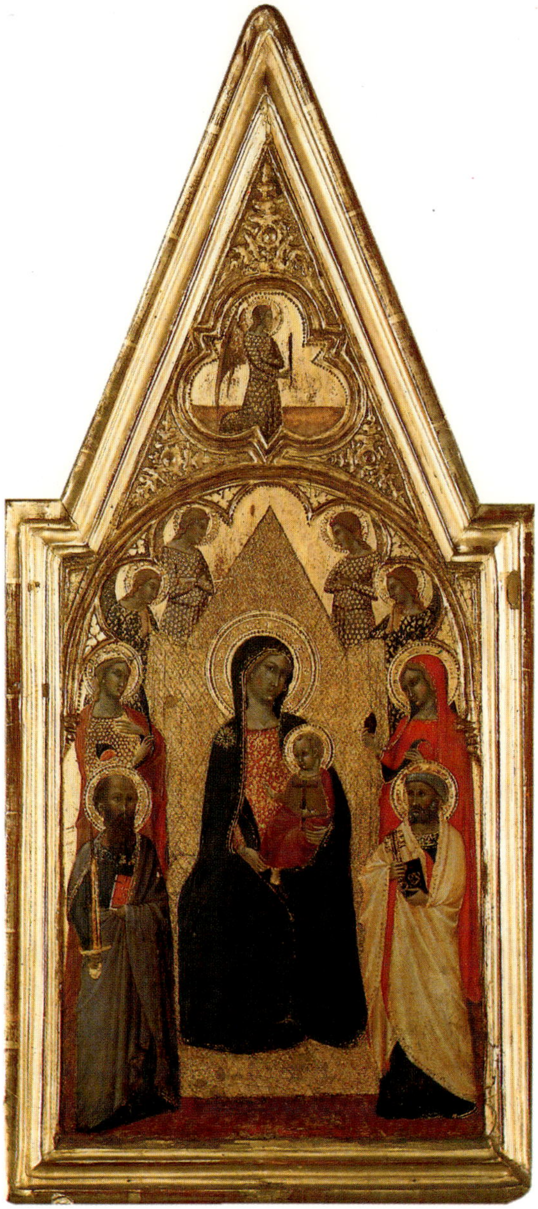

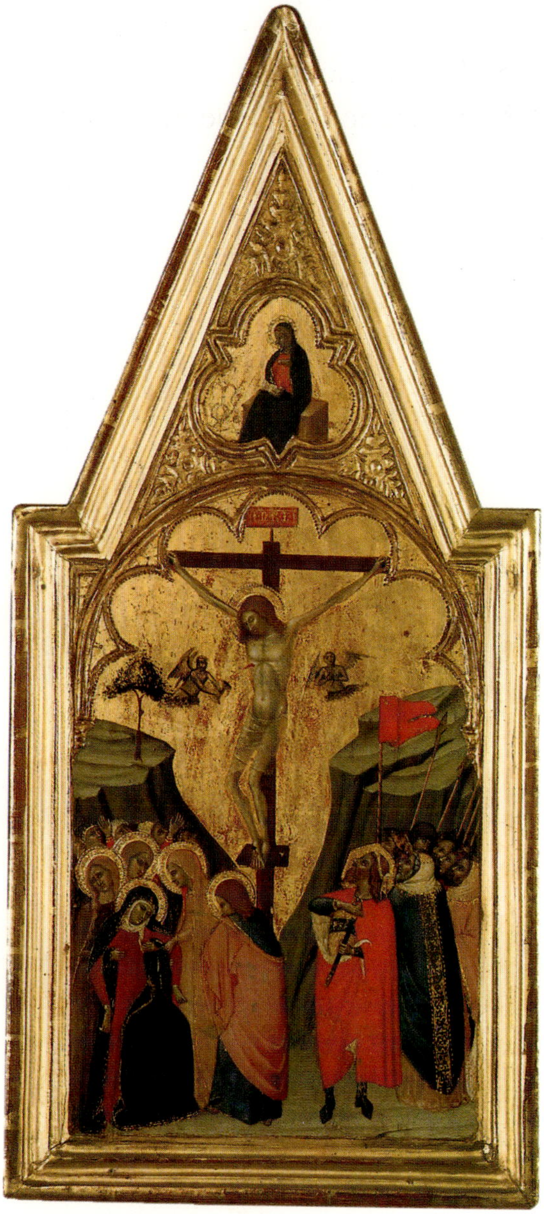

Pietro di Giovanni called Lorenzo Monaco
circa 1370 Siena - 1425 Florence

11 The Lamentation

1408
Wood. 67 × 28.5 cm
Before 1805 in the collection of Tommaso degli Obizzi, Catajo.
D'Este collection, Konopiště castle. Acquired in 1939.
Inv. n° O 11911

Lorenzo Monaco was one of the most significant artists of the international Gothic style in which the art of Bohemia holds such an important place. Whereas Gentile da Fabriano and Pisanello interpreted in Gothic style the refined culture of the north Italian courts, Lorenzo Monaco devoted his art to the monasteries of Tuscany. In fact he spent most of his life in that of Santa Maria degli Angeli in Florence. The monks here lived the severly ascetic life of hermits, and made use of Lorenzo's paintings in their solitary prayers. Most of these paintings were scenes from the Passion of the Lord, and the present example is now divided between Paris and Prague.

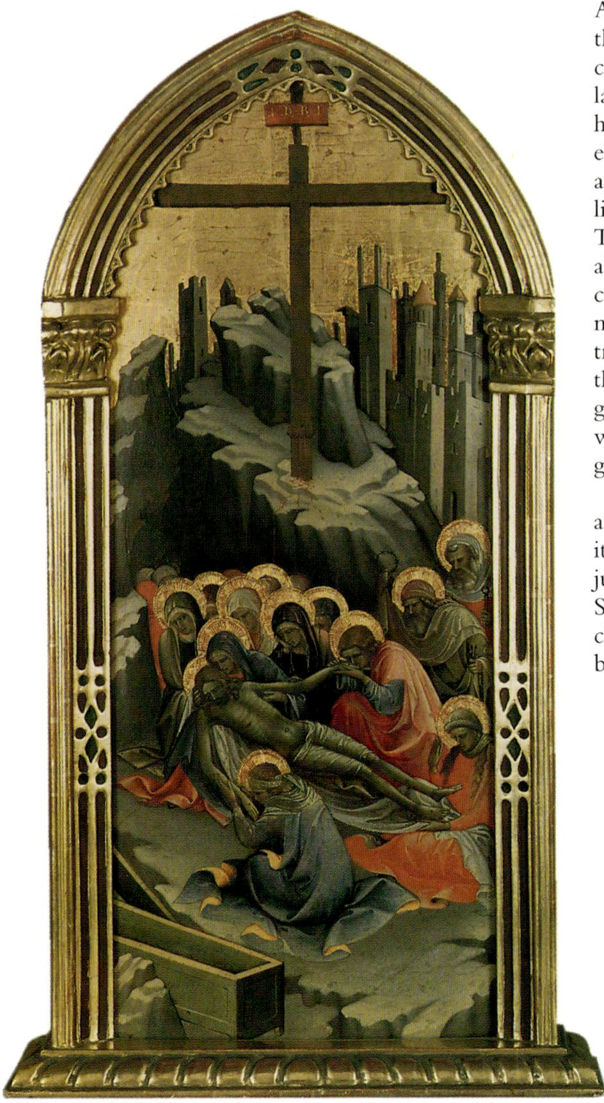

This work by Lorenzo Monaco in the National Gallery is the central panel of a triptych of which the two others (*Christ on the Mount of Olives* and *The Three Maries by the Tomb*) belong to the Louvre. The panels in Paris have been brought together and bear the date 1408, which is therefore also the date of the Prague *Lamentation*. The treatment of the theme is in the Tuscan tradition, with Christ lying on the knees of the Virgin like in Giotto's *Lamentation* in the Arena chapel in Padua, or in the fresco version of this theme which is in the Upper church of San Francesco in Assisi. Lorenzo Monaco has however translated Giotto's scene into a different register: the human drama, in his interpretation, becomes an elegant tragedy. The profound grief of the scene appears to be fixed in ice-like immobility, underlined by the solitary cross in an empty landscape. The figures, the draperies, the crystal-like rocks — all are subjected to the linear rhythm of continuous curves, the nobility of their execution and the harmony of their tones: clear lapis-lazuli surfaces contrasting with reds and olive greens, and the gold of the background and the haloes set off against the grey of the rocks and the architecture. The light which floods the whole scene models the forms and gives them their volume.

This painting, preserved in Prague, is one of the artist's best works. Noble in character, exquisite in its refinement and perfect in execution, it amply justifies the claim of Ambrogio Traversari, abbot of Santa Maria degli Angeli and connoisseur of the classics, when he rejoiced in the elegance his monks brought to their painting.

O.P.

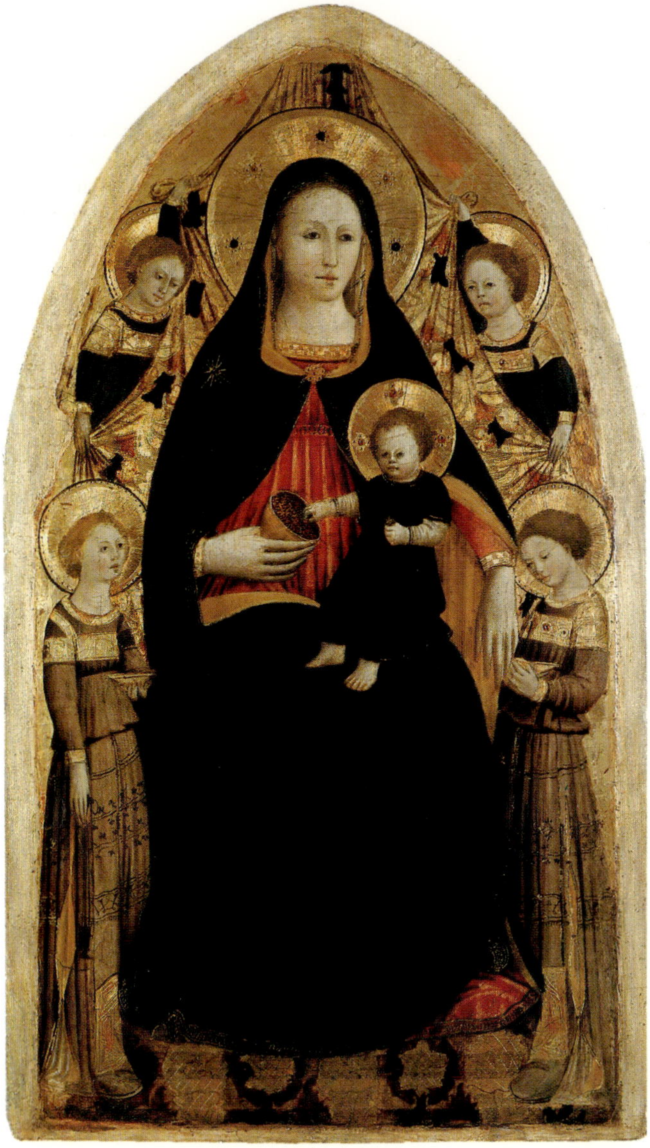

Andrea di Giusto liked to find inspiration in the works of his contemporaries. This Child Jesus and the elegant little angels seem to come straight out of Fra Angelico's paintings, though the angels also remind one of Masolino: the elongated figures bend at the waist and their robes fall in undulating folds characteristic of Gothic sensitivity. By contrast the Virgin is treated more in relief: full-faced and rounded brow, her body clearly outlined beneath the folds of her dress. The spread of her robe and her monumental air evoke the Madonnas of Masaccio, the founder of Renaissance painting. But although the entire artistic production of the late 20's and 30's of the fifteenth century bears Masaccio's stamp, his erudite, sophisticated style and composition were not properly grasped by his contemporaries. Even those artists who worked alongside him, such as Masolino da Panicale or Andrea di Giusto, went back, in their own works, to the well-tried procedures of Gothic. Andrea di Giusto worked in the rather conservative studio of Lorenzo di Bicci; but in 1426 he assisted Masaccio in the execution of an altarpiece for the Carmelites' church in Pisa. This was a highly significant experience for him, as the Prague painting demonstrates. It probably dates from the late 20's, when the strictness of Masaccio's pictorial construction was still fresh in his mind.

O.P.

Andrea di Giusto
living in Florence in 1424, died in 1455

12 Virgin and Child with Angels

Wood. 100 × 58 cm
Acquired in 1947
Inv. n° O 9488

Medieval paintings expressed certain ideas by means of symbols. In this picture, the pomagranate which the Virgin is holding out to the Child Jesus was considered already in antiquity a symbol of fertility and immortality. In Christian art it symbolizes the Resurrection.

Paolo di Giovanni da Visso
1447-1481 living in the Marches

13 Saint John the Baptist and Saint Bartholomew

Wood. 138 × 48 cm (each panel)
Before 1805 in the collection of Tommaso degli Obizzi, Catajo.
D'Este collection, Konopiště castle.
Acquired in 1939
Inv. nº O 12009, O 12010

Paolo di Giovanni da Visso is one of the little known, though numerous, artists of the Marches. His birthplace Visso, unlike its neighbour Camerino, was never a creative artistic centre. Separated by its hills from the outside world, local artists worked in peaceful isolation. Most of them were simple artisans who usually remained anonymous. Paolo di Giovanni da Visso was the exception. One of his best works is the *Virgin in Majesty* of the Campana collection (Petit Palais Museum in Avignon); it is the only one which bears his signature. It formed the centre of an altarpiece to which these two panels, representing Saint Bartholomew and Saint John the Baptist, probably belonged. All three panels have decorative volutes of acanthus leaves executed with the same characteristic precision. The style of the work would tend to place it in the latter period of the artist's activity, when he was beginning to adopt Renaissance principles. This is particularly evident from the positioning of the two saints to dominate the mountainous landscape. This type of composition enabled the artist to integrate the figure into the landscape while attributing special importance to him.

The Siennese composition of these two Prague panels, which were earlier attributed to the Sassetta circle, is one of the many proofs of the interest that Paolo di Giovanni showed in the painting of Siena. Throughout the Quattrocento there were intense and reciprocal cultural exchanges between Siena and the Marches. The Siennese painter Nicolo da Siena was active in Norcia, a neighbouring town to Visso, whereas Nicolo di Naldo, from Norcia, was one of the team of painters working on the Duomo of Siena under the direction of Sassetta and the Maestro dell'Osservanza. Paolo da Visso probably studied their work in Siena in order to complete his training. Once back in his home town he gave a more provincial interpretation to these models, more in tune with the local, less demanding taste. But in some particularly important commissions he managed to preserve the mystical atmosphere of his exceptional models: the underlying melancholia and hesitancy emanating from the figures of Saint Bartholomew and Saint John the Baptist.

O.P.

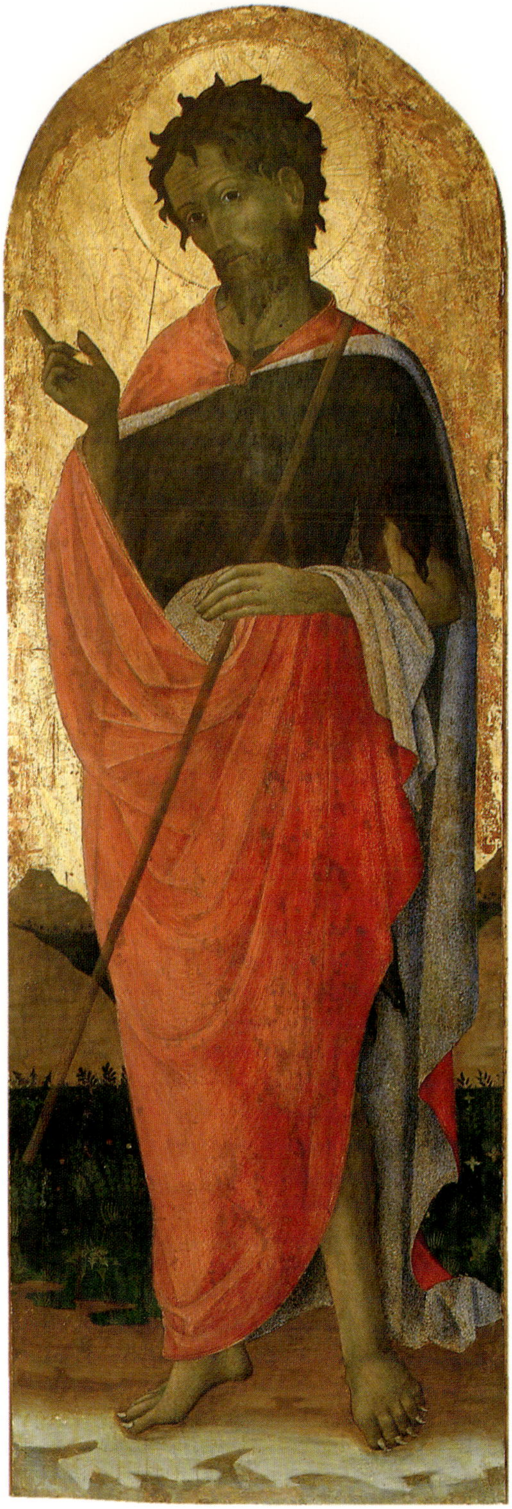

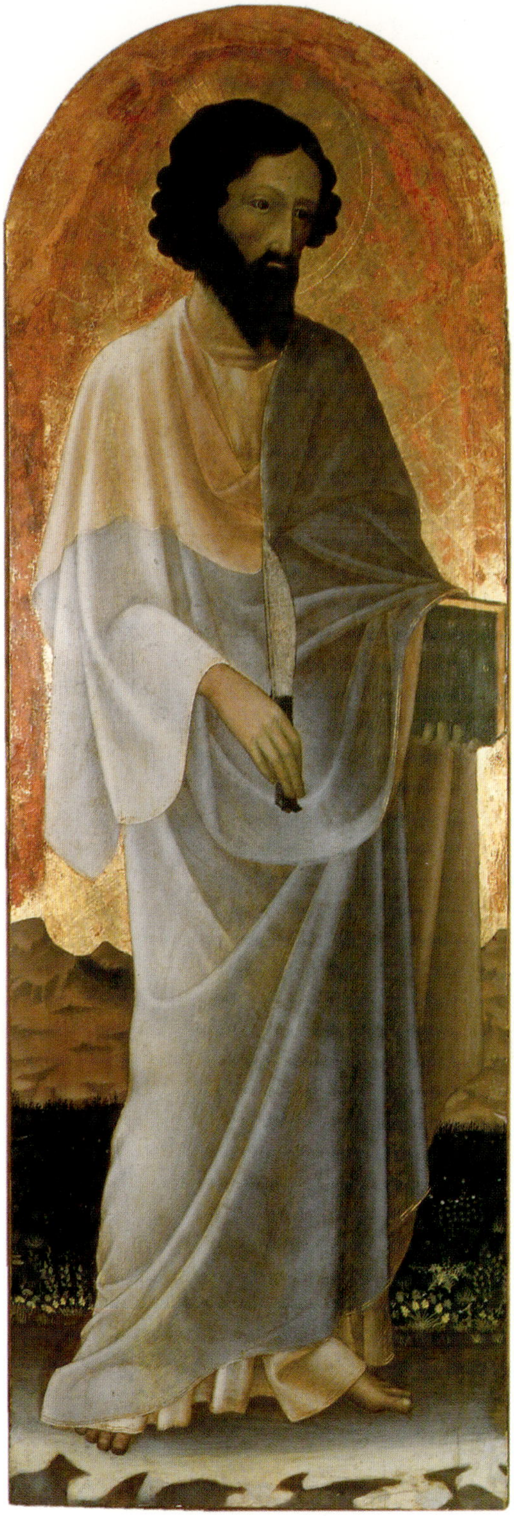

Giovan Francesco Caroto
living c. 1480 in Verona, died after 1555

14 Saint John the Evangelist on Patmos

Wood. 92 × 77.8 cm
Acquired from the Saint Lucas Gallery in Vienna, in 1923
Inv. nº O 1394

Giovan Francesco Caroto grew up in Verona but he was born in Santa Maria in Organo and it is there, in the church of San Zeno, that he will have seen the works of Andrea Mantegna that impressed him so strongly. However this painting preserved in Prague is more strongly influenced by Lombard painting, especially that of Bramantino, and probably dates from the late 20's of the Cinquecento, when he had spent time in Milan. It certainly reflects in its iconography the art of north Italy. Saint John the Evangelist is represented writing the Apocalypse on the island of Patmos. His only companion is the eagle which is to become his attribute. Italian art usually presented the saint in this scene as an old man, as described in the Bible, but north of the Alps he was depicted as a young saint in a state of ecstasy (W. Suida). Caroto's Saint John is a grave young man deep in his thoughts. In front of him the eagle is standing on the open book, head tilted, as though trying to read the unwritten pages. This poetic motif, whose exact meaning still escapes us, is furthermore an unusual iconographic element of the scene, and yet, with Caroto, it is no surprise. Not a few of his works contain unusual motifs whose meaning has not yet been satisfactorily elucidated, and which lend the work an air of genre painting. There are for example *The Madonna sowing* (Modena, Estense Gallery) or the *Portrait of a Boy with the drawing of a Puppet* (Verona, Castelvecchio Museum).

The Prague work is so original that expert opinion as to its author is divided and its attribution has changed several times. Not even X-ray photography has been able to settle the question, and all it has proved is that the little white leaf which figures in the picture bears neither the artist's name nor any other information, as had been hoped. Placed as it is on the rock against which the saint is leaning, the little leaf only adds to the mystery of the scene. Sunlight floods the landscape, creating a powerful cohesion between the ample figure of the saint and the seashore. This *Saint John the Evangelist on Patmos* is undoubtedly one of Caroto's most important works.

O.P.

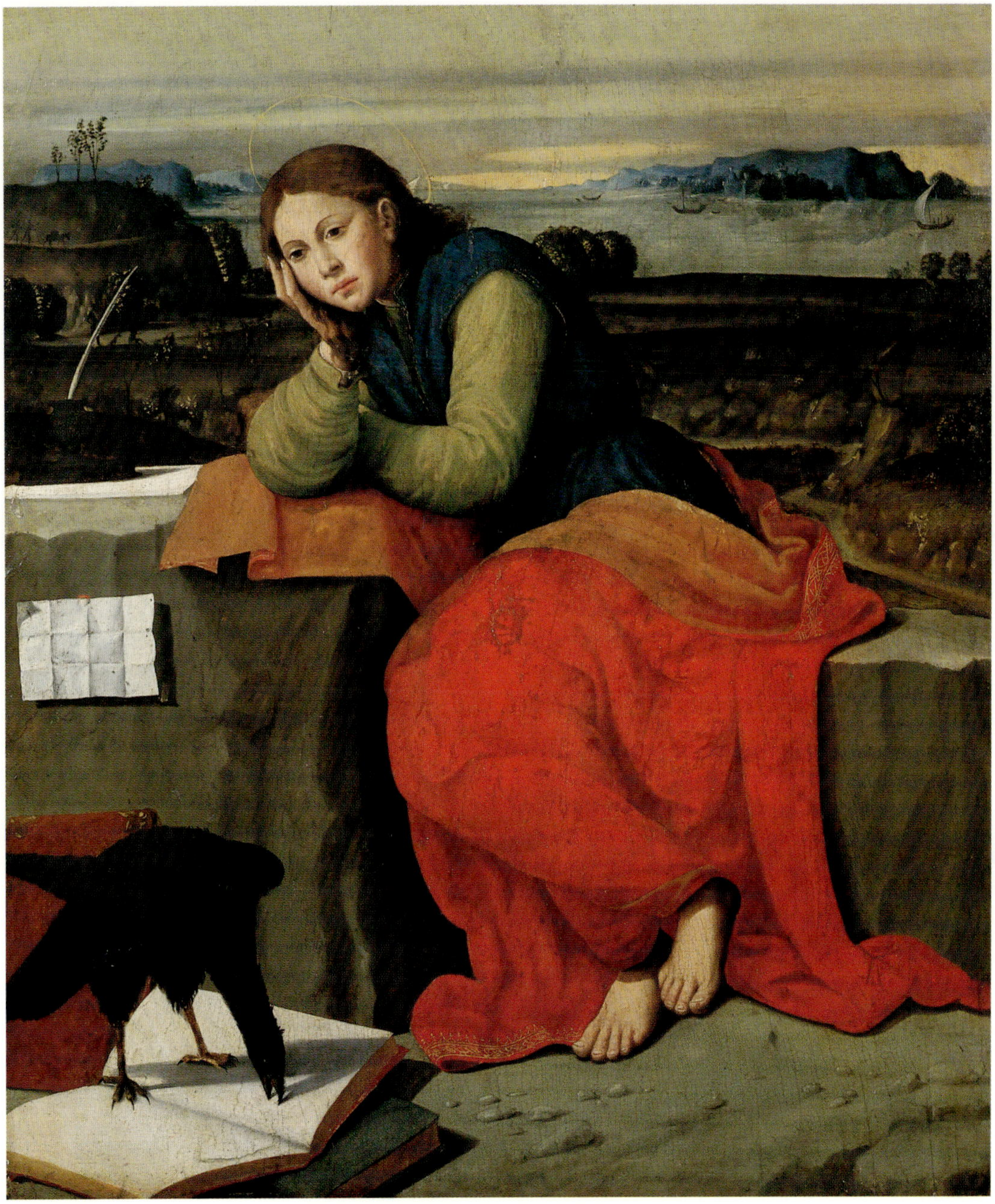

Antonio Vivarini da Murano

living c. 1415 in Murano, died before 1484
in collaboration with

Bartolomeo Vivarini da Murano

living c. 1432 in Murano, died after 1495

15 # Saint Peter

1451
Wood. 114.5 × 41 cm
Church of San Francesco in Padua.
Before 1805 in the collection of Tommaso degli Obizzi, Catajo.
D'Este collection, Konopiště castle.
Acquired in 1960.
Inv. n° O 8302

In his guide to North Italy Giambattista Michiel mentions, around 1530, two altarpieces by the Vivarini in the church of San Francesco in Padua. His account tells us of a large polyptych of 1451 at the High Altar and a smaller one adorning one of the side altars. When these two works were removed from the church they were acquired by Tommaso degli Obizzi for his collection in Catajo castle, near Padua. (see Jacopo del Casentino) The smaller work, dated 1477, represents the Adoration and is signed on the frame as the joint work of Antonio Vivarini and his brother-in-law Giovanni d'Allemagna. This is the only medieval Italian polyptych which the National Gallery in Prague possesses complete (Inv. n° 0 11983 - 0 11987). The large polyptych of the High Altar, however, was dismantled and its various sections dispersed. Fortunately G. Rosetti left us a description of it in 1675.

It consisted of two registers surmounted by a pinnacle with an *Imago Pietatis* (Prague, National Gallery). In the centre of the upper register there was a picture of the *Virgin and Child* (Prague, National Gallery). To the left of this there were panels representing Saint John the Baptist and Saint Clare (Vienna, Kunsthistorisches Museum). To the right, next to a picture which is now missing, there was Saint Bernard of Siena (Prague, National Gallery). In the centre of the lower register there was a painting, now lost, of Saint Francis. Next to him there were Saint Peter and Saint Paul (Prague, National Gallery), and at either end, Saint Anthony of Padua and Saint Louis of Toulouse. These last two were auctioned off in 1974 at the Dorotheum in Vienna. Now that all these fragments are part of a single whole is proved not only by their stylistic unity but also by their common provenance. It seems likely that they all belonged to the d'Este collection, and when this collection was moved from Modena to Austria part of it remained in Vienna and another part, which includes the majority of the pictures, went on to Konopiště. These were later incorporated into the National Gallery in Prague on the eve of the Second World War.

For the execution of the polyptych in the church of San Francesco in Padua, Antonio had the help of his younger brother Bartolomeo. At this time, 1451, the two brothers worked in collaboration, later they worked sometimes together, sometimes apart. During the sixties Antonio gradually gave up his work, whereas Bartolomeo became one of the most significant personalities of the early Renaissance in Venice.

O.P.

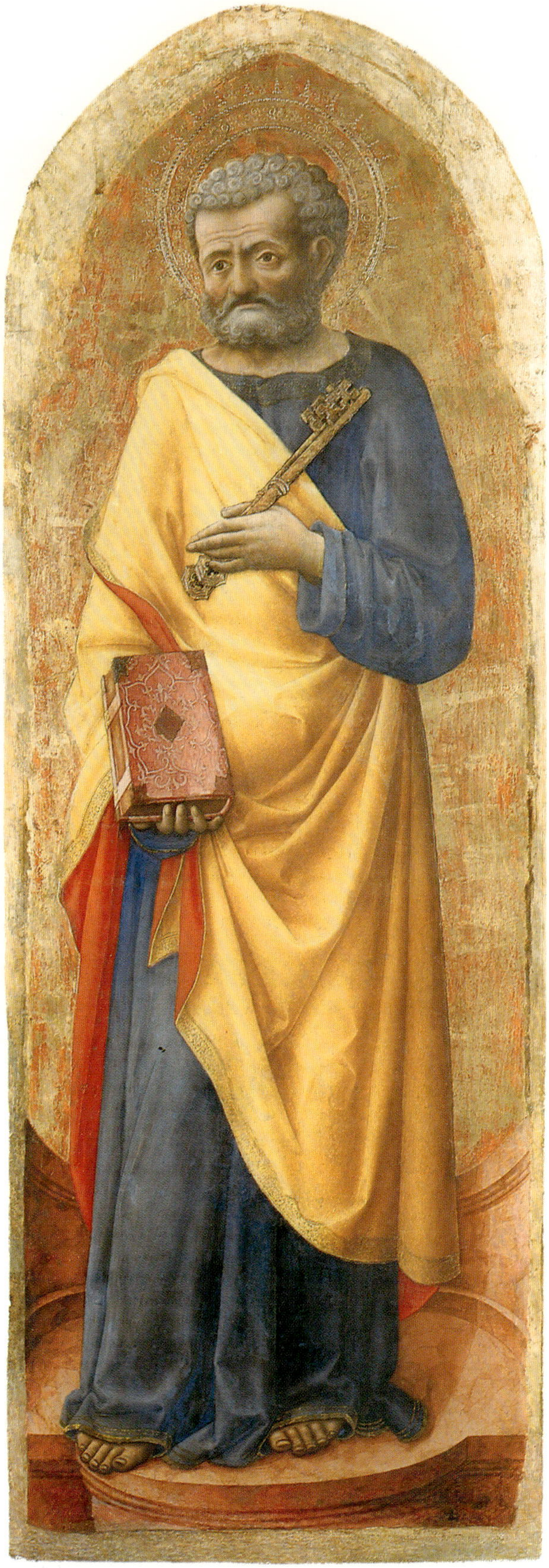

Lorenzo Costa
1460 Ferrare - 1533 Mantua

16 Triumph of Federico II Gonzaga

1522
Canvas. 267 × 639 cm
San Sebastiano Palace in Mantua.
1630 Marechal Aldringen collection, Prague.
Clary Aldringen collection, Teplice castle.
Acquired in 1961.
Inv. n° O 8274

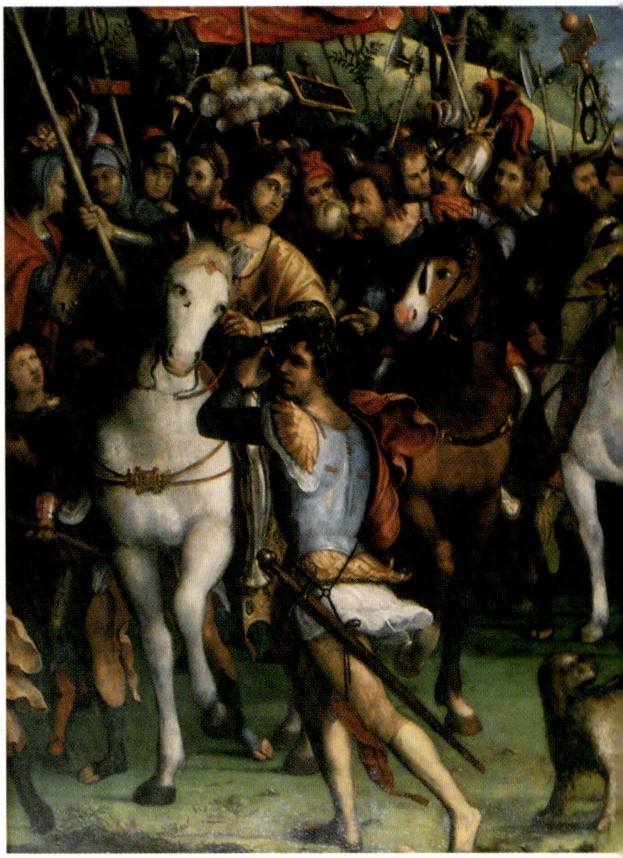

The numerous Italian paintings of the Trecento which glorify saints, allegorical personages or various personalities are generally known under the title *trionfi*. In the Quattrocento they frequently recall a Roman military triumph. Such works show the influence of the statuary of antiquity, which also inspired the famous *Triumph of Caesar* by Andrea Mantegna (c. 1486-1494), painted by the artist while in the service of the Gonzagas in Mantua. This cycle of large canvasses was set up shortly before 1512 in the San Sebastiano Palace. Its original siting is unknown but we know it was moved around on various occasions to decorate the theatre, which is probably what caused it some damage. Mantua's chronicler, Equicolo (in the *Commentari Mantuani* of 1521) remarks that this canvas lacks the crowd which usually marches through Rome behind the Chariot of Triumph. When after the death of Mantegna (1506) Lorenzo Costa became court painter to the Gonzagas it fell to him to make good this lack. At the time he was working on the decoration of the new San Sebastiano Palace and he painted two canvasses intended to be placed alongside the *Triumph of Caesar.* The first is lost. According to Vasari's description it represented the sacrifice of Hercules and included portraits of Francesco Gonzaga and his three sons, Federico among them. The second canvas, kept in the National Gallery, shows Federico with his suite. Even though at first sight these two canvasses seem to have no direct relation to the *Triumph of Caesar,* they could in their time substitute for those expected from Mantegna's brush. The first scene is an allusion to the sacrifice made to Jupiter, which, according to classical tradition, was the climax of the ceremonial. The second canvas, held by the National Gallery, with its crowd of men under arms, was eminently suited to close the procession accompanying Caesar's chariot. Costa had probably begun to paint it in Francesco Gonzaga's lifetime. But after his patron's death in 1519 he made modifications. The new lord of Mantua, Federico II, wanted this work to commemorate a military success of his own, his nomination by Pope Leo X as Commander of the Papal Guard in 1520-1521.

The grandiose work is dated 1522. It is one of the latest of Costa's authenticated paintings.

O.P.

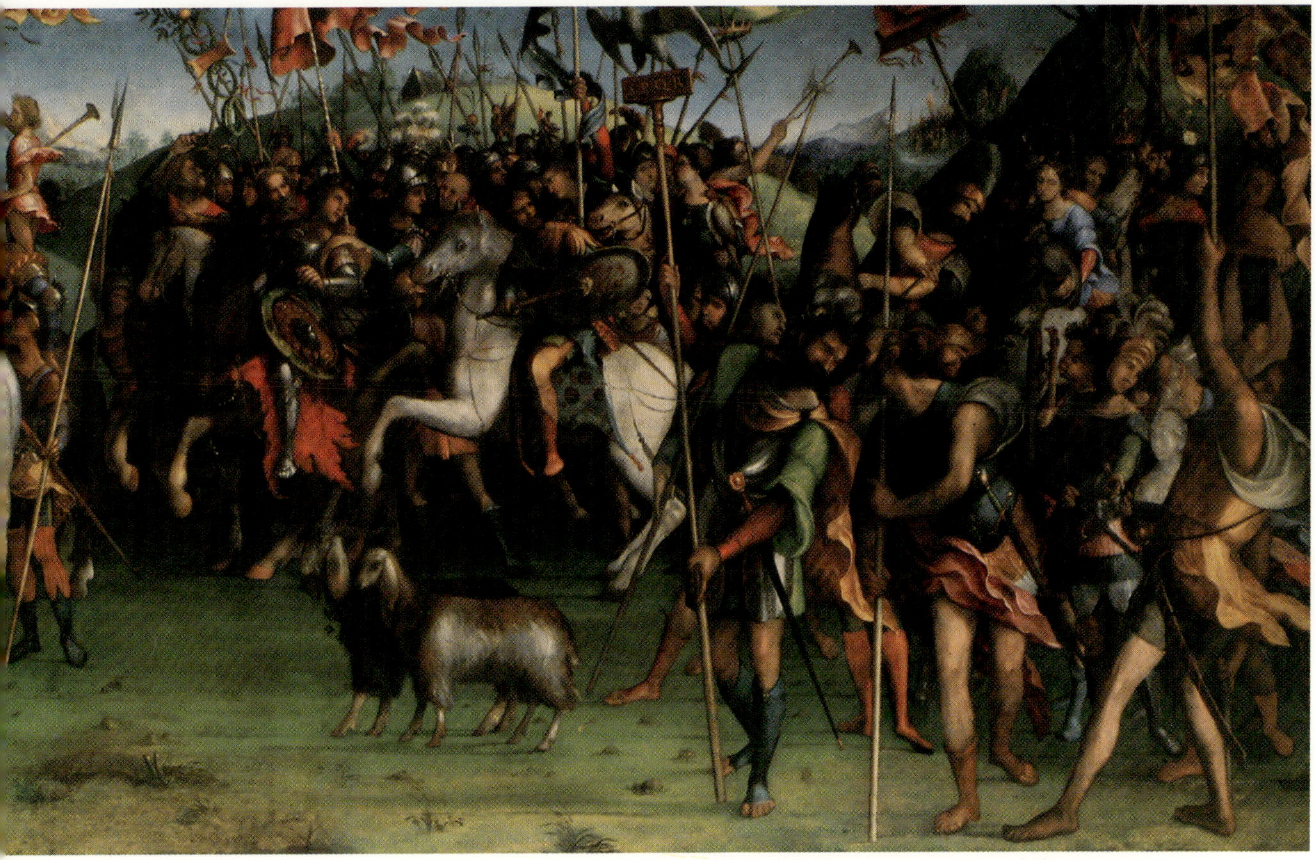

Cosimo Rosselli
1439-1507 Florence

17 Saint Catherine of Alexandria

Wood. 53 × 27 cm
Before 1805 in the collection of Tommaso degli Obizzi, Catajo.
D'Este collection, Konopiště castle. Acquired in 1939
Inv. nº O 12047

Towards the end of the Quattrocento we find, in addition to very large polyptychs, altarpieces which are monumental but all of a piece, sometimes called *pala*. But they too were sometimes cruelly mishandled, being often cut up into several parts for easier sale. This is what happened to Cosimo Rosselli's altarpiece, of which this fragment representing Saint Catherine combines Verrochio's knowledge of the realism of the Netherlands with an archaic fervour. The painters "techniques and saints" haloes have enabled other fragments of this altarpiece to be traced, whereas for many years the only other panel known was that representing Saint Lucy (now lost). These two saints, Catherine and Lucy, were represented alongside Saint John the Baptist and Saint Bartholomew (private collection, London) flanking the Assumption (Henry E. Huntington Art Gallery, San Marino, California). Two fragments showing the kneeling Saints Ansano and Anthony the Abbot, now in New York (Pietro Corsini Gallery) give us some idea of the lower part of the *pala*. The composition as a whole, the artist's way of representing the figures, influenced by Gozzoli, and the full-front haloes bearing inscriptions, all this leaves no doubt that what we have here is one of the artist's earliest works, probably dating from around 1470. The climax of Rosselli's career was his collaboration on the decoration of the Sixtine Chapel (1481-1483). Apart from this brief sojourn in Rome he worked exclusively in Florence or its environs and made eclectic use of elements and motifs observed in the work of his contemporaries. Although lacking the soaring inspiration of Botticelli or Ghirlandaio, he was nonetheless their equal in point of pictorial mastery and technical precision, both characteristic of the panel preserved in Prague.

O.P.

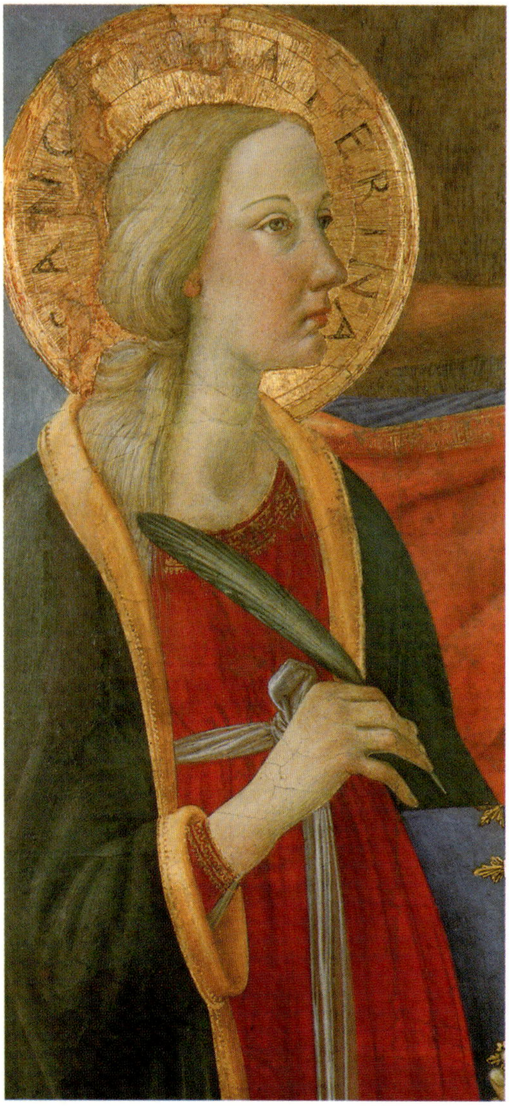

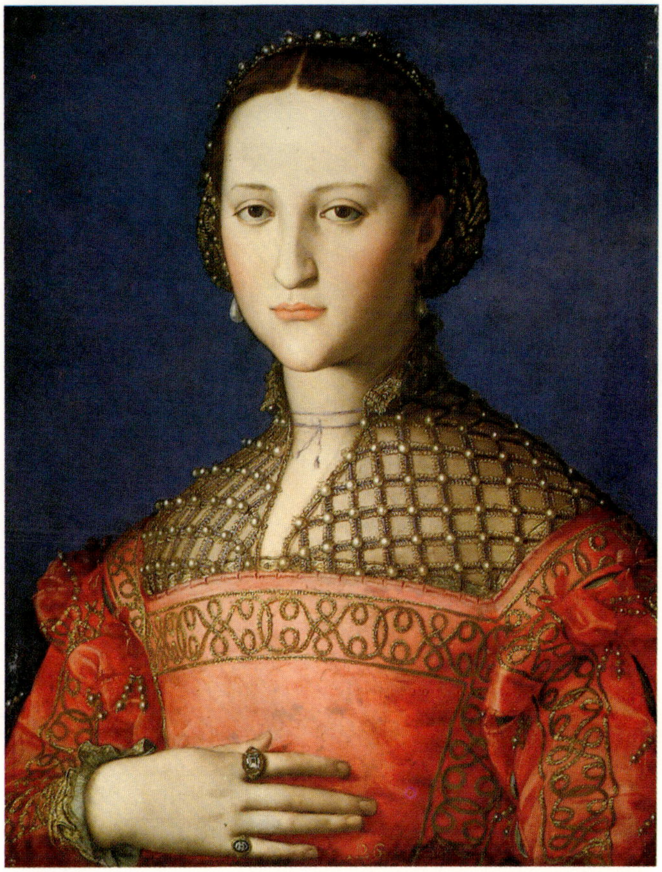

Agnolo Bronzino
1503 Monticelli - 1572 Florence

18 ## Portrait of Eleonor of Toledo

c. 1540-1543
Wood. 59 × 46 cm
D'Este collection, Konopiště castle. Acquired in 1939.
Inv. n° O 11971

Agnolo Bronzino, one of the leading exponents of Florentine mannerism is known for his altarpieces, mythological scenes and allegories, but above all for his elegant portraits.

He painted several portraits of the daughter of the Spanish viceroy in Naples, Eleonor of Toledo, after her marriage in 1539 to Cosimo I de Medici. The official portraits of Eleonor were intended, like those of the Duke of Tuscany, for purposes of state and ceremonial functions, and have been copied many times. In most of these variants the duchess is shown half-length, as is also the case in the painting kept in the National Gallery. She appears here in a dress which is adorned with pearls. It is a fresh face, with no trace of the grief that later portraits reveal. The right hand held to her waist is probably Bronzino's hint that she is pregnant. She gave birth to eight children, of which the first four were born between 1540 and 1543. One of these occasions may well have called for this portrait to be executed. One detail distinguishes it from the others: Eleonor is wearing two rings, a point which has not yet been elucidated. The background is bright blue, reminding one of the large portrait of Eleonor with her son Giovanni which is in the Uffizi: most of its background is taken up with an azure blue sky. Although the work preserved in Prague is very different from that to be seen in Florence, both in its dimensions and more especially in its overall conception, the two paintings have a common theme: Eleonor's fertility, much praised by Vasari.

O.P.

Italian, Spanish and French painting from the second half of the 16th century to the early 19th century

Jacopo da Ponte, called Bassano

circa 1515 - 1592 Bassano

19 Annunciation to the Shepherds

circa 1575
Canvas. 126 × 175 cm
From 1718 in Prague Castle, acquired by the National Gallery in 1960.
Inv. n° O 9026

His minute observation of reality led Jacopo Bassano, around 1575, to paint night scenes, a theme taken up and developed by his sons Francesco and Leandro. Bassano was anticipating on what painters of the next century were going to be doing. The idea of painting a scene which is happening in the dark and is illuminated by a non-natural light-source came to Italy from 15th century paintings of the Netherlands. Bassano took inspiration from Titian and Tintoretto. The background of a picture is enveloped in complete darkness, shrouding all the figures and objects, except those parts of the scene receiving direct illumination.

It is the light which marks out the space of this nocturnal scene, the several planes being distinguished by the progressive diminution of the intensity of the light, with the foreground being strongest lit. Here the shepherds and their flocks are bathed in a supernatural light pouring down from an open sky: "the Glory of the Lord enveloped them in light". Through an opening in the clouds an angel leans out to announce the birth of Christ. The shadow cast by the figure of the angel on the clouds makes the distinction clear between the radiant light shed by the "glory of the Lord" and the natural light of the moon on the horizon. On the most strongly illuminated surfaces there are shining pasty touches fraying at the edges: so it is not only the composition of the light but also the execution of the picture which create the illusion of radiating light. Delicate brush strokes touch up the cheeks and fingers of the shepherds, to be echoed more softly in a scintillating cascade of shrubbery behind the figures.

In the Albertina collection in Vienna there is a study for this painting which shows a boy kneeling and a seated shepherd asleep. Replicas have been preserved of night scenes representing the *Annunciation to the Shepherds*, but they are not the work of Jacopo although modelled on the prototype preserved in Prague, one of the most beautiful and most lyrical creations of the artist's beginning old age.

L.D.

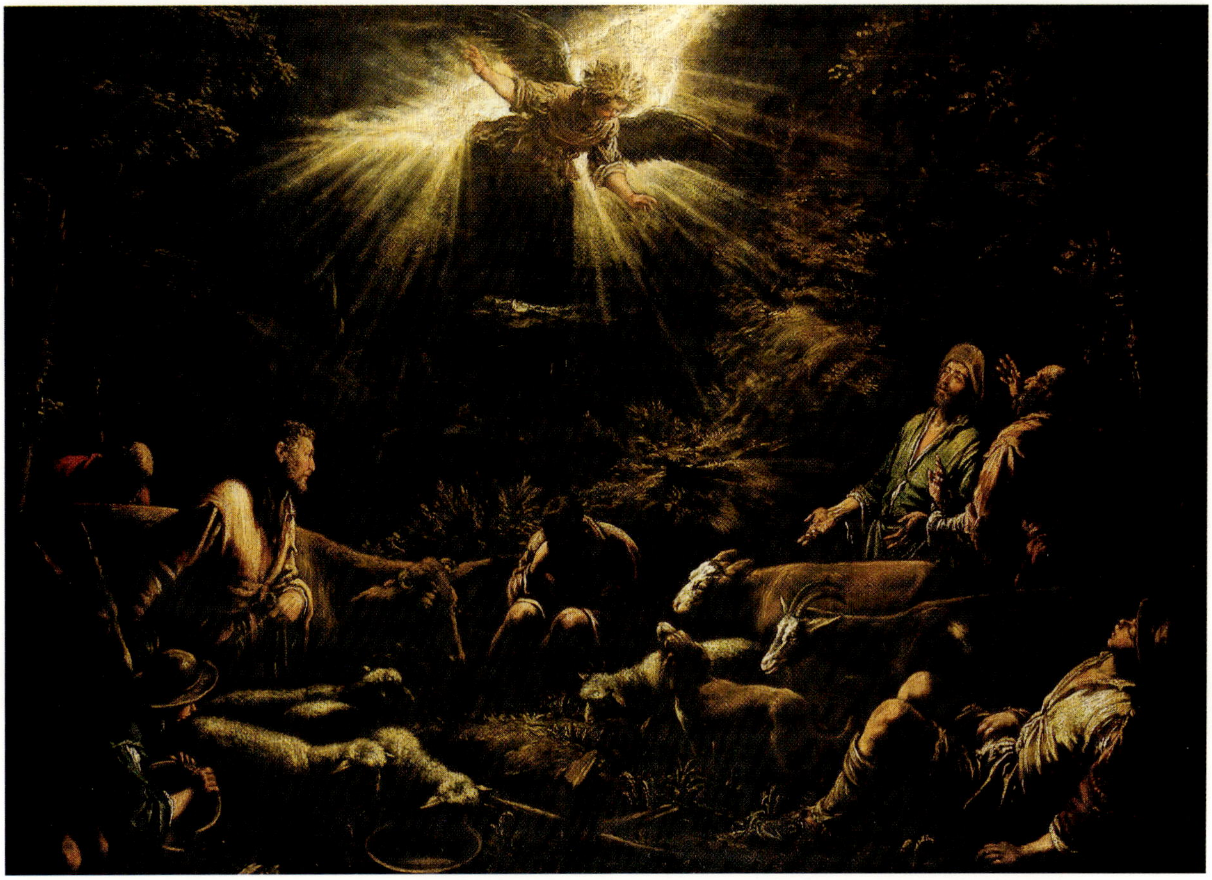

Andrea Boscoli
circa 1560 Florence - 1607 Florence

20 Virgin and Child with Saint John the Baptist

circa 1594
Wood. 91.5 × 69.5 cm
The first owner, from 20th December 1594, was Luca di … Potenti from Borgo San Jacopo in Florence. In 1922 the picture was auctioned at the Kassirer Rooms in Berlin.
Acquired from a private collection in Prague in 1950. Restituted in 1992. Now on loan.
Inv. nº O 10297

Shortly before Christmas 1594 the Florentine painter Andrea Boscoli noted in his accounts that "master Luca di … Potenti, cabinet-maker, is to pay … forty-two lire … for two paintings measuring one cubit and one third" (i.e. circa 90 cm); one of them was to represent "Our Lady with a little boy in her arms holding out a cross to the little Saint John". The picture thus described is very probably the one preserved in Prague which shows the Virgin and Child with Saint John the Baptist, a painting which is stylistically very close to Boscoli's works of this period.

Boscoli has painted this scene with a mannerist mixture of virtuosity able to capture the most fleeting emotions, symbolic meaning and dematerialized pictorial means. The Christ child is holding in his left hand one end of a ribbon bearing the inscription ECCE AGN(US) DEI while the fingers of his right hand let go of his mother's sleeve to seize the apple, symbol of world dominion which John is holding out. The transparency of the veils, the acid, broken, "alchemist" colours, the clear flesh tints of the oval faces with their close-set eyes, all this and the complexity of the curves are inherited from the early Florentine mannerism of Andrea del Sarto, Jacopo Pontormo and Rosso Fiorentino, who are Andrea Boscoli's references, in conformity with the international mannerism which was dominant around 1600, e.g. at the Prague court of Rudolph II.

L.D.

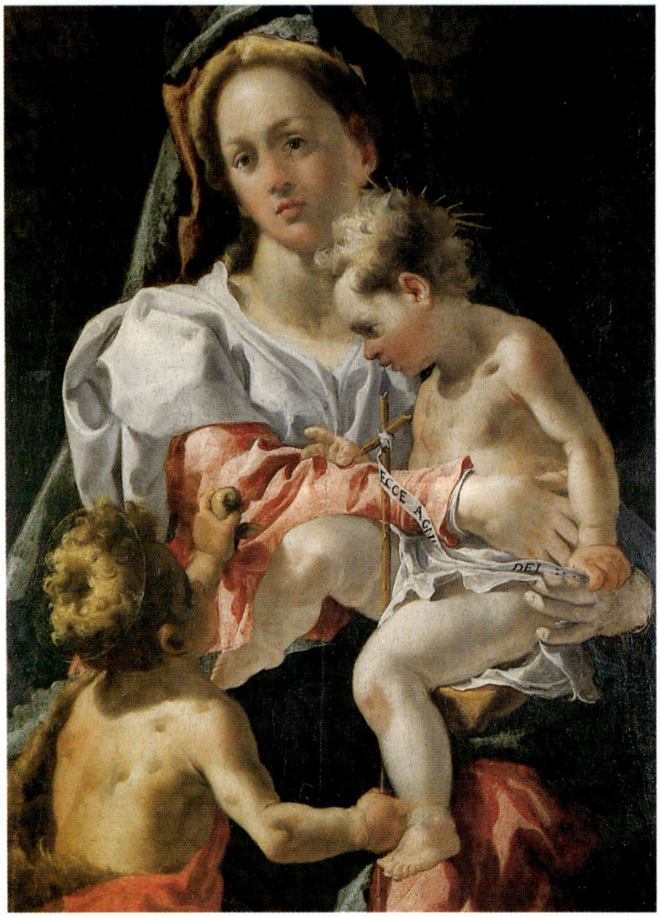

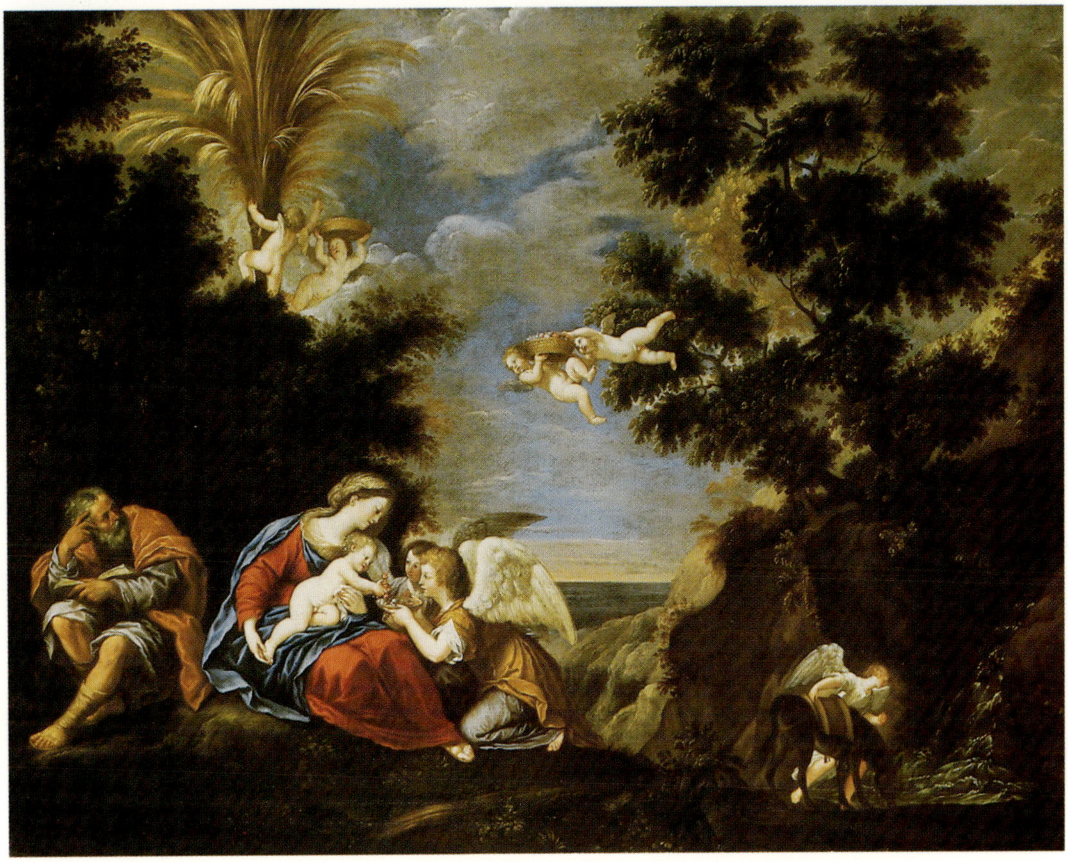

Francesco Albani
1578 Bologna - 1660 Bologna

21 Rest on the Flight into Egypt

circa 1640
Canvas. 79 × 100 cm
At least from 1864 in the Stroganoff collection in Saint-Petersburg, State property after the 1917 revolution; in 1931 sold by auction at the Lepke rooms in Berlin. Acquired by the Prague National Gallery in 1949.
Inv. nº O 10627

Albani "usually painted on a small scale, his paintings are scattered like precious gems throughout Europe..., and being learned and enjoyable, they please everyone". This is how, in 1699, Roger de Piles expressed his estimation of Albani's best works, his little landscapes with biblical or mythological scenes. Composed with realistic detail - following in "ideal landscape" his venerated Bologna-Rome master, Annibale Carraci, - Albani's works are transposed into a more lyrical register with a pictorial softness inspired by Titian.

The raphaelesque figures interact harmoniously with the landscape: the Holy Family and the angels find in nature a worthy and idyllic frame, and give her in return their intimacy and grace. The basic story of the flight into Egypt of Joseph, the Virgin Mary and the new-born Child is taken from the Gospel of Saint Matthew, but the details derive from the Pseudo-Matthew's Gospel of the childhood of Jesus: the fugitives taking rest at the foot of a palm-tree which, on a sign from the Child, bends down to allow the Virgin to take refreshment from its fruit; the miraculous spring of water; the angel holding a palm branch.

The picture which is preserved in Prague, like the related ones belonging to a private collection in Lucerne and to the castle of Fontainebleau, is an example of the brilliant works Albani painted in his old age. Other variants are in the Dresden Gallery, in the Ringling Museum in Sarasota and in the reserves of Florentine galleries.

L.D.

Domenico Fetti

1588 or 1589 Rome - 1623 Venice

22 Christ on the Mount of Olives

circa 1617-1619
Canvas. 170 × 130 cm
Probably positioned, from the time of its creation, in the conventual church of Santa Maria della Presentazione, known as La Cantelma, in Mantua, where its existence was confirmed in 1763. After the church was deconsecrated in 1797 the picture was acquired by an unknown collector of Mantua and later exported from Italy. On loan from the Valdštejn collection to the Picture Gallery of the Society of Patriot Friends of the Arts (noticed in 1822, 1825). Acquired by the Prague National Gallery from the Valdštejn collection in 1949.
Inv. n° DO 5356

Christ kneeled and prayed: "Father, if you are willing, take this cup way from me. Nevertheless let your will be done, not mine." Then an angel appeared from heaven to lend him strength. Saint Luke is the only one of the evangelists to mention that the prayer on the Mount of Olives was said kneeling, also the presence of the angel, before Christ is taken prisoner. The diagonals created by the figures, the contrasting darkness and supernatural glow, the drapery billowing in the wind above the angel's head, Christ's shining robe with its gently agitated folds, all become the means of expressing the dramatic tension of the scene. No artist before Caravaggio had given physical expression to a psychological state with a force to equal that given by Fetti to his fainting Christ. Gripped in mortal anguish, the face of Christ is covered in sweat which, according to Luke, "falls to the ground like drops of blood". The look of empathy in the boy-angel's eyes and his embrace demonstrate his compassion with Christ's suffering, which is portrayed in accordance with that ardent mysticism which Theresa d'Avila in particular exalted. The symbolic chalice is really in the angel's hand, and the withered olive branch - a symbol of death - succinctly indicates the scene of the action. The gold of the supernatural light contrasting with the bluish glow of night reminds us of Bassano's nocturnes. In Fetti's painting the naturalist features are absorbed into a pictorial execution which develops from the Venetian tradition of Titian, Tintoretto, Veronese, and the works Rubens executed in Mantua, where Fetti was active between 1616 and 1621. This Prague canvas was painted between 1617 and 1619 at the instigation of the Andreini family, friends of the artist, probably for the church of Santa Maria della Presentazione, known as La Cantelma.

L.D.

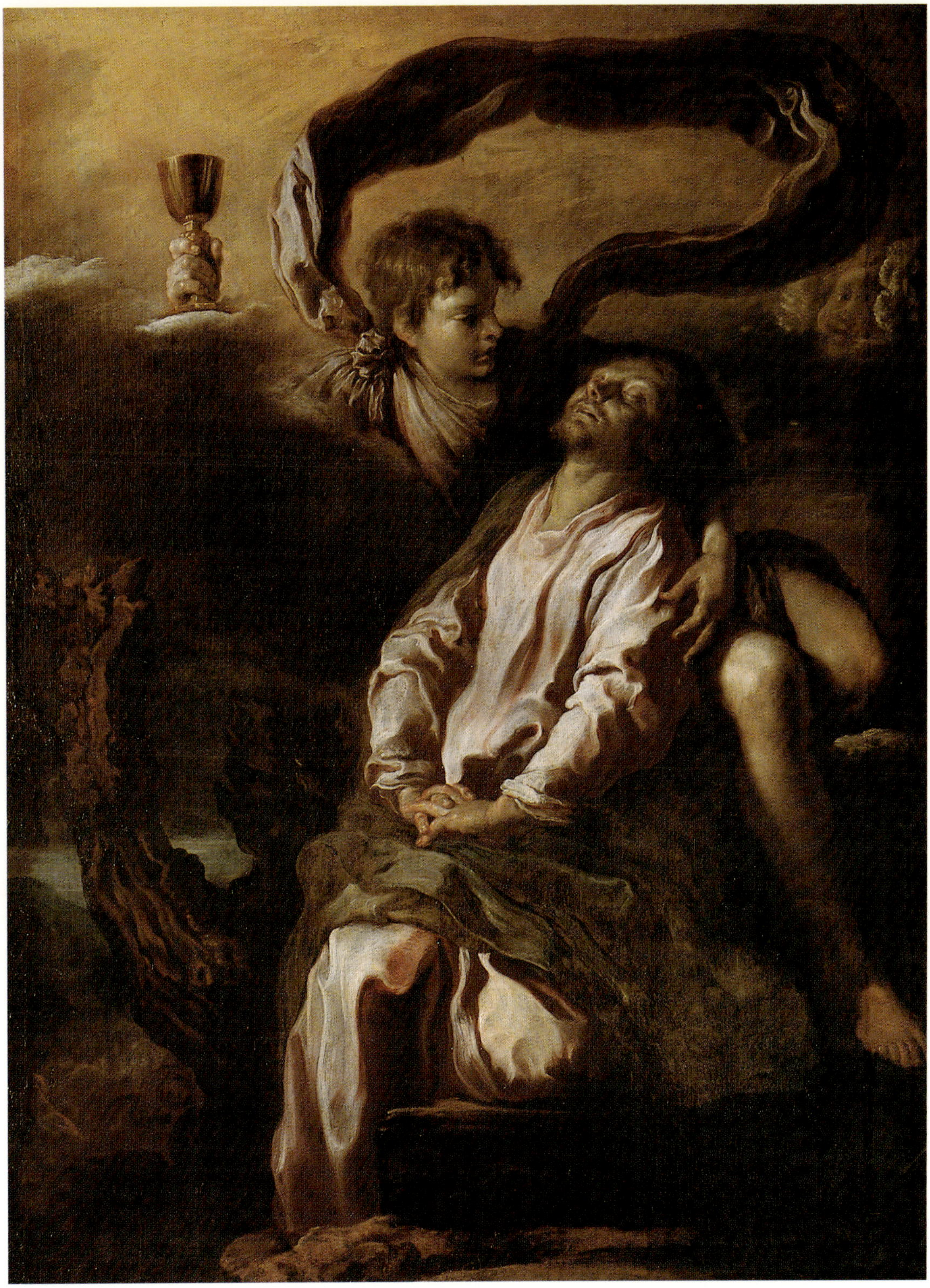

Giulio Carpioni

1613 Venice - 1679 Verona

23 Venus and the Nymphs lamenting the death of Adonis

Canvas. 71.5 × 88.5 cm
From 1692 at latest in the collection of Count František Antonín Berka of Dubá; bequeathed in 1706 to the collection of Count Anton Johann Nostitz.
Transferred from the Nostitz collection in 1945.
Inv. n° DO 4202

"Adonis gives weak moan
with failing strength he fights for breath
The pale nymphs, sobbing,
their faces bathed in tears,
murmuring the sweet name, tear at their hair,
bewailing the youth's death."
"He is no more.
Death has passed the portals of his eyes.
Weep for the springs, weep for the banks.
May the goddess weep, and from the heavens, should she wish
to see the loved one, let her make haste!"

The poem *Adonis* by the great Italian baroque poet Giambattista Marino (1569-1625) was a powerful influence on Italian culture in his day. Its popularity probably explains why the legend recounted by Ovid of Venus' love for Adonis was so often represented in painting. According to Ovid Adonis disregards the warnings of Venus and continues to hunt until at last "death grasps him by the wild boar's tusks". Marino's highly ornate and exalted verses exactly suited the taste of an aristocratic society which was fond of identifying with the characters of his poems and equally with those of the mythological paintings of the period.

The work of Carpioni which is kept in Prague is inspired not only by Ovid's *Metamorphoses* but also by Marino's poem. Carpioni is a rare phenomenon among Venetian painters of this century. While the neo-Venetian trend harks back to the later Titian and Tintoretto, with their free pictorial expression and colour effects, Carpioni opts for the classicism of Poussin and takes after Albani's smaller-scale compositions, which evoke Titian's "poesie". In fact in the inventary of Count Berka of Dubá's collection this painting is attributed to "un discipulo del Alban". While taking on the classical discipline Carpioni allows himself enough freedom to give his work that personal note which will distinguish him from his contemporaries. He works with a minute touch which has all the airy lightness and poetic impulse of the Venetian tradition. The canvas preserved in Prague has that degree of restraint in its expression and that melancholy tonality and harmonious ordering which link it to the paintings of his full maturity, dating between 1650 and 1665.

L.D.

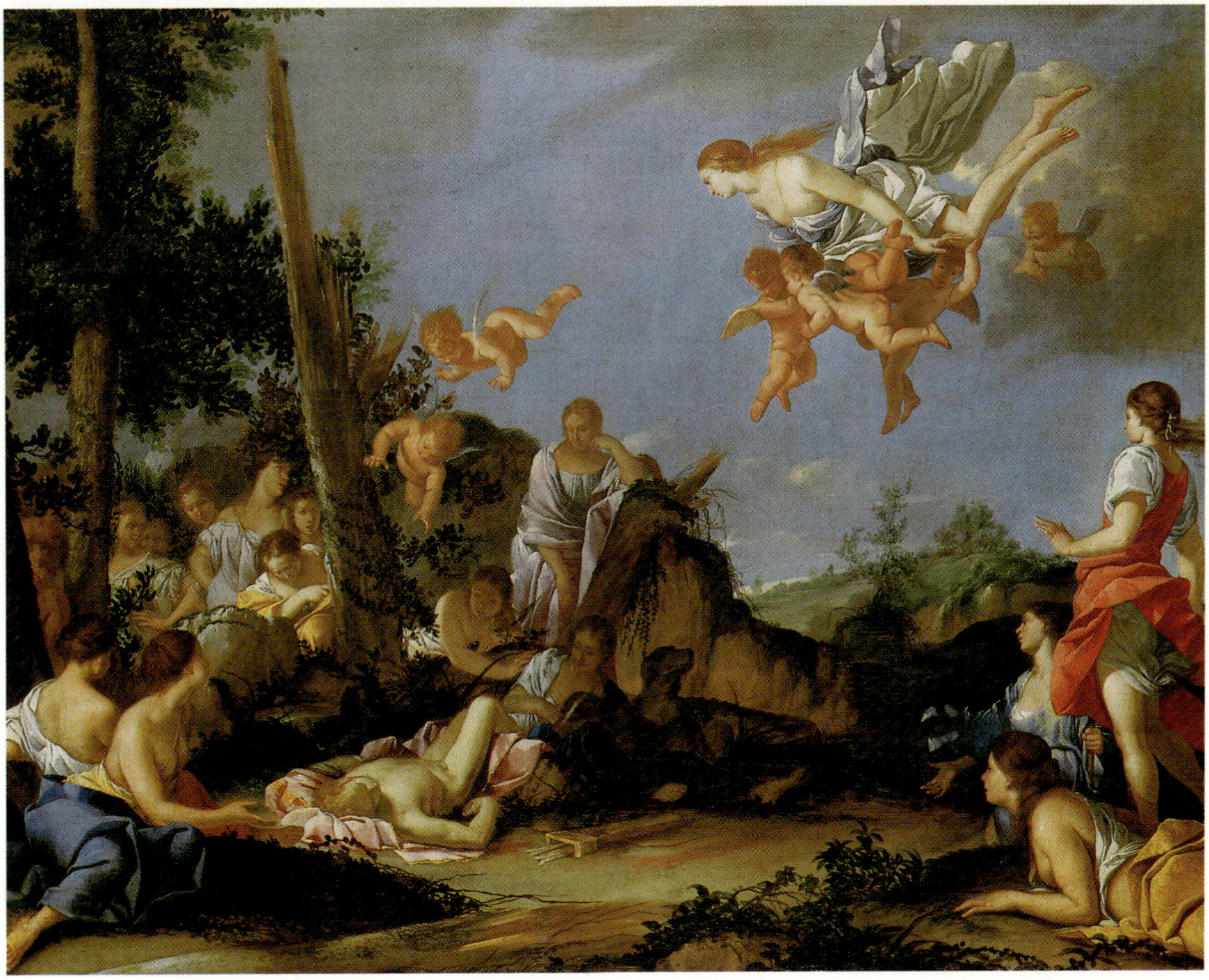

Sebastiano Ricci
1659 Belluno - 1734 Venice

24 Bacchus and Ariadne

after 1725
Canvas. 105 × 140 cm
Before 1796 this painting was in the collection of František Josef Vrtba; later loaned to the Picture Gallery of the Society of Patriot Friends of the Arts; in 1852 it came by inheritance into the collection of Prince Jan Karel Lobkowicz, whence it was sold in the second half of the 19th century into a private collection in Prague. Bought by the Prague National Gallery in 1979.
Inv. nº O 14422

Ovid's verses have taught us the legend of Ariadne abandoned by Theseus on the Island of Naxos, and the *Metamorphoses* tell how "Bacchus found her in tears, opened his arms to her and promised his protection". In his *Ars amatoria* Ovid describes the betrothals of Bacchus and Ariadne: "And the god said to her: I will vow you a faithful love, do not fear, daughter of Crete, become the spouse of Bacchus." The *Ars amatoria* is likewise the source of "the vigorously beaten resounding drums", the bacchantes, satyrs and crowd marching ahead of Bacchus and his team of tigers. Venus makes a gift to Ariadne of a diadem of pearls which she sets on her brow, and in the *Metamorphoses* "are transformed into stars, set in the heavens in the shape of a crown". In Ovid's *Fasti* Bacchus gives Ariadne this prediction: "When you become a goddess your name will be Libera". In Ricci's painting Bacchus, looking rather like John the Baptist, comes towards Ariadne with a gesture of benediction which is already known to the iconography of Netherlands paintings. The most striking influence here is not the famous Titian which is in the London National Gallery, nor the well-known *Coronation of Ariadne* by Tintoretto belonging to the Doges Palace, but rather a work by Giulio Carpioni belonging to a private collection in Treviso. The significance of Carpioni as Ricci's model is that it shows that his composite style was forged according to pictorial principles peculiar to Venice but that he also adopted those of classicism. Ricci's style in fact became the point of departure of Venetian painting of the eighteenth century.

The Bacchus and Ariadne theme, so popular in painting, also invaded Venetian theatre and opera of the 17th and 18th centuries. Sebastiano Ricci himself took up the subject at least five times before he undertook the canvas which is preserved in Prague. We know of a study for one of these compositions, but none of the anterior versions includes the figure of Venus or the scene of Ariadne's coronation. In harmony with his portrayal of the diadem of stars the artist has created an overall silvery atmosphere, between day and night, and used softly muted colours to transpose Ariadne's apotheosis into the dream-like realm of myth.

L.D.

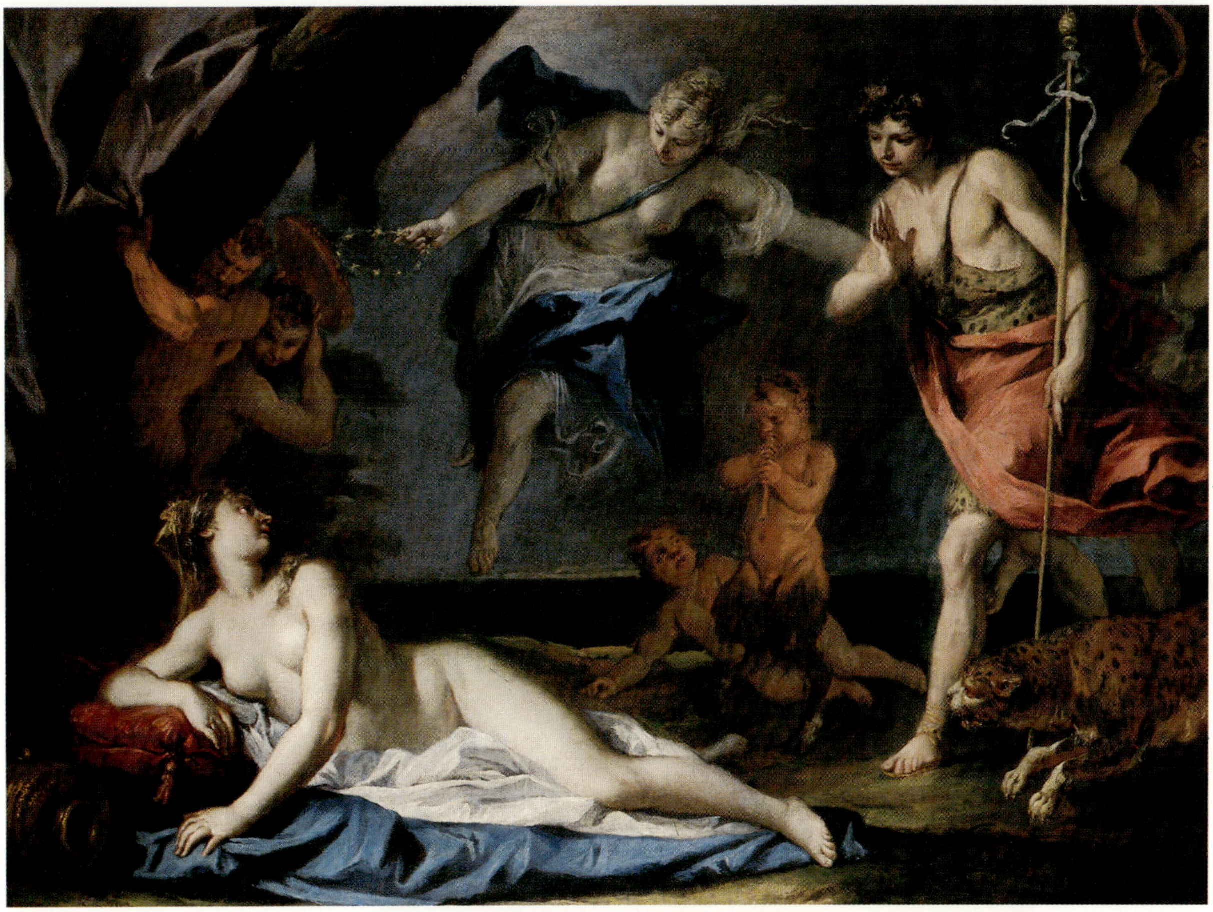

Giambattista Piazzetta
1683 Venice - 1754 Venice

25 Saint Joseph with the Child Jesus

circa 1729
Canvas, oval. 69 × 56.5 cm
Acquired in 1950.
Inv. nº O 10655

In the course of the 17th and 18th centuries the cult of Joseph the Carpenter "of the House of David", foster-father to Jesus, grew, and more and more churches and altars were consecrated to him. His figure appears with increasing frequency on church altars and adopts an iconography which shows him carrying the Child, whereas in older representations he is no more than present in scenes of the Holy Family. For this new type of Joseph, Piazzetta seeks inspiration from the impressive painting of Saint Jerome by Johann Liss which is at the altar of the San Nicolò dei Tolentini church in Venice. (There is a replica in the archbishop's pinakothek in Kroměříž castle.) Chiaroscuro was now rediscovered, having been reintroduced into Italian painting by Giuseppe Maria Crespi of Bologna, under the influence of northern artists, such as Eberhard Kheil. A pupil of Crespi, Piazzetta uses it as the very foundation of his pictorial expression. Late seventeenth century Venetian academicism was revivified by Piazzetta's works, which marked a new manner of observing reality, especially scenes from daily life. This was to play an important part in the success of Venetian Settecento.

For this oval-shaped painting, which was probably meant to fit into the architecture of an altar, the painter makes effective use of contrasts between Joseph's plebeian face and the smooth, plump body of the Child, between the head thrown back of the old man and that of Jesus, tilted forward, and between the strongly lit elements and those which are plunged in the dark, all of which provide the basis for the composition. Charged as it is with emotion and tenderness, this painting is one of the most beautiful religious works that Piazzetta achieved in his full maturity.

L.D.

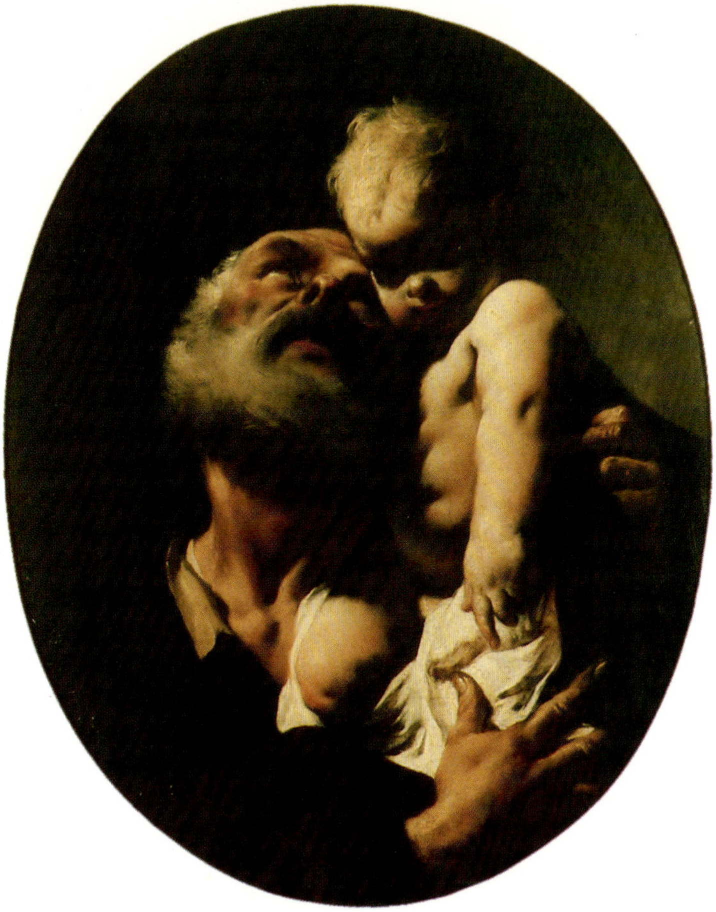

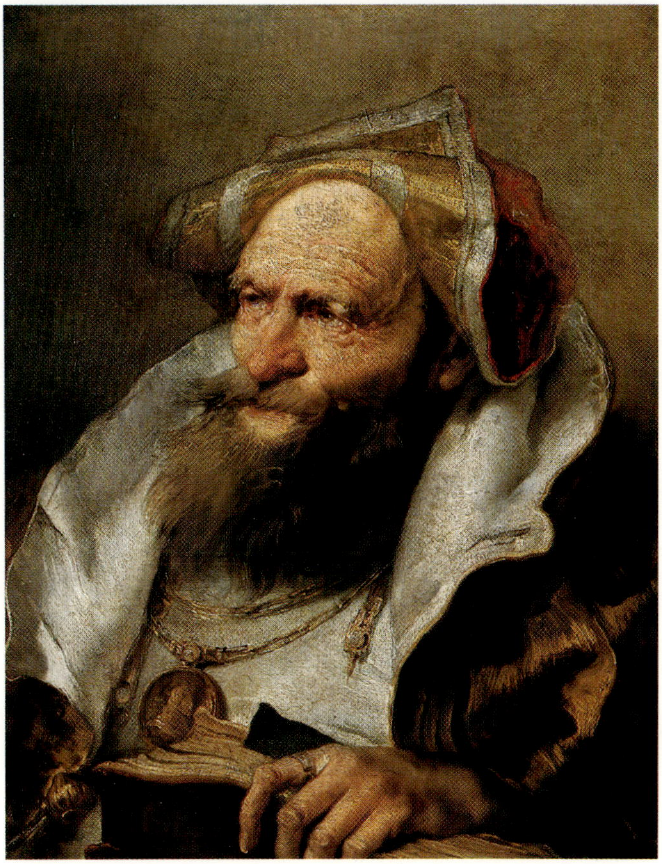

Giovanni Battista Tiepolo
1696 Venice - 1770 Madrid

26 Bust of an Old Man

circa 1755
Canvas. 61 × 50.5 cm
Probably originating from the collection of Yuri Vladimirovich Orloff, collector of Tiepolo's drawings. Included in the sale of the Alexis Orloff collection in Paris in 1920. Acquired by the National Gallery in 1945 from an unknown collection.
Inv. DO 4628

Tiepolo balanced the theatrical magnificence and enchantment of his brilliant spectacles of colour with a matter-of-fact expression and, on occasion, a biting wit. His keen sense of observation and the ingenuity with which he catches the unfamiliar realist detail found impulse and support in the interest his contemporaries had in Dutch painting of the preceding century. Tiepolo was fascinated by the paintings and graphic works of Rembrandt and his circle. He was inspired by Rembrandt's portrayal of old people to create numerous series of heads which his son Giovanni Domenico Tiepolo then engraved. Sixty engraved sheets, bound into two volumes, make up the *Raccolta di teste* (Collection of Heads, of 1774 and 1775). This "character head" (testa di carattere) conserved in Prague was the model for one of the engravings belonging to the second volume.

Collectors' interest in Dutch painting also took in those of Tiepolo's paintings which figure the heads of orientals and of Venetian patricians. Just as with the rabbis, the scholars, the patriarchs and prophets of Rembrandt, so also Tiepolo's "heads" remain anonymous although they are very clearly portraits. The influence of Dutch painting and especially that of Rembrandt is obvious not only in the choice of theme but also in the effects which the painter uses: the flash of white satin and the golds, though Tiepolo's tones are slightly warmer. For mid eighteenth century taste the chiaroscuro used by Tiepolo in his early works, when he drew inspiration from Piazzetta, was however no longer acceptable under its early form. Also, the remarkable virtuosity of his pictorial manner, while being a mark of Tiepolo's originality, is nonetheless the product of a long cultural tradition common to the whole of Europe.

L.D.

Giovanni Antonio Canal, known as Canaletto
1697 - 1768 Venice

27 View of London with the Thames

circa 1746
Canvas. 118 × 238 cm
Acquired circa 1746 by Prince Philip Ferdinand of Lobkowicz in London. On loan from the Lobkowicz collection in Roudnice nad Labem in 1946.
Inv. n° O 9304

Canaletto probably started on this grand view of London shortly after his arrival in England in May 1746. Prince Philip Ferdinand Lobkowicz came to London in the summer of that year intent on buying thoroughbreds for his stud farm. The young Czech aristocrat, described by Walpole as "a young man of around twenty on his travels", mentions this acquisition in his correspondence.

We can date the completion of this painting by reference to one historical fact: contemporary sources say that the first of the five depicted sets of scaffolding erected for the construction of Westminster Bridge was taken down in September 1746. The bridge was provisionally opened to the public on July 20th before the stone balustrading had been completed. It is therefore likely that the picture was finished at the latest in September. The panoramic view taken from the Archbishop's Palace in Lambeth shows the opposite bank of the Thames from the towers of the church of Saint John the Evangelist, taking in Westminster Abbey as the dominant feature, along to Westminster Hall and as far as the Banqueting Hall of the Palace of Whitehall. Westminster Bridge, bathed in light, leads the eye away up to the horizon, where Saint Paul's Cathedral is visible on the right through the haze.

With its play of light and colour between sky and river surface, in which shore-line buildings and rivercraft are reflected, this work recalls Canaletto's views of Venice, but with the addition of a new experience, characteristic of his pictures of London, that of a northern atmosphere and the delicate veil cast by the haze which gives the scene its unity. The barge flying the Royal Standard, which also floats above Westminster, points to the link between this painting and its companion — *The Lord Mayor's Day*, also included in the Lobkowicz collection (now in Nelahozeves castle), and attributed to Canaletto, which shows a convoy of rivercraft accompanying the Lord Mayor's barge on its ceremonial progress from the City to the Palace of Westminster, where on each 29th of October the Lord Mayor is received by the king.

L.D.

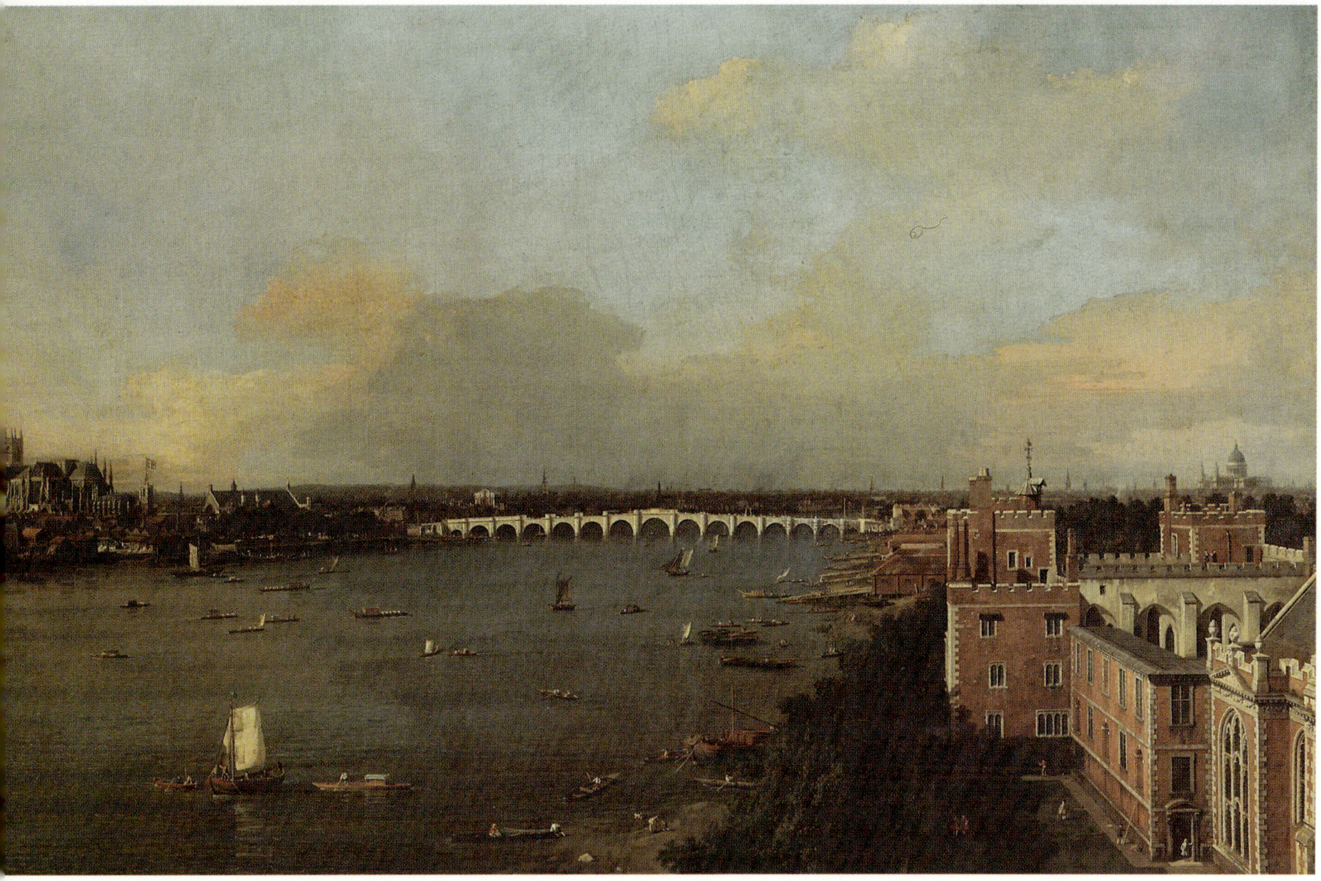

Domenikos Theotokopoulos, called El Greco

1541 Candia in Crete - 1614 Toledo

28 Christ in prayer

circa 1595-1597
Canvas. 61 × 46 cm
This painting was in Spain until the nineteenth century. It was auctioned in Paris in 1879, passing from the collection of the Countess de Quinto into that of baron D. and then that of Leopold II, last archduke of Tuscany. It later found its way to the castle of Konopiště, whence it was loaned to the State Collection of Ancien Art. It was acquired by the Prague National Gallery in 1959.
Inv. n° O 11879

From his Greek origins and years of apprenticeship in icon-painting, to the years he spent in Titian's studio and, after 1576 his life in Toledo: El Greco drew on all these elements for inspiration in forging an original style. The ecstatic sphere of the upper world he renders in luminous tones, while life on earth he depicts with an acute sense for individuality. In this Prague canvas the two realms interpenetrate. Here the Christ in prayer of the Gospel account is beyond space and time. The motionless Pantocrator we know from traditional representations has become animated and the face, portrait-like, is that of a Christ-man, present to us here and now, and vulnerable. In tune as he was with the new forms of religious sentiment inspired by such as Theresa d'Avila, Greco gives delicate expression in the features of his Christ to the depth of emotion of that inner dialogue with God where prayer borders on ecstasy, an expression that is concentrated into the eyes, moist with tears. Here the fine-drawn strokes of thick white outweigh the multiple touches of luminosity animating the composition. The pale face of this Christ reproduces, so it is said, the features of the painter's son, Jorge Manuel Theotokopouli several times painted by his father. The fact that this picture is executed in a manner similar to the artist's portraits and distinct from the anonymous heads of his other Christs and apostles, lends substance to this view, despite the interdiction pronounced by the Church after the Council of Trent against representing living people as divine persons.

L.D.

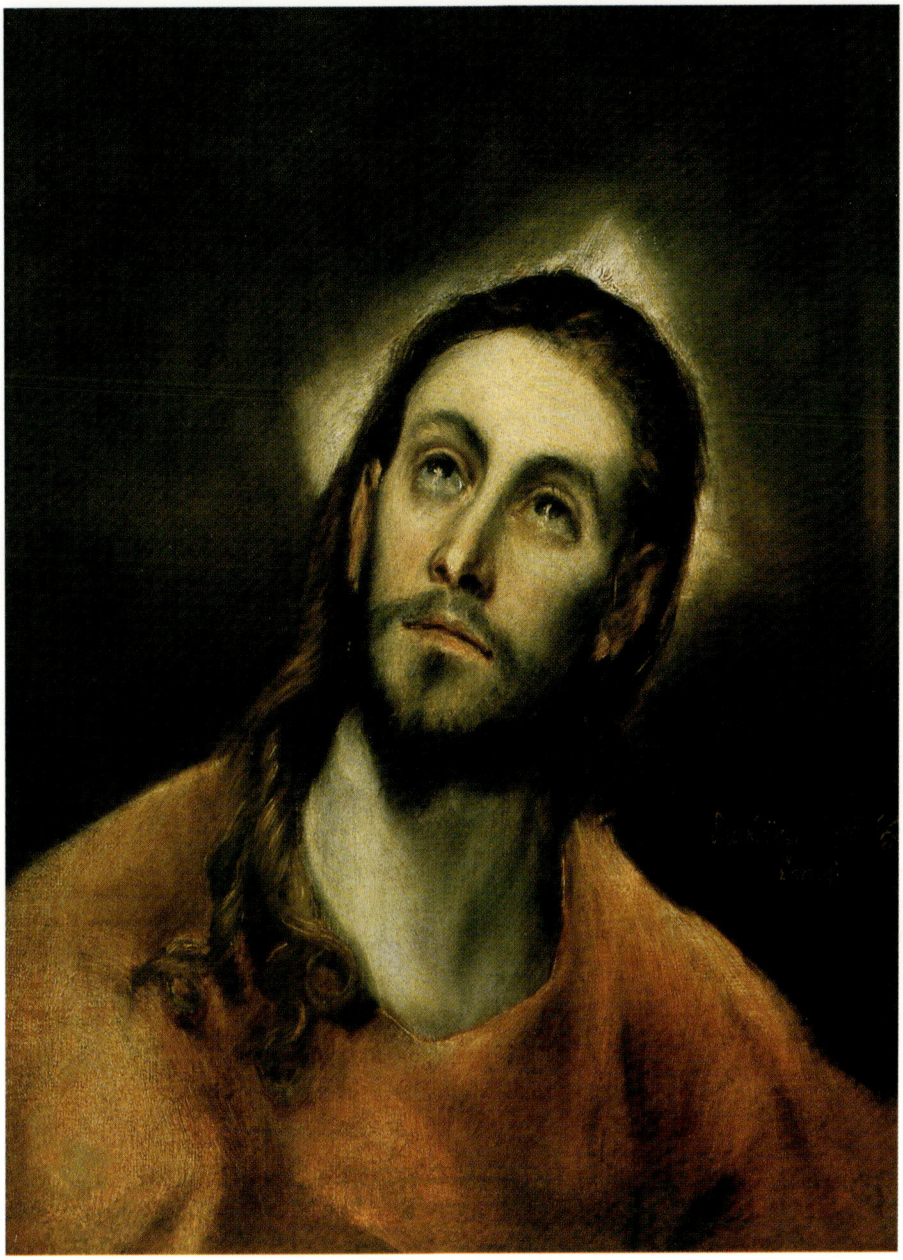

Jusepe de Ribera
1591 Játiva near Valencia - 1652 Naples

29 Saint Jerome

1646
Canvas. 146 × 198 cm
From 1736 in the Nostitz collection
Acquired in 1945.
Inv. nº DO 4374

The Spanish painter Jusepe de Ribera played an equally important role in the development of Spanish painting as in that of Naples, where he was a dominant figure from 1616 until his death. The eighteenth century biographer of the painter, Bernardo de Dominici, has this admiring description of one of Ribera's numerous representations of Saint Jerome, "the texture of the aged saint's body is admirably rendered, dried up with age, tortured by penitence and weakened by fasting, the skin clinging to the bones, creased in the body's folds, especially in the softer parts of the flanks". Dominici also appreciates "the book and the leaves covered with writing, and the death's head, so expressively painted that they seem real and not to come from a brush". The secret of this illusion of reality, which is accentuated by the caravaggesque chiaroscuro and the glow of the coloured surfaces, rests in the treatment of the paint, which trembles and is yet controlled by the brush so that the slightest detail is distinct, completed in subtle touches. The "inner" theme of this work centres on the intensity of the scholar's effort, overcoming old age and mortality.

Saint Jerome in his hermit's cave near Bethlehem is translating the Bible into Latin. Born between 340 and 345 as Eusebius Hieronymus Sophronius to a well-to-do Christian family in north Dalmatia, he was a disciple of the famous grammarian Donatus. Having decided to be baptized, he became a monk and travelled throughout the Christian world of his time. After a stay in Palestine he retired to the Syrian desert to do penance and lead the life of an anchorite. After being ordained he became advisor and secretary to Pope Damasius, and that is why he is often shown as a cardinal, which he never was, since the function of cardinal was not established until much later. He made a second journey to Palestine and worked until his death in 420 in Bethlehem, translating the Bible into Latin from the Greek Septuagint version and from Hebrew manuscripts of the Old Testament. His version, known as the Vulgate, was recognized by the Council of Trent as the official version of the Church and became the basis of church teaching for several centuries.

Saint Jerome defended his opinions vigorously and was an ardent polemicist against the opponents of church authority. A man of the spirit, he was no stranger to physical work, and as an example of a life of contrition and resistance to the temptations of the flesh he became a model for the new "Church combattant". He is traditionally represented with a lion which, according to legend, became his companion after the saint had removed a thorn from its paw. The animal symbolizes, among other things, the victorious strength and power of Christ, and in the composition acts as counterpart to the death's head, which is an attribute of north European origin and usually accompanies penitent hermits as a symbol of earthly vanity and a call to meditate on man's ultimate preoccupations.

L.D.

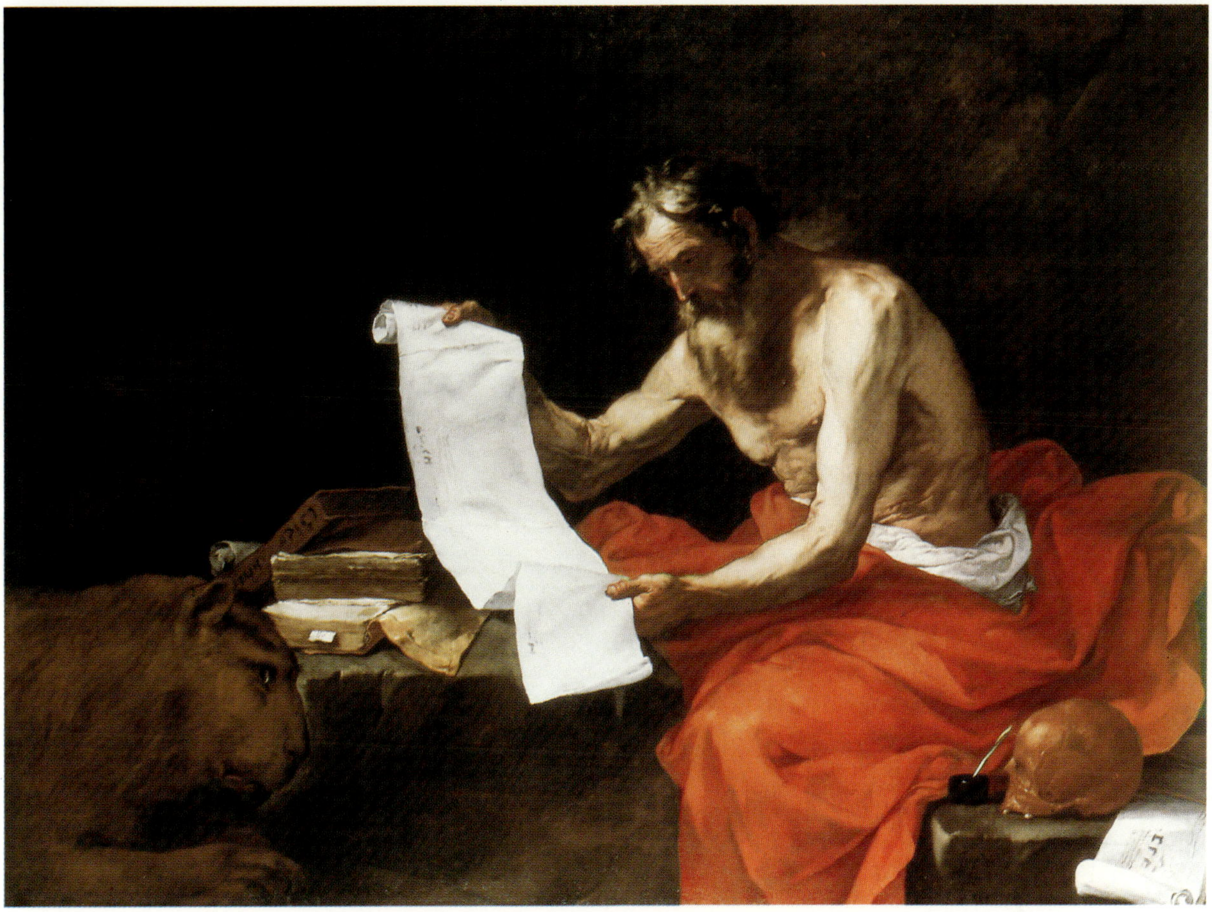

Francisco José Goya y Lucientes
1746 Fuendetodos - 1828 Bordeaux

30 Portrait of Don Miguel de Lardizábal

1815
Canvas. 86 × 65 cm
Between 1883 and 1884 the canvas was in the Ministry of the Navy in Madrid, then in the following collections: Manuel Victoria de Lecca y Parés, Madrid; Enrique O'Shea, Madrid, 1900; Galerie Miethke, Vienna, 1908; Arthur Maier, Karlovy Vary, 1932.
Acquired by the National Collection of Ancient Art in 1937.
Inv. n° O 1577

Don Miguel de Lardizábal (c. 1750-c. 1825) was a politician of Mexican origin and an adversary of the minister Godoy. He supported the claim of Joseph Bonaparte to the Spanish throne but was exiled from Spain soon after Joseph's accession. He shared his exile with Ferdinand II and became an ardent defender of absolutism. For this he was condemned to death *in absentia* by the Cortes in Cadiz. The words written on the letter, *Fluctibus Reipublicae expulsus*, alluding to his exile, became his motto when he became Minister for the Indies, after the return of the king to Madrid, from May 1814 until September 1815, when he again fell from grace.

The minister's calm, assured features are built up with fine touches in light tones that vibrate against the black ground, giving his head an almost sculptural appearance while preserving a life-like air and a natural flesh tint. The delicately modelled face, with the large eyes so typical of Goya, is in sharp contrast with the uniform, the sword hilt, and the hand holding the letter, which have been executed with masterly "negligence". Goya was experimenting with new techniques at this time and sometimes painted, for example, with a split reed. The contrast achieved through a two-fold handling of paint gives his work that fresh immediacy which was so much admired by modern painters.

L.D.

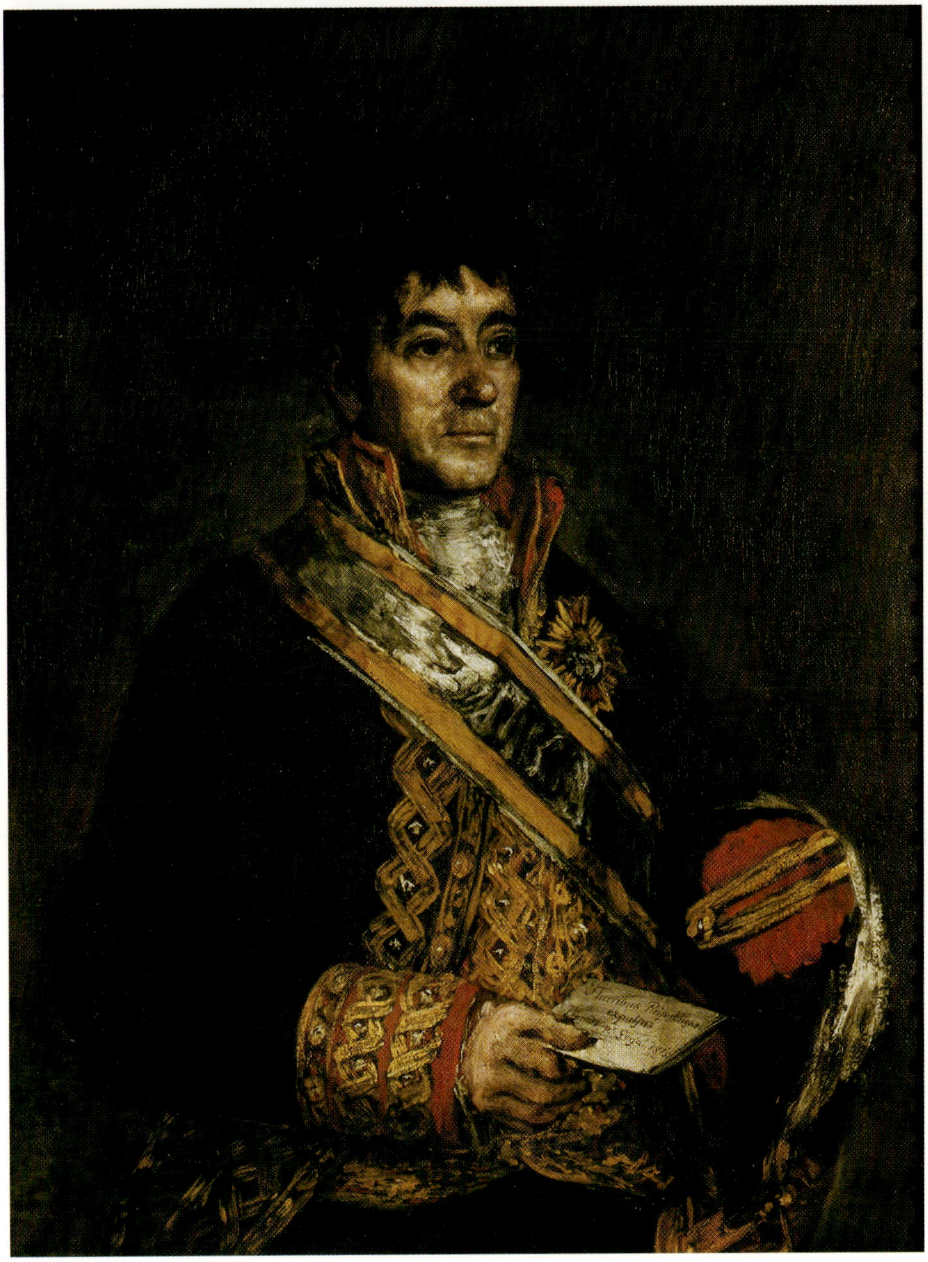

Simon Vouet
1590 Paris - 1649

31 The Suicide of Lucretia

circa 1625-1626
Canvas. 197 × 148 cm
This is probably the picture which was part of Cardinal Mazarin's collection in 1661. After being auctioned in 1918 in Vienna it came into the possession of Josef Váně, in Prague as the work of Guido Reni. It was bought from the heirs of Josef Váně for the Prague National Gallery in 1977.
Inv. nº O 14162

That this work was first attributed to Guido Reni, a mistake which was corrected by the discovery of Claude Mellan's engraving of Vouet's practically identical picture, throws light on the artist's orientation. One of Renis' numerous Lucretias, evidently the Potsdam version inspired this Vouet painting, behind which can be seen an example of Caravaggio and of the works of Artemisia Gentileschi that the latter inspired. The stylistic forerunner most closely related to the Prague *Suicide of Lucretia* is Vouet's *Temptation of Saint Francis* executed in 1624 for a chapel of the San Lorenzo in Lucina church in Rome. This has the figure of a courtesan dressed in furs which is analogous in conception to that of Lucretia, although charged with a different meaning. In the old medieval tradition, and even in modern times, Lucretia is the symbol of feminine virtue. Outraged by her own kinsman, Tarquin, the noble Roman lady chose to die by her own hand in defence of her honour. The model for this Lucretia was probably the Italian painter Virginia da Vezzo, whom Vouet married in Rome in 1626. It was during his stay in Rome that Vouet built his style on Italian principles, after being apprenticed in the style of French Mannerism. The only reminder of the artist's French origins is in the manner of the graceful hand gesture and in the elaborate décor of the scene. On his return to Paris in 1627 as "First Painter to the King", Louis XIII, Vouet inaugurates French classicism, which his disciples carry forward.

L.D.

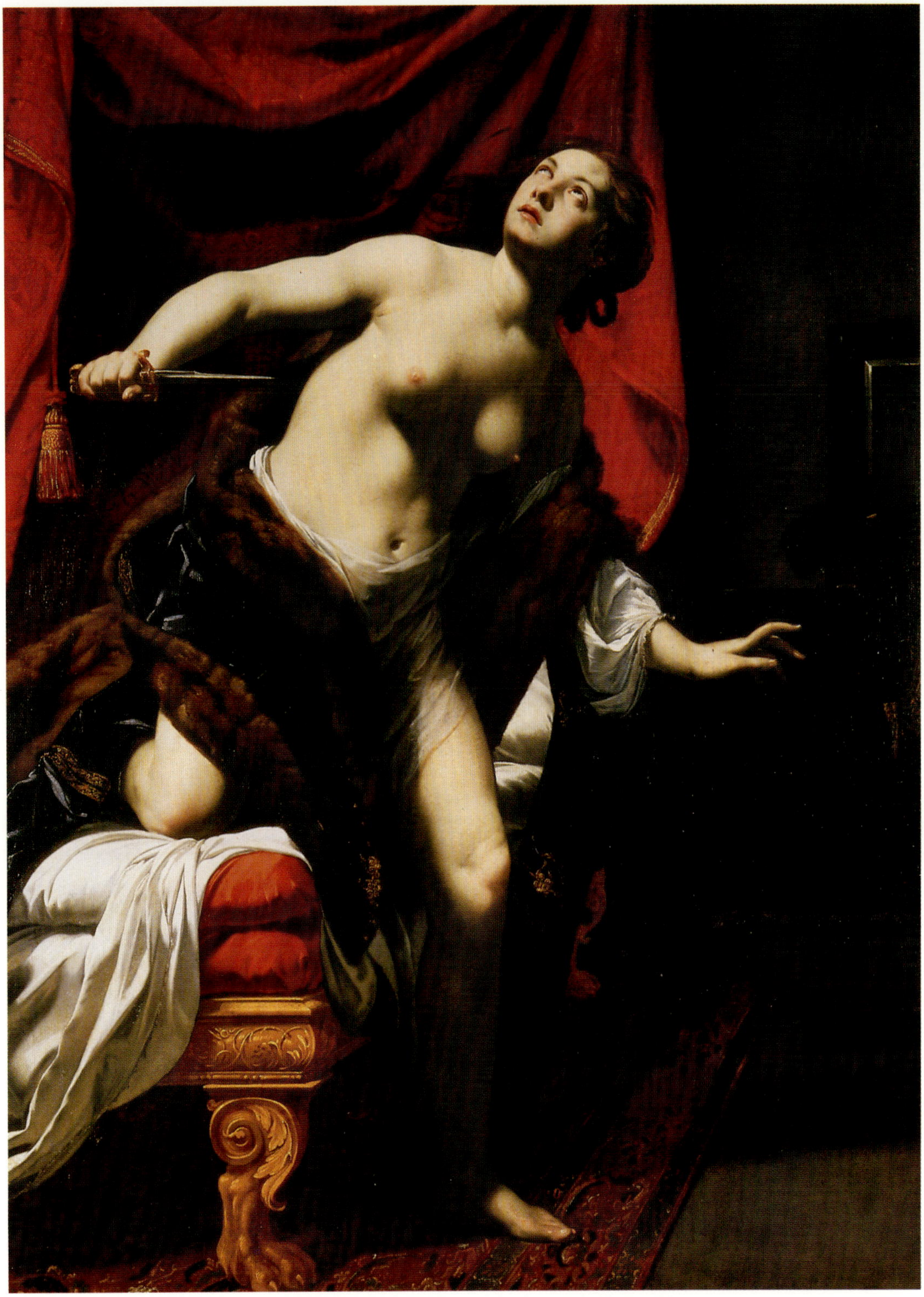

Sébastien Bourdon
1616 Montpellier - 1671 Paris

32 Antique landscape with bowmen

circa 1660-1665
Canvas. 97 × 120 cm
Acquired from a Dorotheum sale in Vienna for the Bělohříbek collection in Vinoř, near Prague, as a work by Poussin.
Acquired by the Prague National Gallery in 1946.
Inv. n° DO 4845

When in Rome as a youth, Sébastien Bourdon had become acquainted with the landscapes of Claude Lorrain and Castiglione, and had later followed Nicolas Poussin's work with great attention. The latter's "heroic landscapes" with their scenes inspired by the ancient world, had a deep influence on Bourdon's later works, which were designed according to an almost invisible geometric scheme in which a succession of horizontal planes creates the space. In this painting, as in others of the last decade of the painter's life, the vertical and horizontal lines intertwine like warp and woof. Trees and buildings are woven into the geometry of the painting, which shows, from the right, first a ship under sail, then a group of bowmen, an antique Herm as quintain and a family seated on the grass watching the exercise.

According to the apocryphal gospel recounting the childhood of Jesus the idols of the heathen were overthrown as the Holy Family passed by on their flight into Egypt. But the evocation of this text hardly makes satisfactory sense of these bowmen, this antique statue or this family at rest. Nor does the enigma of its meaning make up the sum of the painting's mystery, which lies in its internal constitution. This landscape is not laid out openly before our gaze as a stage-setting. The eye must find its way past the texture, through the successive shafts of light and areas of shade. In striving to attain a pictorial clarity we enter a poetic atmosphere, full of hints and expectancy. The human action portrayed acquires a symbolic sub-text, thus producing a fragile equilibrium between tension and calm.

L.D.

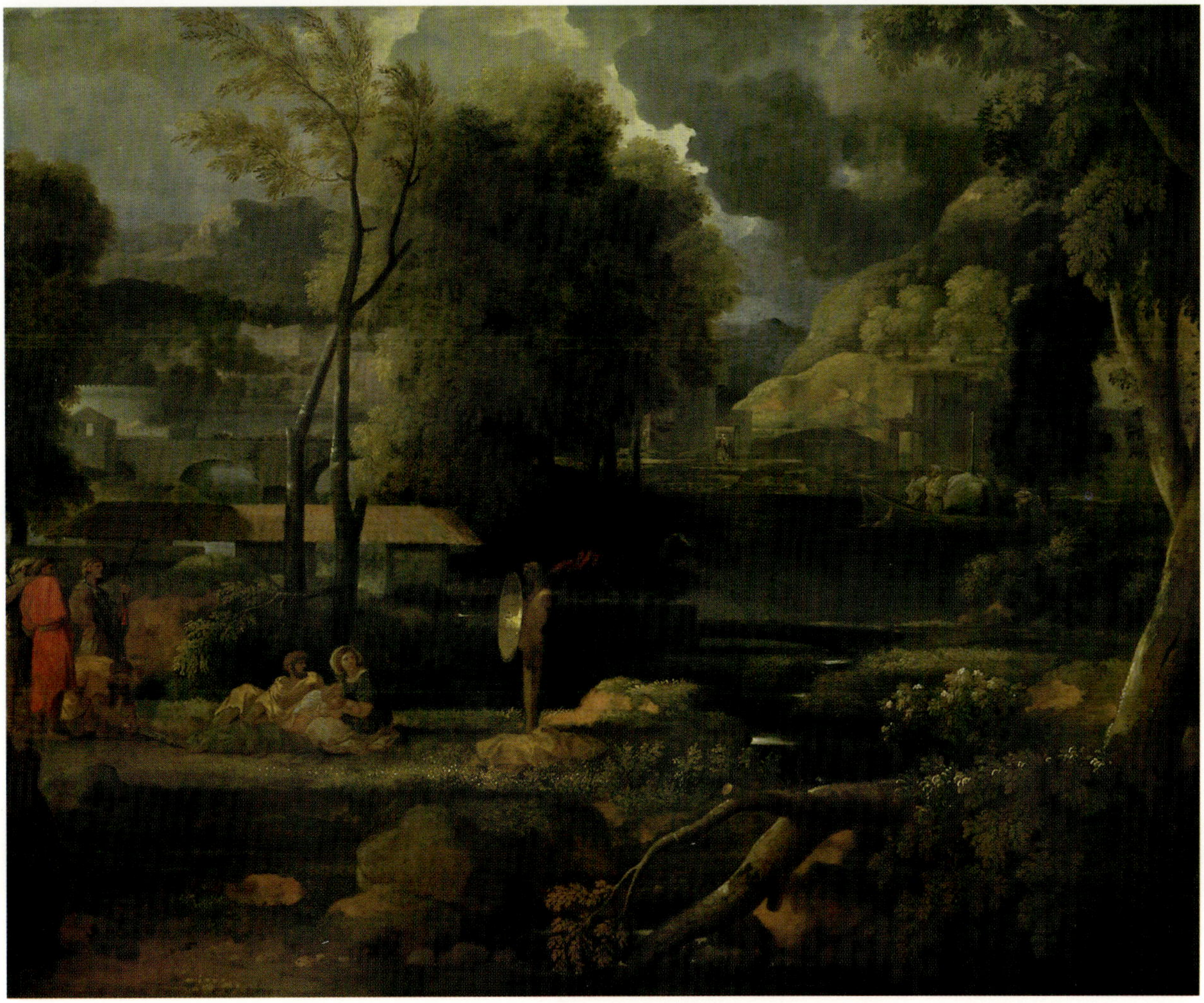

Charles Le Brun
1619 Paris - 1690 Paris

33 The Descent from the Cross

circa 1642-1646
Canvas. 78 × 60 cm
In 1803 on loan from the Sternberg collection to the Picture Gallery of the Society of Patriot Friends of the Arts by Countess Augusta Sternberg-Manderscheid. Bequeathed to Friedrich Wallis and acquired from his estate in 1882 by the Picture Gallery of the Society of Patriot Friends of the Arts.
Inv. n° O 56

Very few artists down the centuries have succeded in changing independently the traditional scenes of Christian iconography. In the case of Le Brun, we can see the frequently very complex pedigree of Christian paintings.

Michelangelo had earlier conceived of a new way of presenting the body of Christ, and his *Pietà* seems to be the first stage of a preparatory study which inspired a *Descent from the Cross* executed in 1541 by his pupil Daniele da Volterra in the Santa Trinità dei Monti church in Rome. This painting was the model for a work by Barocci for Perugia cathedral and for one by Rubens for Antwerp cathedral. Le Brun took over the central scene of Daniele's work during his stay in Rome from 1642 to 1646. The painting he made of the taking down of Christ's body is now lost, though three replicas are known, including the one presently in the Prague National Gallery. The Virgin half lying back is already known before Le Brun from the Barocci work previously mentioned and from Annibale Carracci's *Crucifixion* in Berlin. The theme can be seen in Tintoretto and later in Veronese. Le Brun certainly also knew Tintoretto's mounted centurion pointing to Christ, and the centurion in Veronese contemplating the suffering Virgin. Both Tintoretto, in his *Crucifixion* in the Scuola di San Rocco in Venice, and even more obviously Veronese, the source of Le Brun's inspiration, had borrowed the image of Mary Magdalene, the veiled and weeping figure, from Gian Girolamo Savoldo's.

It is the tragic dignity in the spirit of Poussin that gives Le Brun's portrayal of the scene the unity of a work which draws together motifs borrowed from the most significant creative talents of the preceding century in Italy. Tracing back these connections gives a better understanding of the sources and methods of French classicism. A pupil of Vouet and later "First Painter" to Louis XIV, Le Brun imposed, with the authority of the Academy, classicism as the dominant style of his time.

L.D.

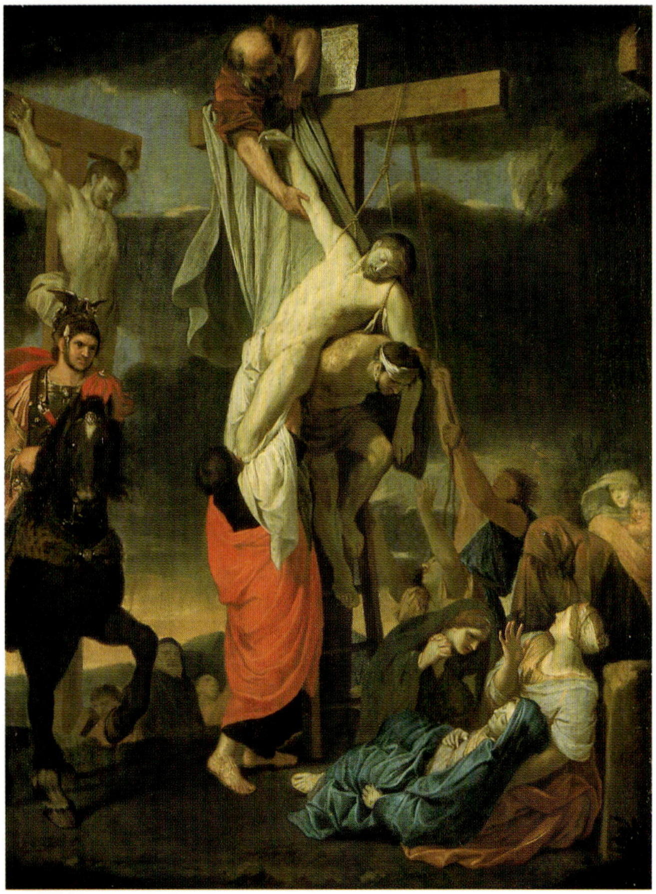

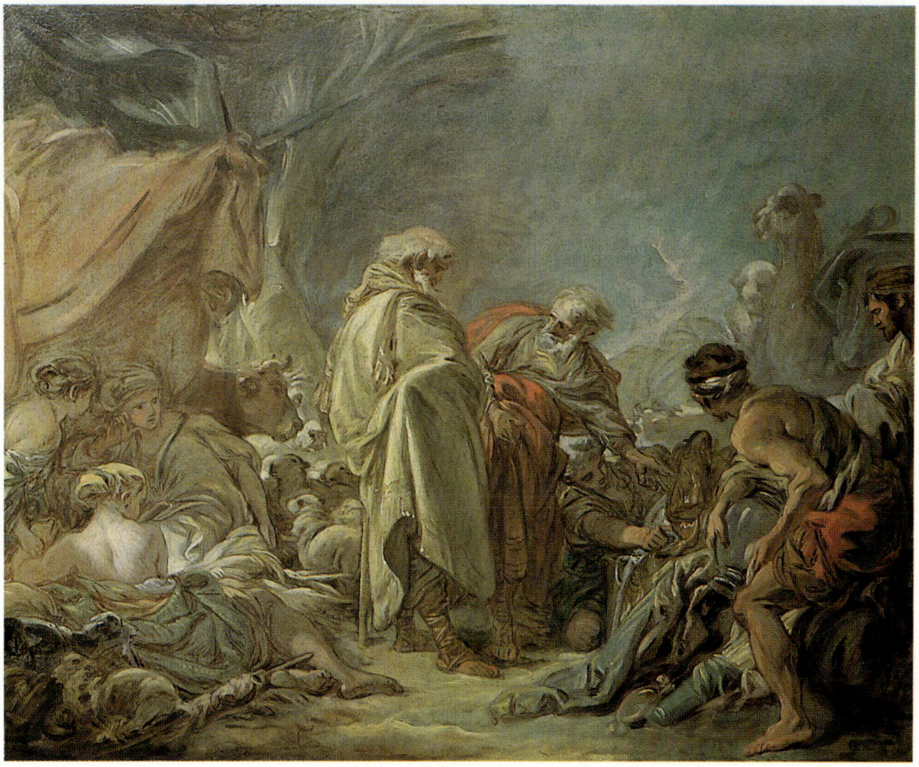

François Boucher
1703 Paris - 1770 Paris

34 Laban searching for his idols

Canvas. 60 × 73 cm
Belonged originally to the collection of Fragonard's friend Bergeret (according to a 1767 auction catalogue), later to the Nostitz collection. Acquired by the Prague National Gallery in 1945.
Inv. n° DO 4626

Having served his uncle Laban for many long years, Jacob flees with Lea and Rachel, daughters of Laban, and all his property. Laban comes in pursuit and demands the return of his household gods. They are not to be found in Jacob's tents. Rachel had stolen them without his knowledge and was hiding them under her, pretending to her father that she cannot rise because it is with her "as it is with women".

In his portrayal of this scene, with its telescoping of the action, Boucher proves that he is a master of the art of scenesetting. His technical skill in sketchy works with delicate contour lines was well suited to the taste prevailing among the collectors of his day. Its pastel shades mark this study off from the works Boucher took as his models: those of Rubens, Castiglione, Sebastiano Ricci, Tiepolo, Watteau. It was their sensibility and relaxed brushwork which he admired. Boucher painted with supreme ease, giving the charm and intimacy of his pastorals and genre scenes also to his mythological and biblical subjects. The grace and charm of his art, as well as its enchanting sensuality, exactly express the gallant life of the court of Louis XV.

L.D.

Painting of the fifteenth and sixteenth centuries in the Netherlands

Geertgen tot Sint Jans

1460/1465? Leyden? - 1490/1495 Haarlem

35 Triptych with Adoration of the Magi

Wood. Centre: 112 × 69.5 cm
Wings: 71 × 38.5 cm
Loaned from the collection of Prague Castle to the Picture Gallery of the Society of Patriot Friends of the Arts
Inv. n° DO 31, DO 14, DO 15

This artist, who in Dürer's words "was a painter before he was born", comes from the north of the Low Countries. After moving to Flanders, where he came to know the works of Rogier van der Weyden and Hugo van der Goes, he settled and worked in Haarlem, and it is there that fairly soon the life's pilgrimage of "little Gerard of Saint John" drew to its close.

This triptych, preserved in Prague, was probably executed in the closing years of the artist's life. His figures are no longer puppet-like, as in his youthful work, his style has matured and the spatial composition is more elaborate. The foreground plane is linked to the middle one by the retinue accompanying the three Magi, and the background has a complex landscape with a town surrounded by ramparts. The three parts of the triptych have been conceived as a whole, which makes it all the more regrettable that it should have been so recklessly mutilated when it was later divided up. That the right wing is continuous with the centre can be seen from the reflection of the main scene in the metal of Saint Adrian's armour and helmet. The reduced size of all the panels upsets the whole composition, since we are deprived of the figure of Saint Joseph, who stood next to the Virgin, and the side panels, showing Saints Adrian and Bavo and the donors, now lack their background landscape. The grisailles with the *Annunciation* on the reverse of the wings have also been damaged. Despite its ill-treatment this triptych is one of the most original creations of the art of the Netherlands. The Virgin's juvenile beauty, the gentle care of the kneeling Magus as he takes the Child's little hand, the horse drinking at the river, all these graceful touches infuse the scene with a warmth and tenderness which have never been equalled.

O.K.

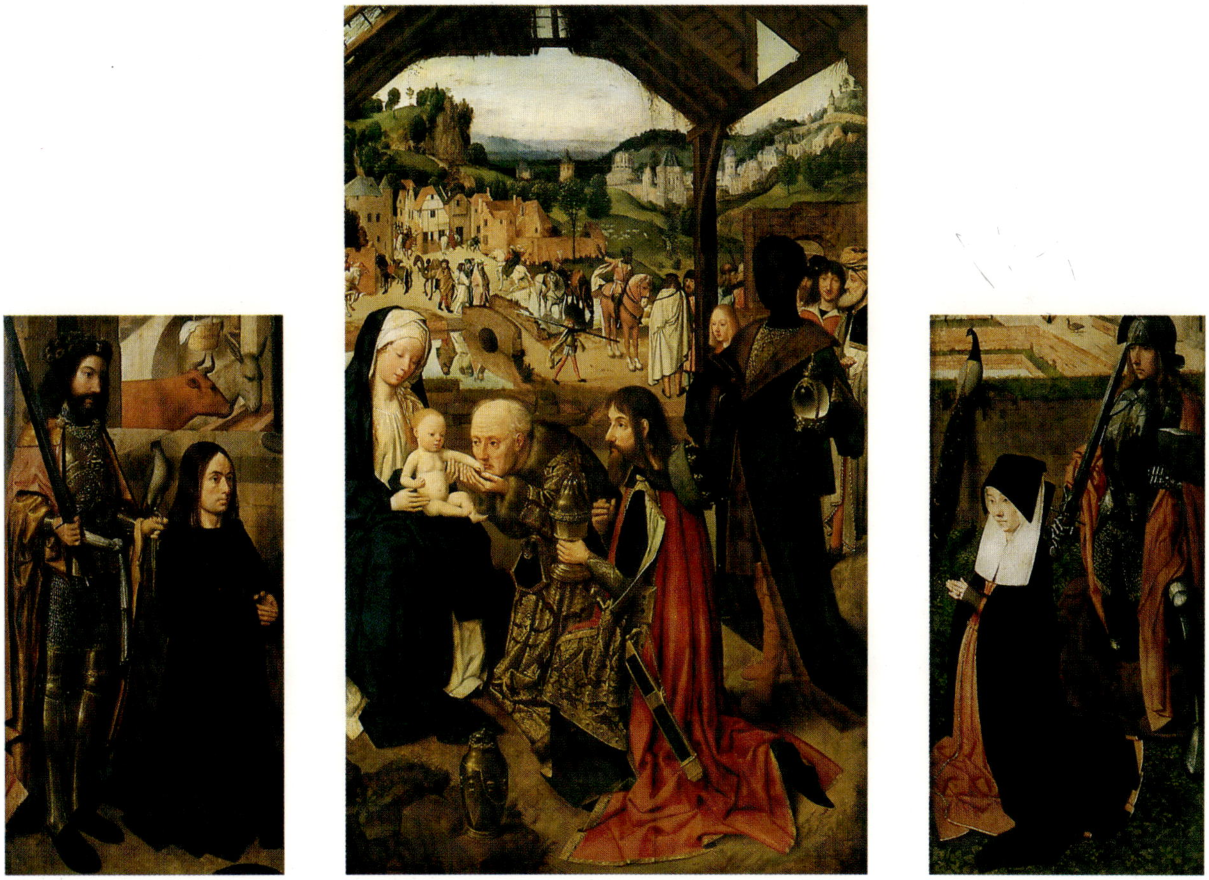

Master of the Fountain of Life

probably active at the beginning of C16 in Utrecht

36 The Fountain of Life

1511
Wood. 90.5 × 73.5 cm
Mentioned in the inventary of the Nostitz collection of 1819.
Acquired in 1945.
Inv. nº DO 4131

The work of an anonymous painter of the northern Netherlands, *The Fountain of Life* is strongly influenced by Jan van Eyck. Three other paintings are attributed to this artist, but it is this one in the Prague collection which gives him his title. Its frame carries representations of the instruments of Christ's passion and the figures taking part in that scene, and an inscription on the lower border indicates that this is a commemorative panel marking the death of Father Clemenssoen of Utrecht in 1511. It can be supposed that the painting dates from that same year. The influence of the *Adoration of the Lamb*, the central panel of the Ghent altar-piece by Jan and Hubert (?) van Eyck, is clear from the composition in three levels and also from the emphasis laid on the idea of the Eucharist, which is the common theme of both works.

The central position in this Calvary, in between the crosses of the two thieves, is taken up by the architecture of the fountain, which is topped by a small cross, the only allusion to the crucifixion of Jesus. The sufferings that Christ had to endure for the redemption of mankind were commonly represented in the Middle Ages by a wine-press, the blood issuing from his wounds being caught up by angels in chalices, which they then held out to the faithful in the hierarchical order of society, first to church dignitaries, then to the representatives of the temporal power, and lastly to the common people, at their head a blind man led by a child. In the *Sémur Passion Play* performed in Burgundy, the blind man recovers his sight after washing his eyes with the blood of Christ, reminding us of the story of the blind centurion who pierced Christ's side on Golgotha, and regained his sight when he touched his eyes with his blood-stained hand.

O.K.

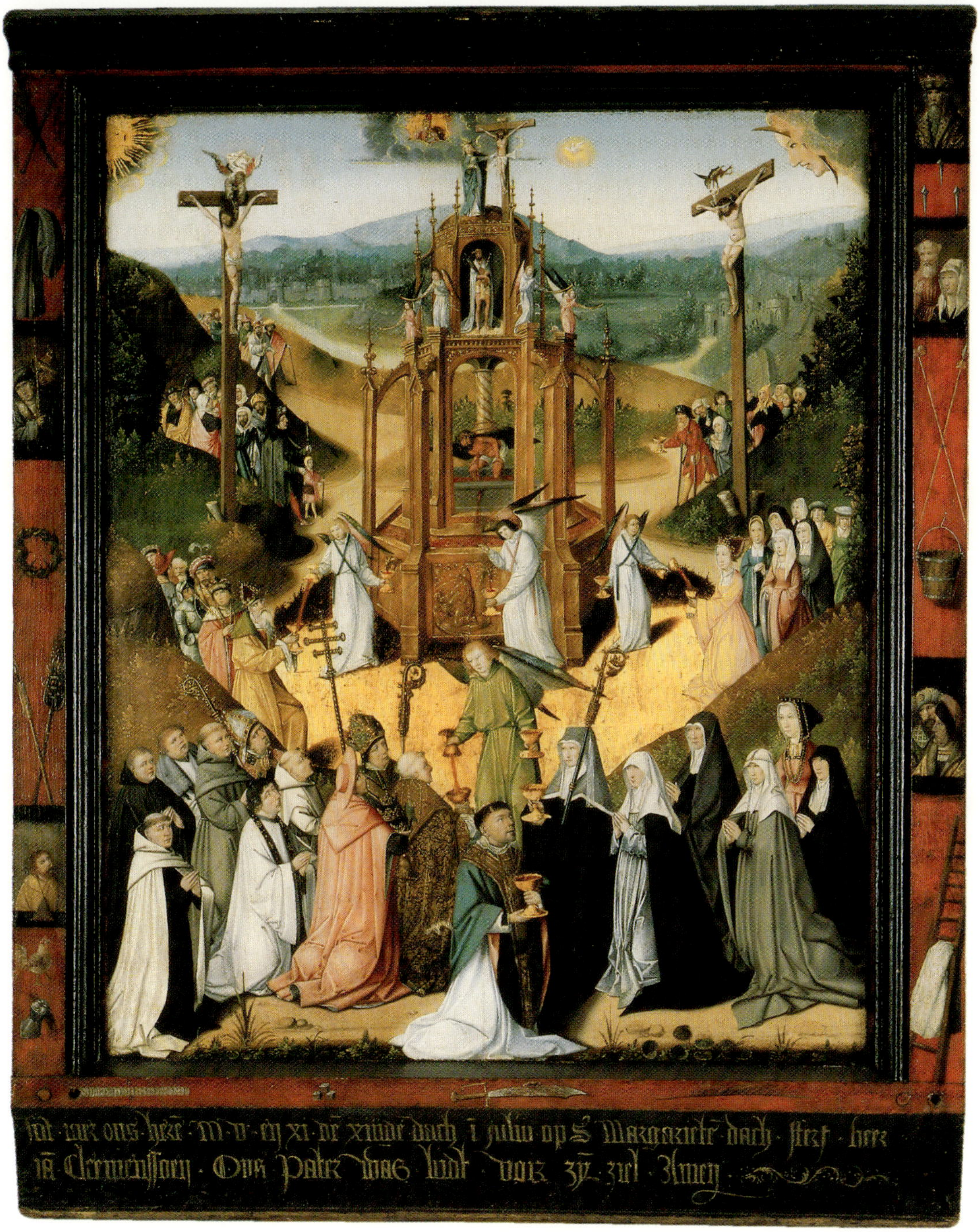
Int iaer ons heere · M · V · en XI · de xiiide dach i julio op S Margarieten dach · sterf · heer
Jan Clemeinssoen · Ons pater was bidt · voor zyn ziel · Amen

Jan Gossaert, known as Mabuse

circa 1478 Maubeuge - 1533/1536 Middelburg

37 Saint Luke painting the Virgin Mary

Wood. 230 × 205 cm
Loaned by the chapter of Saint Vitus in 1870
Inv. n° O 8765

This large-scale panel was originally in the chapel of the guild of painters in the church of Saint Rumbold in Mechelen. When the town was sacked in 1580 this exceptional work of art found its way to the house of Mathias of Habsburg, Governor of the Netherlands, who no doubt saved it from destruction. About this time Michiel van Coxie (1499-1592) painted the two side-panels and the assembled work was transported to Prague. After 1619 the three panels were set up on the high altar of Saint Vitus Cathedral, and in 1870 the chapter loaned them to the Pinakothek of the Society of Patriot Friends of the Arts.

The painters' guild, who commissioned the work, certainly influenced the choice of theme. According to legend Saint Luke painted the first portrait of the Virgin and so became patron of painters. The motif appears frequently in the iconography of the 15th and 16th centuries, and Gossaert could well have simply followed in the tradition of his predecessors. But he had been captivated by Renaissance art, whose charm he had discovered in Italy, being in fact one of the first of his countrymen to travel south of the Alps and to take inspiration from Italian humanism for his work.

The saint is shown as he is drawing the Madonna seated before him, but the artist also alludes to Luke's literary work by placing him in the background, writing the third gospel under the dictation of the Virgin. In his spatial composition Mabuse shows his mastery of perspective and his execution of the palace proves he had made a serious study of contemporary Italian buildings. A noteworthy detail is the placing of the artist's signature on Saint Luke's belt, thereby identifying himself with him in this hallmark of the self-confidence of Renaissance artists.

Nevertheless Gossaert remained essentially a man of the north. The way he combines Gothic and Renaissance morphology is entirely within the tradition of the Netherlands, and as with Jan van Eyck, by portraying different architectural styles varying historical periods can be symbolized. Gowns falling in heavy folds belong to the repertory of the Gothic masters. Gossaert succeeded however in creating a harmony of Renaissance and late Gothic elements, which gives the work preserved in Prague an equilibrium that places it among the artist's masterpieces. We do not know exactly when it was completed, perhaps around 1513. That year was a turning point in the evolution of painting in the Netherlands, marking the first decisive penetration of Italian esthetic into the Low Countries.

O.K.

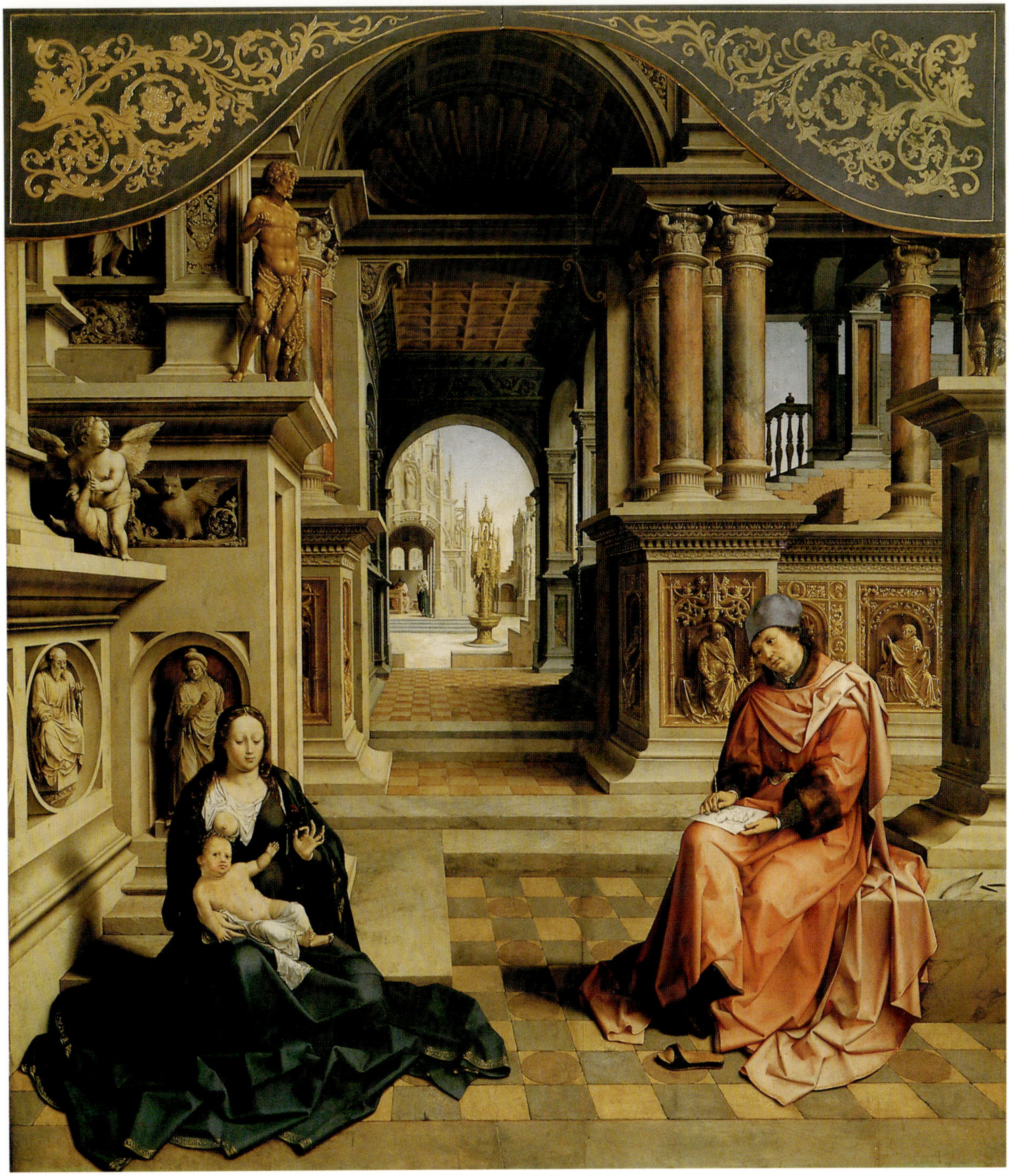

Joos van Cleve
circa 1464 Cleve (?) - 1540/1541 Antwerp

38 Triptych with Adoration of the Magi

Wood. Centre: 71.8 × 69 cm
Side panels: 70 × 31.5 cm
From the collection in Prague Castle; loaned in 1797 to the Picture Gallery of the Society of Patriot Friends of the Arts
Inv. n° DO 28, DO 27, DO 37

The central panel represents the *Adoration of the Magi*, the left-hand one has Saint Jerome, the donor and his sons, while on the right is Saint Lucy, the donor's wife and his daughters. What we have here is a rather traditional work in which many aspects hark back to earlier painting in the Netherlands. However, by placing the scene in a Renaissance palace the artist shows that he is familiar with Italian painting of his day.

The three Magi — Gaspar the European, Melchior the Asiatic and Balthazar the African — have come to pay hommage to Jesus, each bringing a present. They represent the Christians of the whole world, the three continents known to the Middle Ages, signifying that faith in Jesus Christ is now world-wide. But in the foreground the artist has emphasized an additional element, a broken antique column. This feature is to be seen also in the works of earlier painters, as well as in other paintings by Van Cleve. Its presence is not without significance, since Netherlands painters of the period saw in realistically rendered objects a rich means of symbolic expression. An antique ruin, according to the ideas of "disguised symbolism" was a reference to the passing away of the pagan world, whose end is announced by the coming of Jesus, personification of nascent christianity.

O.K.

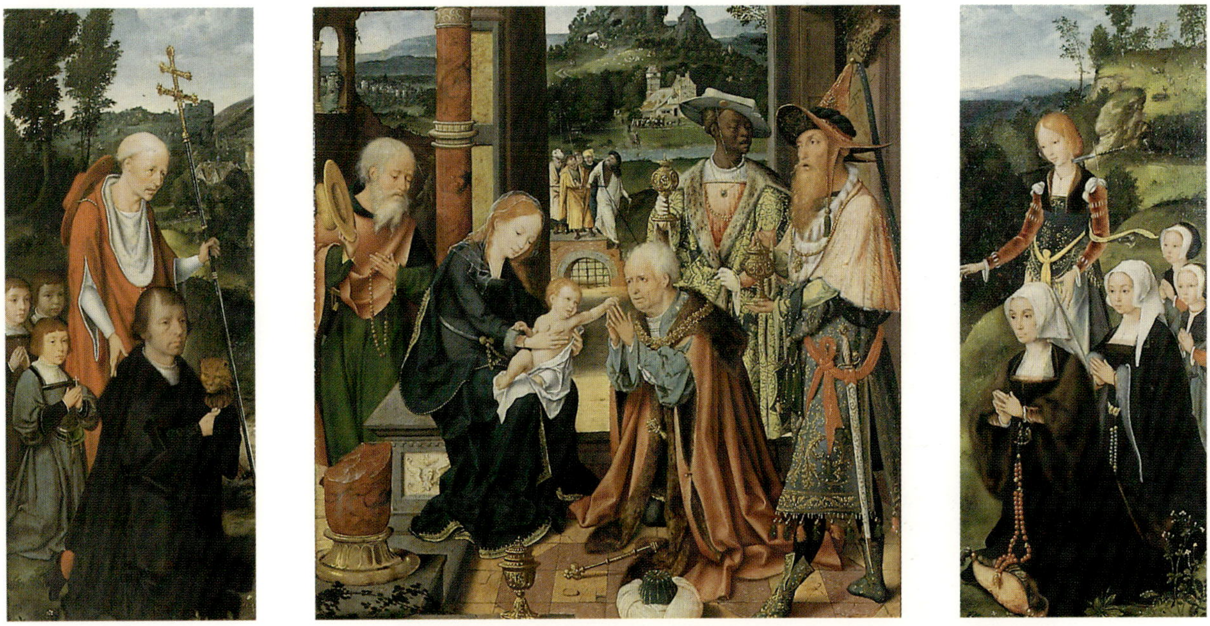

Master of the Legend of the Magdalena

Active between 1480 and 1490 probably in Brussels - died circa 1530

39 Portrait of an elderly man with a ruler

Wood. 43.5 × 31 cm
Acquired in 1945 from the Nostitz collection, which mentions it in the 1819 inventory.
Inv. n° DO 4170

The portrait artists of the Netherlands were already famous in the fifteenth century for their skill in catching their model's characteristics — appearance, social standing, personality. Their art required an acute observation of reality together with a taste for detail. Among the most important portraitists of that century we should mention Jan van Eyck and Rogier van der Weyden, the latter being a source of inspiration for the Master of the Magdalena Legend. Although his name is unknown we know that he worked for the Brussels court and executed several portraits of important official persons.

The portrait preserved in Prague shows an elderly man, grave of countenance, in ordinary burgher's costume. The ruler he is holding suggests he is an architect or builder, and the set-square in the background, near a tree-felling scene, confirms this supposition. But we should not exclude other symbolic meanings to these two objects or to the trees that are being felled. What these might be escapes us, as does also the exact personality of the model.

O.K.

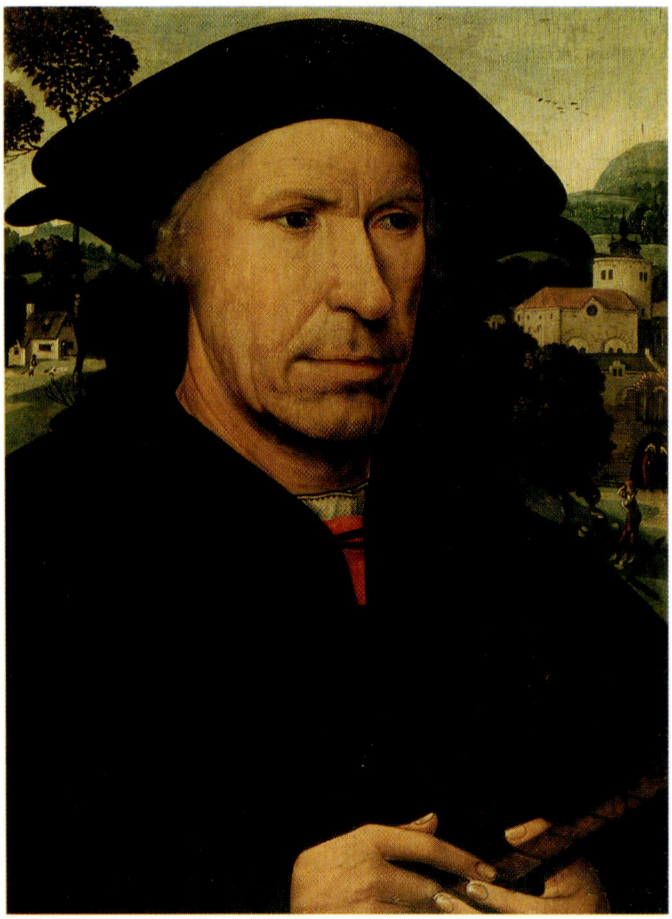

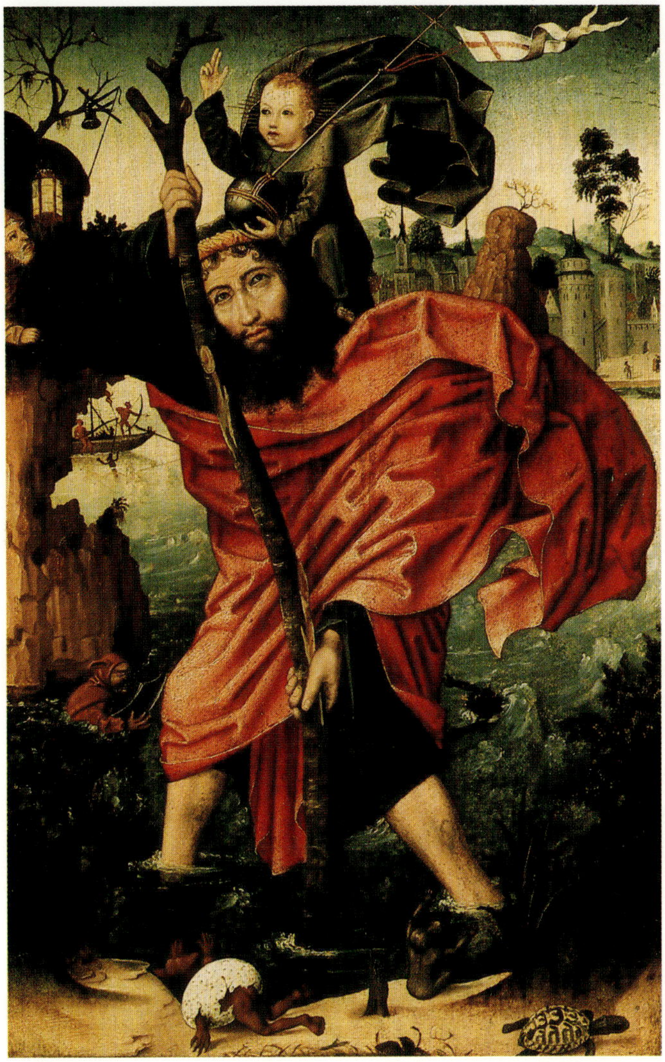

Master of Frankfurt
1460 Antwerp - 1533 Antwerp
Master of Frankfurt-follower

40 Saint Christopher

Wood. 84 × 55 cm
Acquired from a private collection in 1947
Inv. nº O 2684

The author of this Saint Christopher is one of the followers of the Master of Frankfurt, active in Antwerp around 1493-1520. He is so named from two altars which he painted for churches in Frankfurt.

According to legend Saint Christopher, the Christian giant, helped travellers across dangerous rivers. He was a favourite object of devotion in the 15th and 16th centuries, a period which has left us numerous paintings representing this saint.

The artist of this Prague Saint Christopher adheres to the usual iconography founded on the text of the *Legenda aurea*, well known to the Middle Ages, whose author, says tradition, was a Dominican monk, Jacobo Voragine, from the vicinity of Genoa. This text dates from circa 1260 and tells the lives of many saints, including Saint Christopher. It relates how the Child Jesus asked the saint to help him over a river and was carried across on the giant's shoulders. A hermit guides them with his lantern. He may have symbolic meaning, since it is he who charged Christopher to help travellers. The dangers facing the giant and child are evoked by the churned up waters of the swollen river and its monsters, which recall those of Bosch's paintings. This is probably why the late 19th century attributed this work to him.

O.K.

Jan Swart van Groningen

circa 1500 Groningen - after 1553 (?)

41 # Triumph of Death

Wood. 33 × 54 cm
Acquired from the collection of Václav Butta in 1959
Inv. n° O 7922

This artist, named by Karel van Mander "The Master of Frisia", owes his reputation above all to his wood engravings and to his designs in various branches of the applied arts. In his paintings he modelled himself on the Venetian masters and on contemporary north European artists (for example he was strongly influenced by the landscape artist Joachim Patinier, a few years his senior), as well as German master engravers.

The *Triumph of Death* panel preserved in Prague presents a subject which is both poignant and central to the middle ages, a time of great plagues, wars and peasant rebellions, which sufficiently explains the numerous representations of death which we find in the plastic arts of the period. We need hardly mention the fresco of the *Triumph of Death* at Campo Santo in Pisa or the terrifying scene of this name by Peter Bruegel the Elder (Prado, Madrid). Death mows down, without distinction of status, age or sex, every living thing - the theme was common at the time of the German Reformation, as we can see from the engravings of Albrecht Dürer or Hans Holbein.

Van Groningen heightens the drama of his scene by placing it amid a merry-making company given over to carefree indulgence in this world's delights, while a young girl tries desperately to escape the pitiless arrow of Death. The inherent contradiction of the scene recalls the words inscribed on Albrecht Dürer's engraving of a similar subject: "so much happens in the course of a man's life, but the end comes upon him all too soon."

O.K.

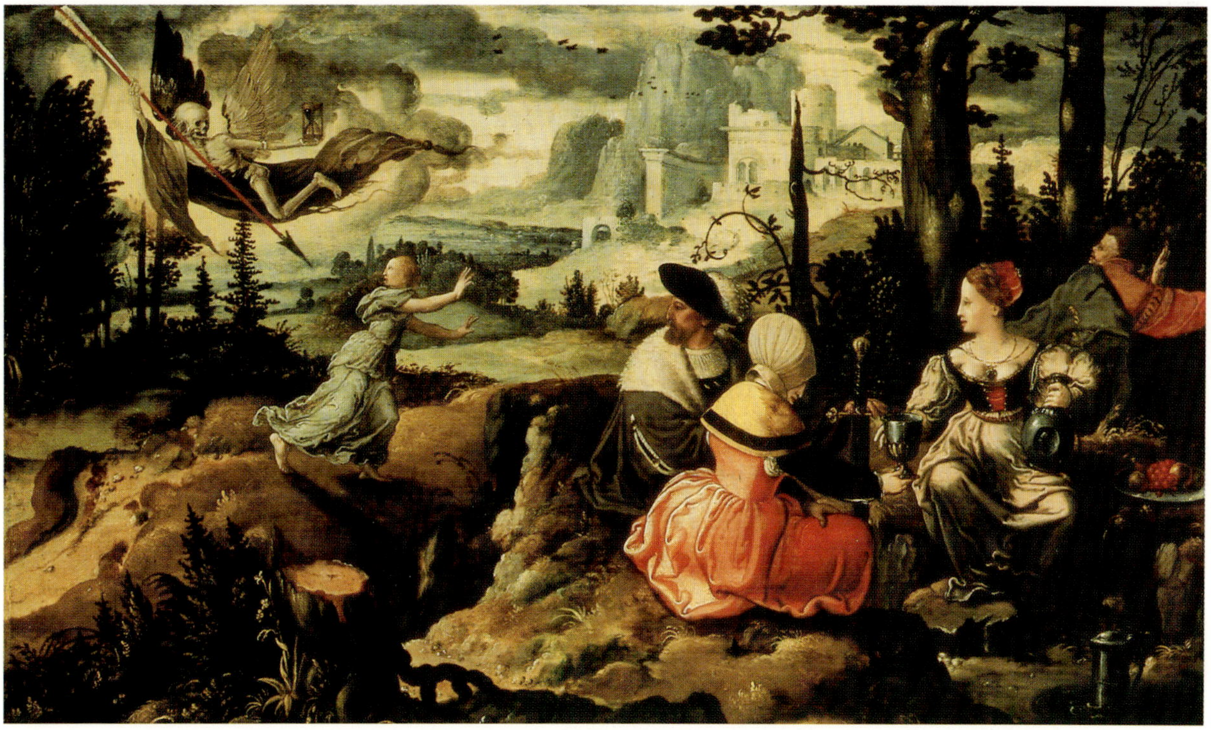

Jan Sanders van Hemessen

circa 1500 Hemiksen near Antwerp - 1563 Haarlem

42 # The Weeping Bride

1540?
Wood. 52 × 63 cm
Acquired from the Sanct Lucas gallery in Vienna in 1937
Inv. n° O 1576

Several titles have been allotted to this painting by Van Hemessen in the course of the 20th century, the most recent being *Old Woman inebriated.* Hesitation about a title shows how difficult it often is to grasp the painter's intention. However recent comparison with literary works of the period and with paintings of contemporary artists (for example Maerten van Cleve or a follower of Jan Massys) has made it clear that the theme in question here is that of the *Weeping Bride.* Although largely forgotten nowadays, it was familiar to Netherlanders of the 16th and 17th centuries and several times rendered by their painters and engravers during those centuries, often accompanied by a short text explaining the significance of the scene. Typically, a very plain girl with a coronet of flowers on her brow, weeps bitterly, while her mother and fiancé try to calm her. Usually the bride, fearful of the wedding night, puts a candle and a chamber pot next to her bed. These two indispensable accessories of the matrimonial bedchamber are often met in Dutch genre painting of the 17th century. They symbolize the life of the married woman, no longer innocent.

This is probably the scene which Van Hemessen's painting portrays, although the bride here is far from young. The artist's treatment of his figures is close to caricature, recalling some of Leonardo da Vinci's drawings, and his merciless realism only adds to the ugliness of the old woman, not that her partner fares any better, as far as looks go. On the left a young man of resplendent beauty is offering the bride a receptacle which could be a pitcher, ancient symbol of innocence. But in this case it is more likely a chamber pot, with rather different symbolic value. If they were old and ugly, lovers were the laughing stock of the people of the time, who treated them with undisguised contempt. Yet they too are worthy of love for, as the poetess of the Netherlands Anna Bijns (1493-1575) teaches us, even the ugliest among us can be lucky and find a partner: "Gheen zoo slimmen scheelken, ten vindt zijnen pot"; which means "no lid is so bent there's no pot to fit it". Folk tradition can also interpret the coronet of cherries the old woman is wearing on her brow: ripe cherries often figure in folk songs as an allegory of beauty, so their presence here adorning an ill-featured bride adds insult to the injury Nature has done her, thereby accentuating the satirical stamp of this work.

O.K.

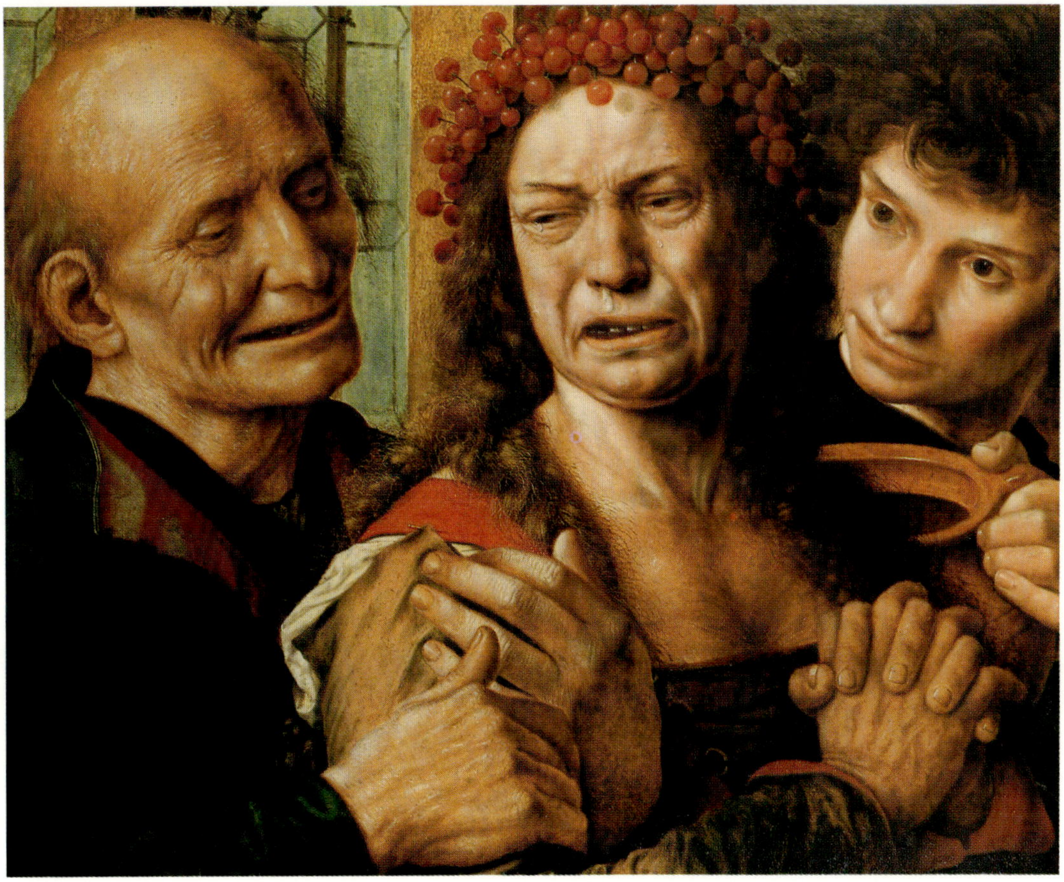

Pieter Bruegel the Elder

between 1525 and 1530 Bruegel near Breda? - 1569 Brussels

43 # Haymaking

1565
Wood. 117 × 161 cm
Loaned from the Lobkowicz collection in Roudnice in 1946
Inv. n° VO 1172 (0 9299)

The series of *Months* which includes *Haymaking* was probably painted by Bruegel the Elder within one year. It was commissioned by the Antwerp merchant Nicolas Jongelinck, an enlightened humanist. In addition to the panel which is now in Prague four others of the series have been preserved: *Gloomy Day, Return of the Herd* and *Hunters in the Snow,* all in the Vienna Kunsthistorisches Museum, and *Harvest,* which is in the New York Metropolitan Museum. It is not known whether the original series consisted of twelve or only six paintings, to correspond with the former division of the year into six periods. In that case *Haymaking,* which tradition relates to the month of July, would represent the beginning of summer. But although the archives for the year 1566 are no help in determining how many paintings belong to this series, they do trace the history of Bruegel's *Months.* In 1594 the six paintings were in the possession of Archduke Arnold, Spanish Governor of the Low Countries. From 1659 to 1809 five of them are listed in the inventory of the collection of Archduke Leopold-William in Vienna. Then *Haymaking* turns up in the collection of Leopoldine Grassalkowich, née Esterhazy, and then in the Lobkowicz collection in Roudnice.

The work associated with each of the changing seasons of the year was a common theme in the *Books of Hours,* which were so numerous in the fifteenth century. The artists of the illuminated manuscripts of the middle ages treated the landscape as a mere background to man's activity, whereas with Bruegel the Elder nature and its seasonal variations become the source and power determining all human action.

Central to the *Haymaking* is a summer landscape bathed in sunshine, seen from afar and high up. With his clear, vivid greens and his sombre blues Bruegel catches the atmosphere of a warm, soft day. Intent on his harvest, man's role in nature is important but not predominant. This picture, probably the first of the series, shows Bruegel the Elder still conforming to the traditional representation of the world: he plays out his scene in a landscape containing an entire world. Right down to the middle of the sixteenth century landscapes can be found which contain, in one and the same painting, towns, fields, woodland and even, in the background, the sea. German has coined the term "Weltlandschaft" to designate this manner of composing an unreal landscape. Later works of the 1565 series of *Months* reveal that the artist, influenced perhaps by his humanist and cartographer friend Abraham Orteli, gradually abandoned this conception and aimed to represent the real world, and the changes it undergoes in the course of the year.

O.K.

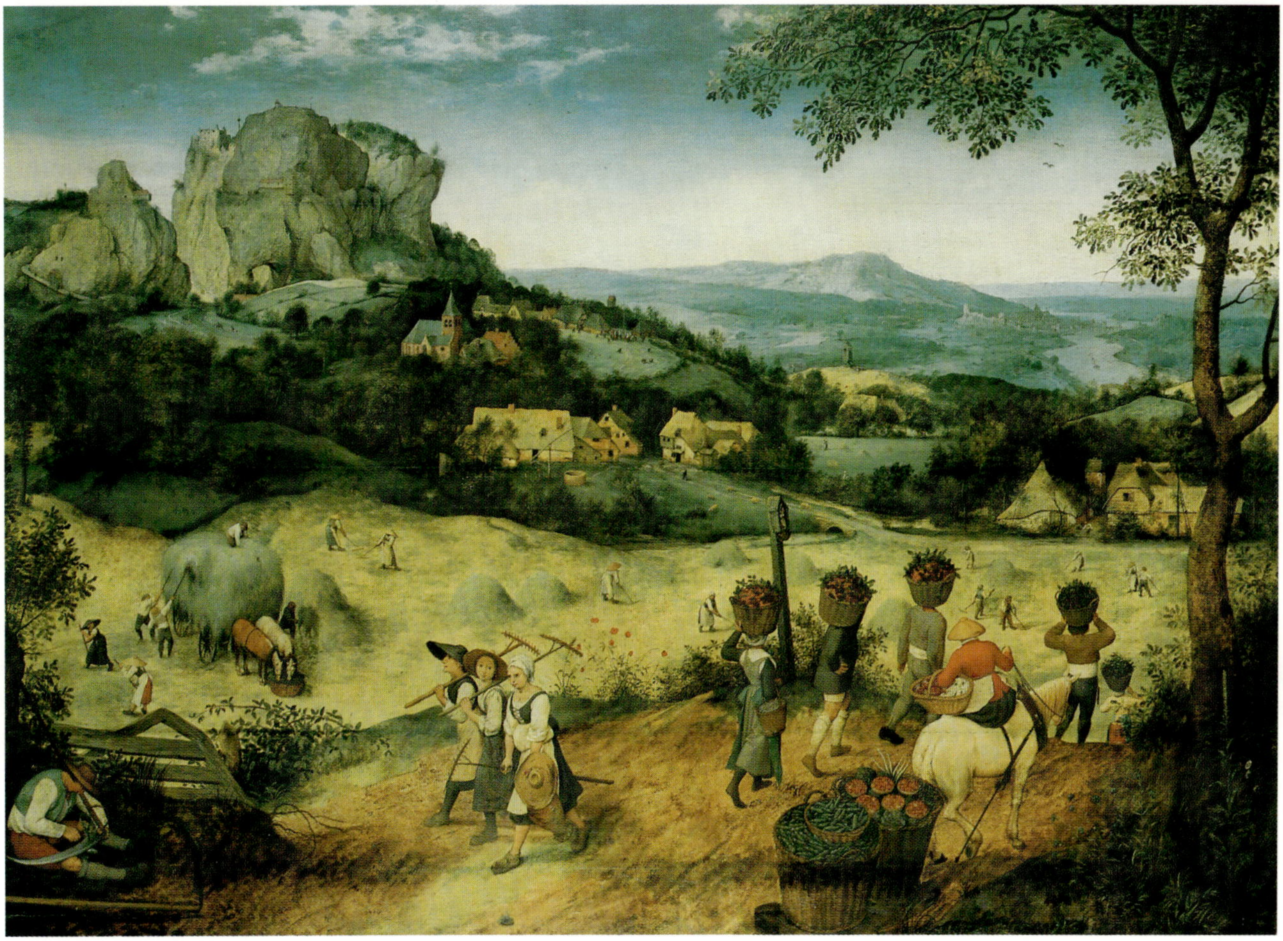

Gillis Mostaert
1534 Hulst - 1598 Antwerp

44 Town Market

1579
Wood. 41 × 68.5 cm
Acquired in 1945 from the Nostitz collection, where it is mentioned in 1765.
Inv. n° DO 4237

This painting presents a typical Flemish town with its bustling market, set in a panoramic landscape. There are scores of persons busy at their trade, or at games, or in animated discussion with passers-by. The painter's feeling for all this agitation reminds one of Bruegel the Elder's *Children's Games* (Vienna, Kunsthistorisches Museum), which also gives him the wide-open street diminishing into the distance. But unlike the elder Bruegel and the painters who followed his example, Mostaert gives his figures elongated, elegant postures, in accord with the then fashionable *maniera italiana* which Frans Floris among others had introduced to Antwerp. Mostaert's Italianate figures suited the Netherlandish taste of the time, witness the fact that he sometimes added "extras" to other painters' landscapes, Jacob Grimmer's for example. Grimmer and Mostaert are much alike in style, which has led more than once to mistaken attribution. Although *Town Market* carries Mostaert's name as author on the back, it has sometimes been attributed to Grimmer.

O.K.

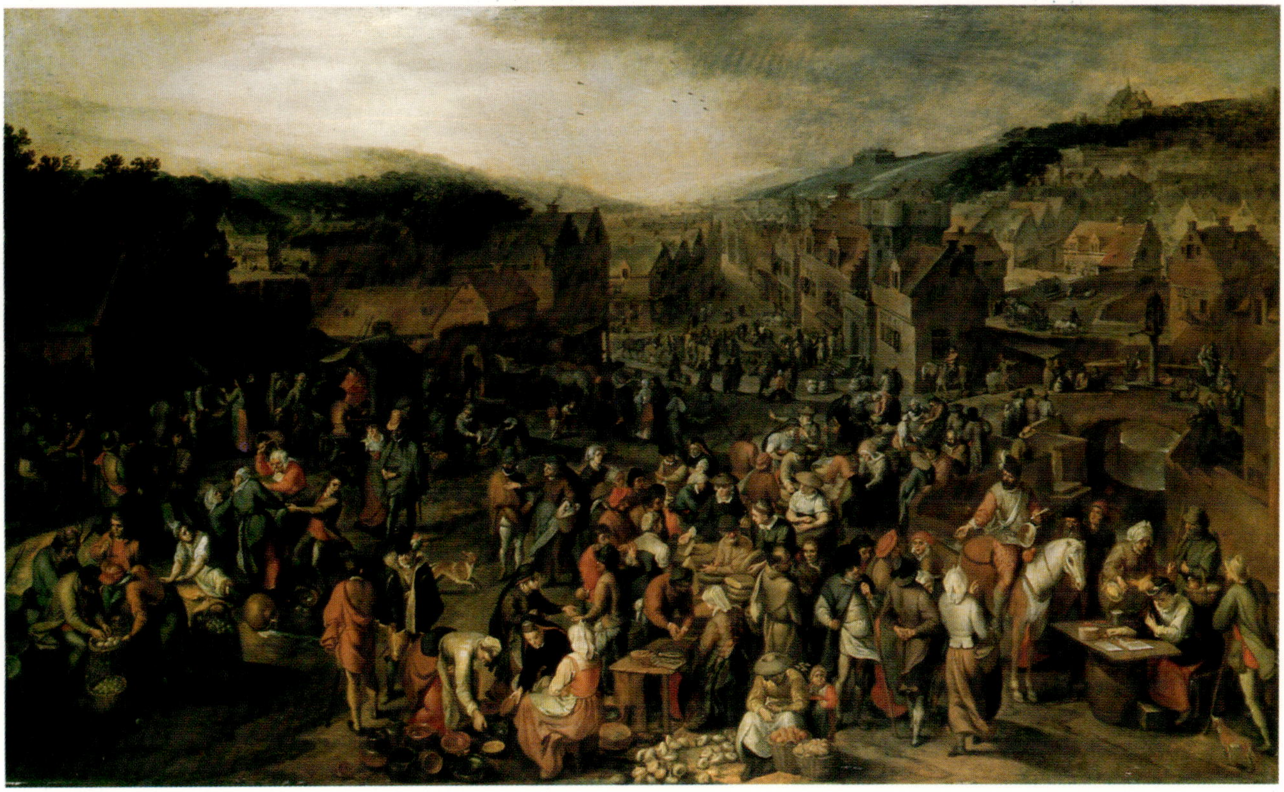

Seventeenth century Flemish painting

Pieter II Brueghel

1564 or 1565 Brussels - 1638 Antwerp

45 Spring, Brook, River, River-mouth

Oak. Diameter 16.5 cm
On loan from the Valdštejn collection to the Picture Gallery of the Society of Patriot Friends of the Arts from 1821 to 1885
Acquired in 1885.
Inv. n° O 77, O 78, O 79, O 80

Netherlandish landscape artists of the second half of the 16th and early 17th centuries frequently painted landscapes changing with the seasons, and were influenced in particular by Pieter Brueghel the Elder's series of *Months*, which enjoyed a great reputation (see cat. n° 43). These pictures were often formed into cycles. These four works by Brueghel preserved in the National Gallery in Prague are an example of the genre. Until the late 19th century they were held to be the work of his father, Pieter Brueghel the Elder. The son often executed replicas, at times with variants, of his father's most famous works. With these four round panels the artist has caught four transformations of a current of water, from its source amid rocks down to the outflow in to the sea. It is more than likely that these paintings showing successive stages of a river, like the landscapes portraying the changing seasons, have a deeper meaning, that they are an allegory or a metaphor of the life-cycle.

When examined as a whole, these four panels, certainly among the best of this painter's abundant output, reveal a striking lack of stylistic unity. Whereas the *Brook* and the *River-mouth* have indubitably been painted from personal observation of nature, the *Spring* and the *River* take over and make use of landscape formulas which are conventional with Pieter Bruegel the Elder. These sheer jagged rocks, the castle perched high above a river are motifs often found in the drawings of Pieter Bruegel the Elder around 1560.

L.S.

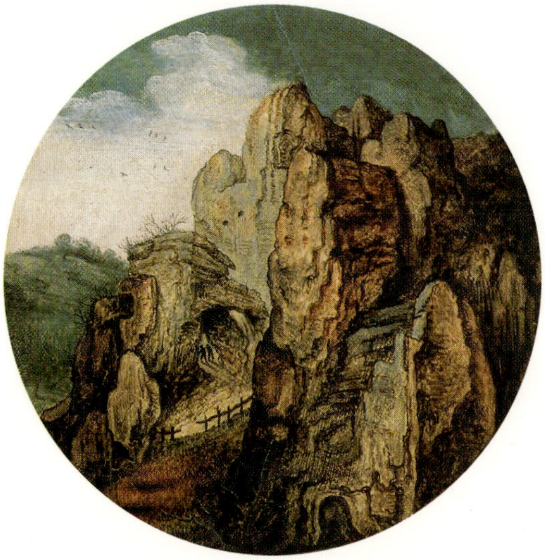
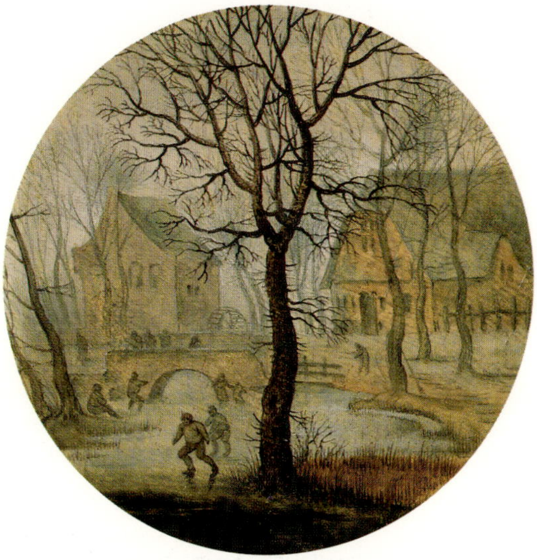
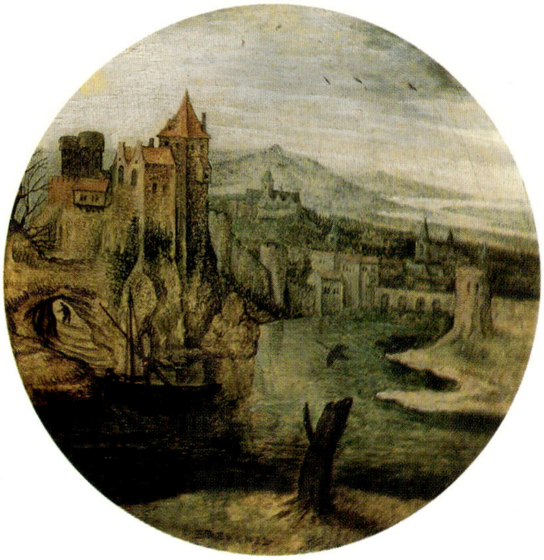
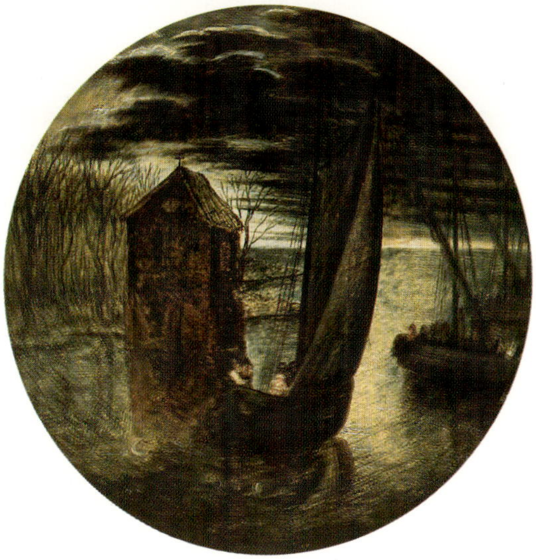

Jan I Brueghel
1568 Brussels - 1625 Antwerp

46 Landscape with Diana and Acteon

between 1606 and 1609
Oak. 51 × 89.5 cm
Acquired from the Nostitz collection in Prague in 1945.
Inv. nº DO 4130

This painting results from the collaboration of two outstanding representatives of Flemish cabinet painting: Jan I Brueghel, the author of the landscape and Hendrick de Clerck, who peopled it with figures in accordance with the canons and colour schemes of mannerism. The work preserved in Prague is one of the lesser known examples of the creative cooperation of these artists between 1606 and 1609, when they were working for the court of the governors of the Netherlands in Brussels.

This very fine landscape is executed with all the precision of a miniature, while presenting us with a view which opens out into the distance. To the left there is a mythological scene taking place in a deep forest. In the legend, as retold by Ovid, Diana with her retinue is discovered bathing by the huntsman Acteon, who is therefore chastized by being turned into a stag (*Metamorphoses* 3, 138-253). The view towards the right opens out onto a broad valley. The lay-out of coulours conforms to the tradition of the day: the three planes of the picture are distinguished by colour — brown for the foreground, green for the middle ground and blue for the background. A similar relationship between a dominant landscape and a narrative scene of secondary importance is to be seen in other paintings which are the fruit of collaboration between Hendrick de Clerck and another Flemish landscape artist, Denys van Alsloot (see for example their *Landscape with Cephalos and Procris*, circa 1608, National Gallery in Prague).

L.S.

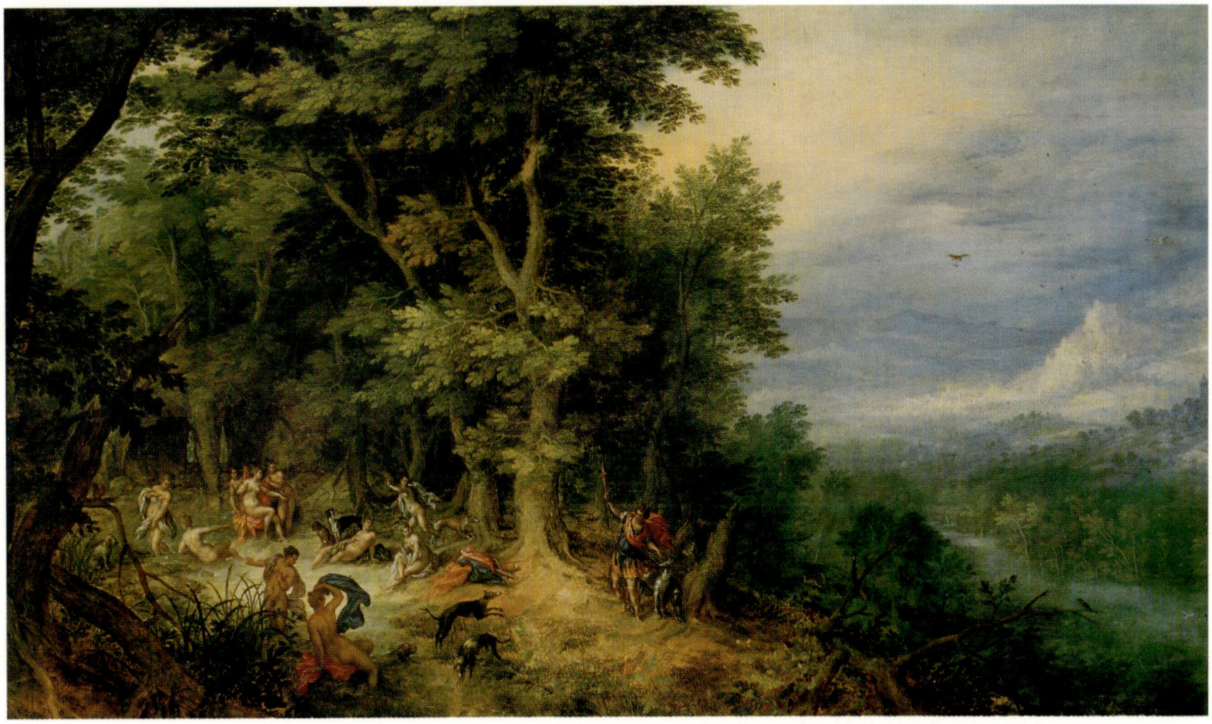

Jacob Jordaens
1593 Antwerp - 1678 Antwerp

47 Study for an Old Man with clasped hands

1620-1621
Oak. 68.5 × 51.5 cm
Acquired in 1944.
Inv. nº O 2814

Around 1620 Jordaens drew a large number of studies of heads showing an old man with well marked features. Abraham Grapheus modelled for them, himself a painter (died 1624) and patron of the Antwerp Guild, who was used several times by Jordaens for various figures in his paintings and altar-pieces. Grapheus was much in demand to model for Antwerp painters of the late sixteenth and early seventeenth centuries, particularly for Marteen de Vos, Anthony van Dyck, Cornelis de Vos. The study which the Prague National Gallery holds is of a quality which classes it among the best of Jordaens' studies. Other works of this type are to be found in many museums in Europe and the United States (Douai, Chartreuse Museum; Detroit, Institute of Arts; Ghent, Museum voor Schone Kunsten; Brussels, Musées Royaux des Beaux-Arts de Belgique; Hamburg, Kunsthalle).

The old man's face seems to have been sculpted out of the thick coats of paint by an energetic but carefully controlled use of the brush, creating a complex of layers especially around the eyes. A very effective disposition of the colours creates a striking contrast between the warm, rich tones of the face and clasped hands, and the cold, grey-green shades of the robe and the neutral background.

The earliest works of this artist, and the Prague example is to some extent representative of them, are marked by the efforts Jordaens made to break free from the influence of Van Dyck, who was a few years younger. Comparison of the two artists' work, especially certain studies of heads, shows that this influence was reciprocal, and their pictorial styles, above all in paintings executed around 1620, reveal affinities which lead us to suppose that they worked together.

L.S.

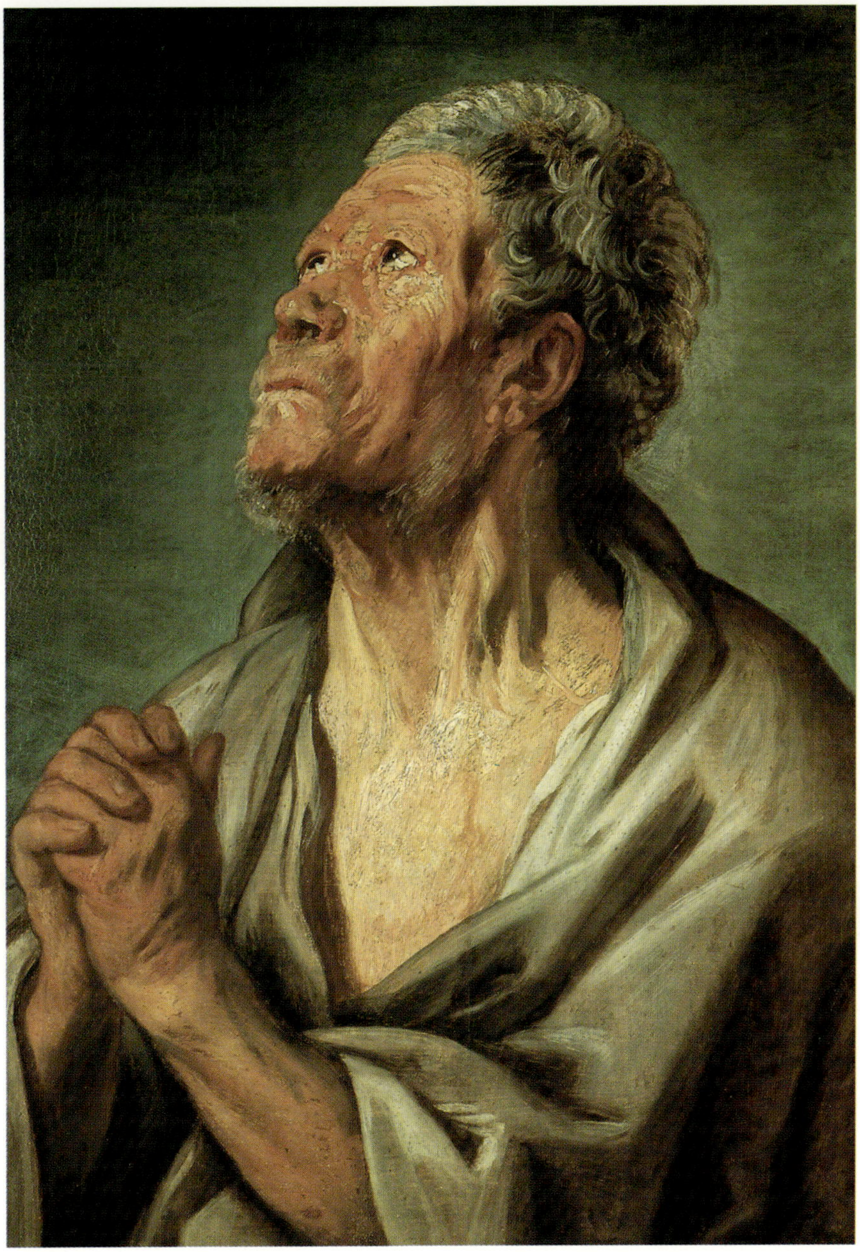

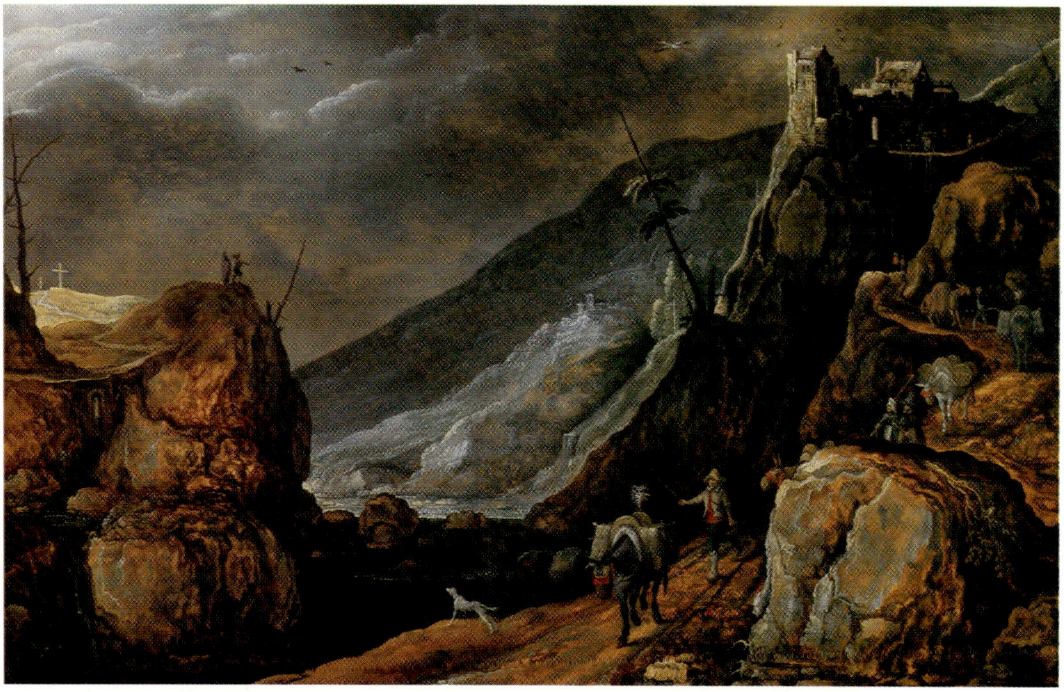

Joos II de Momper
1564 Antwerp - 1635 Antwerp

48 Mountain Landscape with the Temptation of Christ

after 1600
Oak. 51 × 83 cm
Acquired from the Nostitz collection in Prague in 1945.
Inv. n° DO 4188

Joos de Momper is one of the most striking exponents of Flemish landscape painting at the turn of the 16th century when earlier mannerist conceptions began to give ground to a realistic representation of nature. He is well represented in the National Gallery in Prague by several works deriving from the Nostitz collection, which are the perfection of landscape conceived, as in most of his abundant production, to accord with the 16th century tenets already adopted by Pieter Bruegel the Elder. So much can be clearly seen in the *Mountain Landscape with the Temptation of Christ*, where the artist harks back in a very personal manner, to the traditional schemata (composition, colours) used by landscape painters of the second half of the 16th century. In this case the landscape is viewed from a slight rise and is bordered by rock formations which disclose a valley watered by a stream. Ever since Joachim Patinier, founder of the landscape tradition in the art of the Netherlands, these lowland painters have been unforgettably impressed by Alpine peaks and rocks. The present work is a case in point. The traditional disposition of the colours, the colder tones being reminiscent for us of neon lighting, and the lightness of touch subtly hinting at foliage and distance, together with the effective play of light, all give this landscape its dream-like quality. Down the path that twists and turns on the right of the scene a caravan of pilgrims with their mules makes its way, while high above them a medieval fortress crowns a rocky peak.

The main narrative scene presents an episode from the New Testament, the *Temptation of Christ* (Mt 4. 1-11; Lk 4. 1-13). Conceived in the spirit of Brueghel the Elder, it has been removed into the background. The artist at work here is from Antwerp, Sebastian Vrancx (1573-1647), who frequently collaborated with Joos de Momper.

L.S.

Anthony Van Dyck
1599 Antwerp - 1641 London

49 Saint Bruno

before 1620
Canvas. 97.5 × 78 cm
Acquired from the Nostitz collection in Prague in 1945.
Inv. n° DO 4207

Saint Bruno is the founder of the Carthusian Order. He was never canonized but in 1514 the Holy See authorized members of the order to observe his cult, which was extended in 1674 to the universal church of the southern Netherlands. Van Dyck's canvas represents the saint (circa 1030-1101) half-length, at prayer. Several details lead one to suppose that it is a commissioned portrait, not only in the treatment of the saint's face but in elements of composition which are typical of portraits of the time: a window opening onto a landscape, or high up in the picture, the heavy folds of a hanging. Van Dyck often used analogous motifs in his early portraits, executed before 1620, during his stay in Antwerp. Other clues are given by the pictorial means employed, in particular the lightly coated canvas, which allows the texture to show through, or the strong light cast on certain anatomical details, clues which enable us to date this painting to Van Dyck's first creative period. The same elements can be seen in a series of canvases executed before he left for Italy.

This work by Van Dyck, like a great number of excellent Flemish paintings preserved in the National Gallery in Prague, once belonged to the renowned Nostitz collection, to which it was transferred in 1706 with the collection of Count František Antonín Berka de Dubá.

L.S.

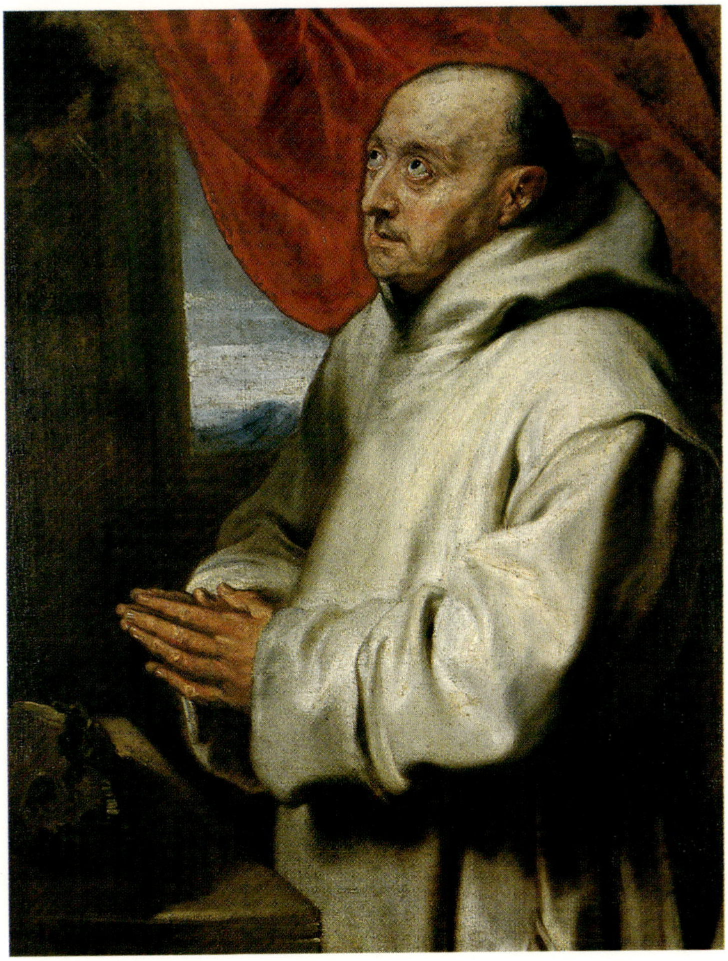

Roelant Savery

1576 Kortrijk - 1639 Utrecht

50 Landscape with Birds

1622
Oak. 54 × 108 cm
Acquired from the Nostitz collection in Prague in 1945.
Inv. nº DO 4246

An entirely new vision begins to come into Roeland Savery's landscapes after 1613, subsequently affirmed through a whole series of paintings where landscape becomes a paradise, peopled with the most varied animals. This vein had been assiduously worked, in the same period, by Velvet Bruegel, whose example seems to have powerfully influenced Savery. *Orpheus playing to the Beasts* and *Noah's Ark* are among the subjects which enabled painters to include within a mountain or forest landscape, often inspired by the Tyrol or the environs of Prague, the representation of a whole host of the most varied animals, in response to the naturalist interests of Dutch people in those days.

In its composition and pictorial quality, this *Landscape with Birds* stands out as the most effective of all Savery's works. Within this wild landscape, backing onto a river, there is a ruined portal and the heavily inclined trunk of a great tree, around and against which the painter has pictured every kind of bird. Dominating them all is the eagle, perched with wings deployed on the tree-trunk. The ruins of an imposing building, surmounted by a dome, can be seen in the distance on the right.

This architectural motif is found, with variants, in others of Savery's landscapes with animals, and it is probably a reminiscence of the journey he (supposedly) made to Istria. *Orpheus playing to the Beasts* (National Gallery in Prague) is another example.

In his minutely faithful rendering of both European and exotic birds Savery demonstrates with what assiduity he studied them, both in the wild and in the aviaries of Emperor Rudolph II, who engaged him as court landscape painter between 1604 and 1612. Savery could have been familiar with the superb Persian miniatures, which were the gift of the Shah to the emperor famed for his love of the arts.

L.S.

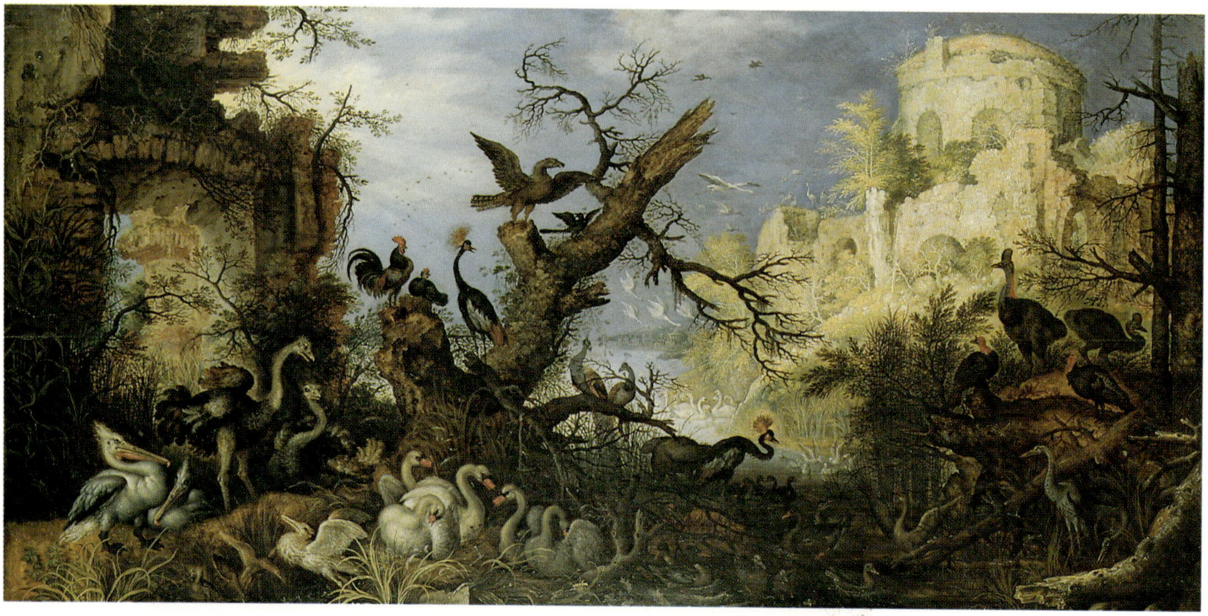

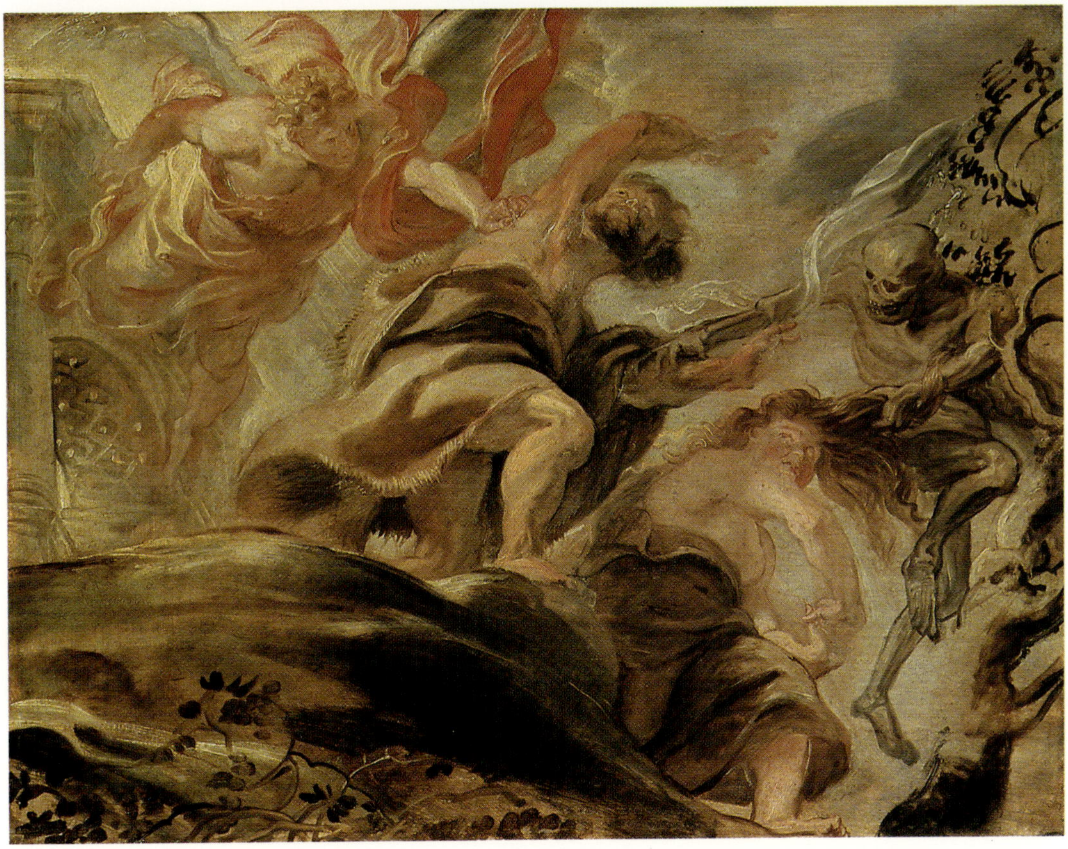

Petrus Paulus Rubens
1577 Siegen (Westphalia) - 1640 Antwerp

51 The Expulsion of Adam and Eve from Paradise

1620
Oak. 49.5 × 64.5 cm
On loan from 1802 to 1932 to the Picture Gallery of the Society of Patriot Friends of the Arts. Acquired in 1950.
Inv. n° O 1950

The sketch preserved in Prague is one of the finest of Rubens' preparatory studies for the prestigious commission he was given in the 1620's, which was for the ceilings of the two galleries of the Jesuit church in Antwerp. Altogether thirty-nine canvasses were to decorate the ceilings with illustrations of episodes from the Old and New Testaments and from the lives of several saints. Although the scene of Adam and Eve expelled from Paradise is listed among the themes mentioned in the contract passed on 29 March 1620 between Rubens and Father Jacobus Tirinus, Superior of the Jesuits in Antwerp, it was nevertheless not realized. These adornments to the Jesuit church, marking the canonization in 1621 of the Order's founder, Ignatius de Loyola, were destroyed in the fire of 1718.

In this study Rubens penetrates the words of the book of Genesis (3.23) in order to give visible form to their meaning. We are shown an angel with a flaming sword driving our first parents out of the Garden of Eden, a pictorial rendering of the Lord's declaration that henceforth man is mortal. The artist calls on every available pictorial means to transmit the terrible message, the warmth of colour enhancing the vigorous spontaneity of brush-strokes. The composition was conceived to be seen from below, using the perspective principle known as *di sotto in su*. The boldness of the foreshortening testifies how well Rubens had assimilated what could be learnt from the decorative work of Venetian late Renaissance artists such as Veronese, Tintoretto or Titian. And yet in some of its details this sketch reflects a north-European tradition, since it has undeniable affinities with Tobias Stimmer's wood engraving *The Expulsion of Adam and Eve from Paradise,* which he published in his *Neue künstlerische Figuren biblischer Historien* of 1576, and especially with Holbein's wood engravings in the *Dance of Death* cycle of 1538.

L.S.

Petrus Paulus Rubens

1577 Siegen (Westphalia) - 1640 Antwerp

52 General Ambrogio Spinola

circa 1627
Oak. 116.5 × 85 cm
Acquired from the Nostitz collection in Prague in 1945.
Inv. n° O 9688

The Marquis Ambrogio Spinola (1569-1630), a native of Genoa, served for many years as general and counsellor to Archduke Albert and the Infanta Isabella. His professional as well as friendly relations with his portraitist began at the court of the governors of Brussels, where Rubens was both court painter and diplomat. Thus there arose a series of portraits of Spinola painted by Rubens between 1625 and 1628. One of these, now lost, was full-length, representing the general in the ceremonial garb of the Brabant Order of the Golden Fleece, which he received after the victory of Breda. Another, three-quarter length, shows him wearing armour with the insignia of his high military rank. At least three authentic versions of this one are in existence, the finest of them being that preserved in Prague. In composition and basic components it is no different from the general run of military portraits of the period. What makes it remarkable is its painterly quality, the richness of its colours and the acuteness of its portrayal of the aging general's tired features, all of which turns a conventional portrait into one of the artist's master-pieces.

From comparison of the various known portraits of Spinola, and from the artist's correspondence on the subject, it can be affirmed that the Prague version is the one destined for his illustrious model personally, and was completed shortly before Rubens left the Netherlands for good in December 1627. The replica preserved in Brunswick (Herzog Anton Ulrich Museum) was destined for the eminent French scholar Pierre Dupuy; the only difference from the Prague version is in some details of the armour.

The third variant is in Saint Louis (Art Museum) U.S.A., which acquired it from the Leuchtenberg collection in Saint-Petersburg. It is probably the one mentioned in the 1640 catalogue of the Rubens legacy.

The canvas now in Prague belonged to the famous Nostitz collection from 1706 until 1945. Before that it was in an important picture gallery of Bohemia in the baroque period, belonging to Count František Antonín Berka de Dubá, who had himself acquired it in 1675 from the Vienna subsidiary of Forchondt, art dealer in Antwerp.

L.S.

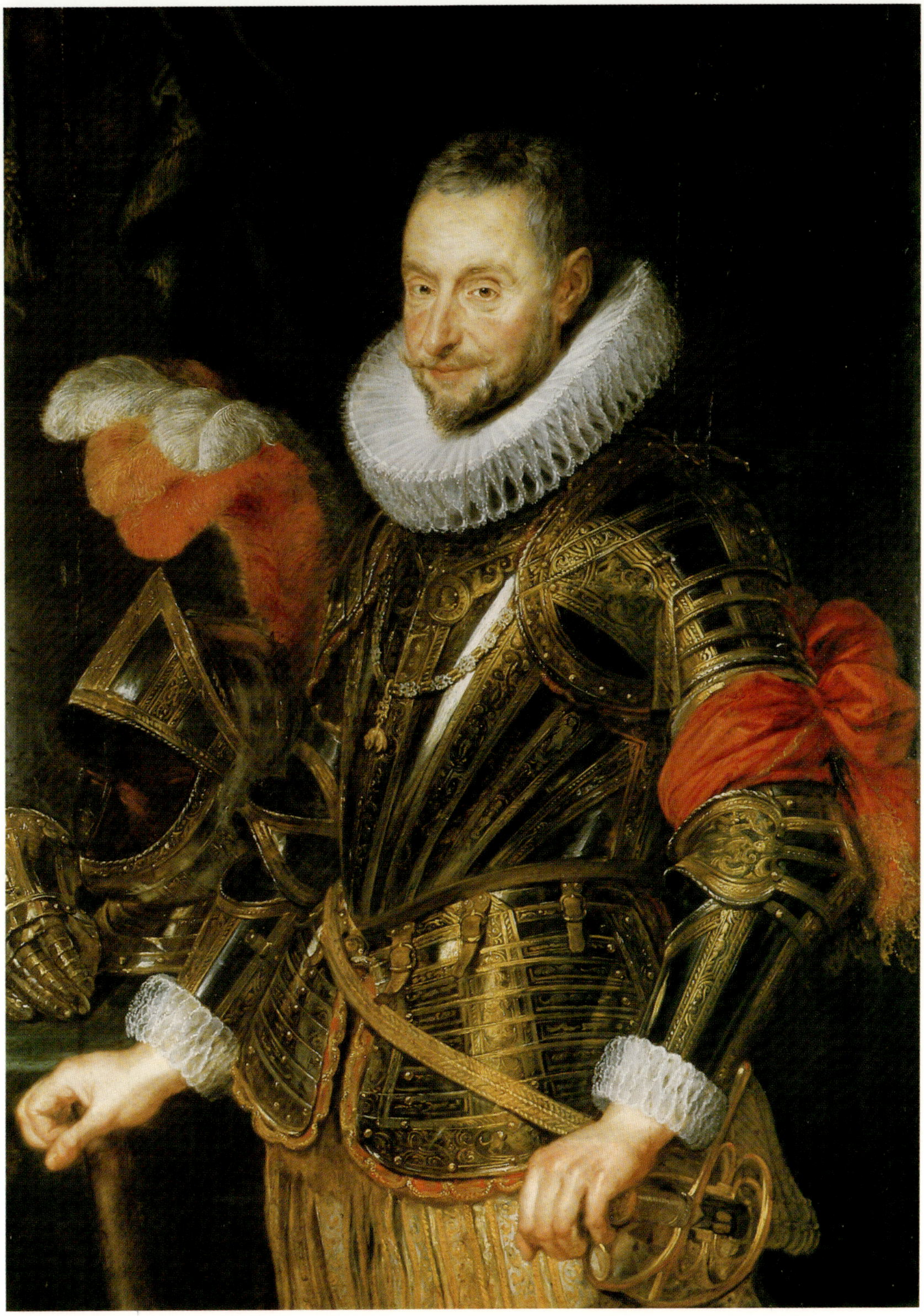

Petrus Paulus Rubens
1577 Siegen (Westphalia) - 1640 Antwerp

53 The Martyrdom of Saint Thomas

1637-1638
Canvas. 380 × 253 cm
On loan from the Augustinian monastery of the church of Saint Thomas in Prague since 1896
Inv. nº O 7597

This is one of the two large-scale canvasses painted by Rubens in his last creative period for Prague, and destined for the church of Saint Thomas of the Augustinian monastery in the Lesser Town. They were commissioned by the Prior, Jean Baptiste Cristelius Svitavský of Bochov (died 1637). These two canvasses, the *Martyrdom of Saint Thomas,* which is a work of great dramatic power, and the peaceful *Meditation of Saint Augustin,* can be dated to 1638. They were delivered in Prague in 1639 and the monastery paid Rubens the sum of 945 florins. On 24 April 1639, in the presence of members of the Czech nobility, the Archbishop of Prague, Ernest de Harrach consecrated the High Altar with the *Martyrdom of Saint Thomas.* Where the Saint Augustin canvas was at that time is not known, and the two works were not brought together at this altar until 1730, when it was replaced by one in the late baroque style.

The two works executed for Prague are remarkable examples of the artist's mature period. Rubens' ecstatic portrayal of the saint's last moments before his martyrdom is fully in accord with the iconographical principles of the Counter-Reformation, and is related in conception and execution to his other works of this period, such as *The Martyrdom of Saint Lievin,* circa 1635 (Brussels, Musées Royaux des Beaux-Arts de Belgique), *The Beheading of Saint Paul,* circa 1637 (Rood Klooster near Brussels, an Augustinian convent), *The Crucifixion of Saint Peter,* circa 1638, (Cologne, Church of Saint Peter), or *The Crucifixion of Saint Anthony,* 1638-1639 (Madrid, Real Disputación de S. Andres de los Flamencos). The martyr's dramatic end and his ensuing apotheosis bring into play the full range of the painter's craft to render all the pathos expressed in gesture, feature and stance.

Judging from the composition and several details it seems that Rubens found inspiration for this work in the 1597 *Stoning of Saint Stephen* by the Florentine Ludovico Cigoli (1559-1640), which belongs to the Pitti Gallery in Florence. One feature which is characteristic of Rubens' method of working is the movement he gives to the central figure, the apostle Thomas, which clearly refers back to the attitude of Laocoon in the antique group of that name, a work he much admired.

The detailed iconographic analysis to which this painting has been subjected by L. Konečný demonstrates that Jacopo Voragine's *Legenda aurea* was not the only source for details of the martyr's death in India. Rubens, the true *pictor doctus* (learned painter), had recourse to the numerous accounts of this martyrdom disseminated by the hagiographic literature of the time, in particular the writings of Pedro de Ribadeneira *Flos sanctorum* (Madrid, 1599 and 1601) and of Laurentius Surius *De probatis Sanctorum* (Cologne, 1570-1575).

L.S.

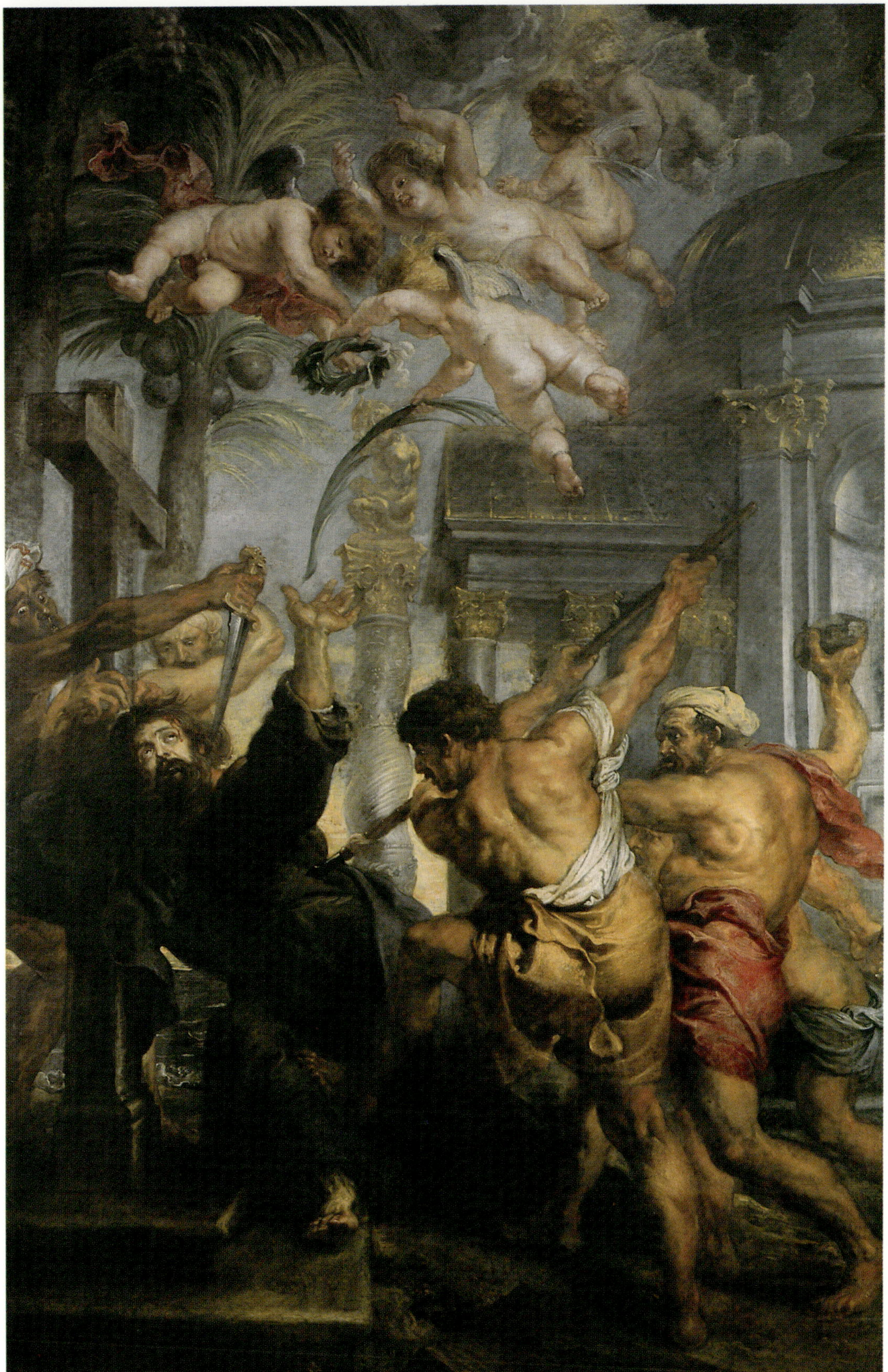

Simon de Vos
1603 Antwerp - 1676 Antwerp

54 Allegory of the Five Senses and the Five Ages of Man

1636
Oak. 49 × 64 cm
Acquired from the Nostitz collection in Prague in 1945
Inv. n° DO 4139

Simon de Vos is very well represented by this work, which is rightly considered the master work of the first period of his intimate painting, and shows the influence of the mannerists (such as Frans Franken the Younger) and especially Rubens. It is a remarkable painting, not only for its undeniable plasticity but also for a wealth of content which has given rise in the past to various interpretations. Unquestionably, the artist conceived his work as a complex allegory, a point confirmed by the presence of Bacchus and by the unreal aspect of the landscape. The five senses, which are the central theme, are personified by their conventional attributes and normal activities: sight by a mirror, taste by food and wine, smell by a rose and a dog, hearing by a musical instrument, and touch by a young couple embracing. We are then led on to secondary themes, for example the successive stages of life: youth is represented by a young couple, maturity by the person of Bacchus and old age by an aging pair warming themselves by a fire. To this articulation of the main theme there is a corresponding lay-out of the landscape in planes behind the grouped figures, showing nature unfolding from its spring-time flowering to the full fruits of summer and the ice and snow of winter. In the spirit of the period the personification of the five senses and likewise the representation of the ages of man carry the connotation of *vanitas,* a notion which is underlined here by the motif of skating, a favourite subject of genre painting that often illustrates the fragility of human life.

L.S.

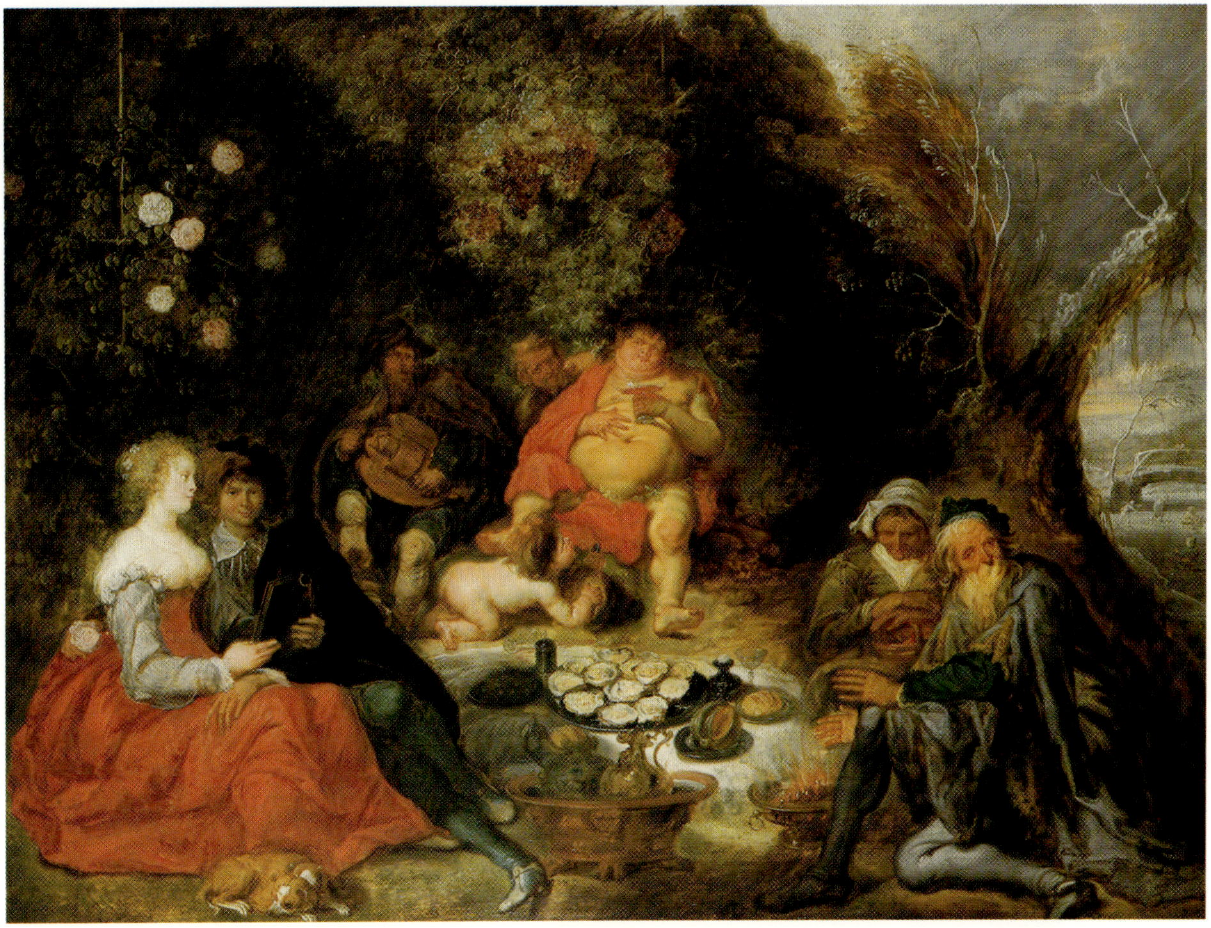

David II Teniers

1610 Antwerp - 1690 Brussels

55 Two Peasants

Oak. 22.1 × 16.6 cm
Donated by Josef Hoser in 1843.
Inv. nº O 115

Genre scenes set among the peasantry constitute the best known element of this artist's diverse production. The paintings of taverns and farms, which mark the beginning of his career, are much influenced by Adriaen Brouwer (1606-1638), a pioneer of the genre who was greatly admired by collectors and artists alike, among them Rubens, and whose influence is no less perceptible in this Teniers painting preserved in Prague and probably dating from around 1640. The two peasant caricatures are particularly reminiscent of Brouwer, and so is the remarkable freshness of execution. Until 1843 this work belonged to Dr Josef Hoser's well-known cabinet, after passing through two Viennese collections, those of Count Friezs and Franz Gabet.

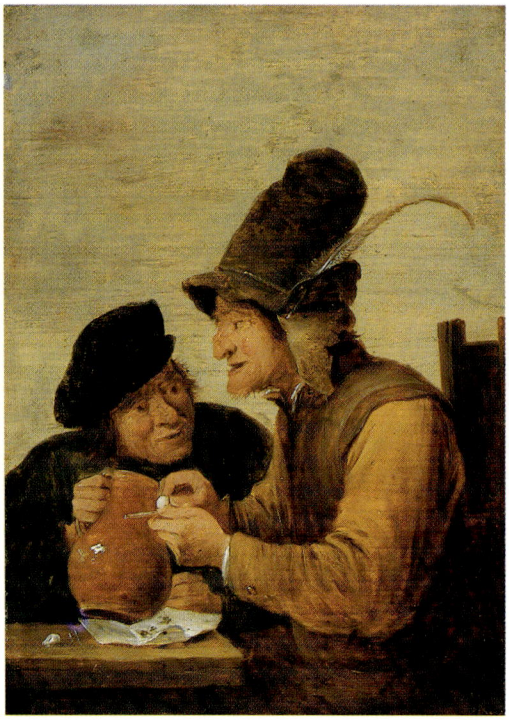

As for the content of this painting, it does not seem likely that the artist's representation of two men drinking and smoking was intended to illustrate the daily life of the peasantry. If we refer to the moralizing and emblematic literature of the time, we can interpret the picture's message as a warning against the evil effects of tobacco and alcohol, which dull the senses and give rise to delusions. It is in any case likely to have been part of a cycle personifying the five senses.

L.S.

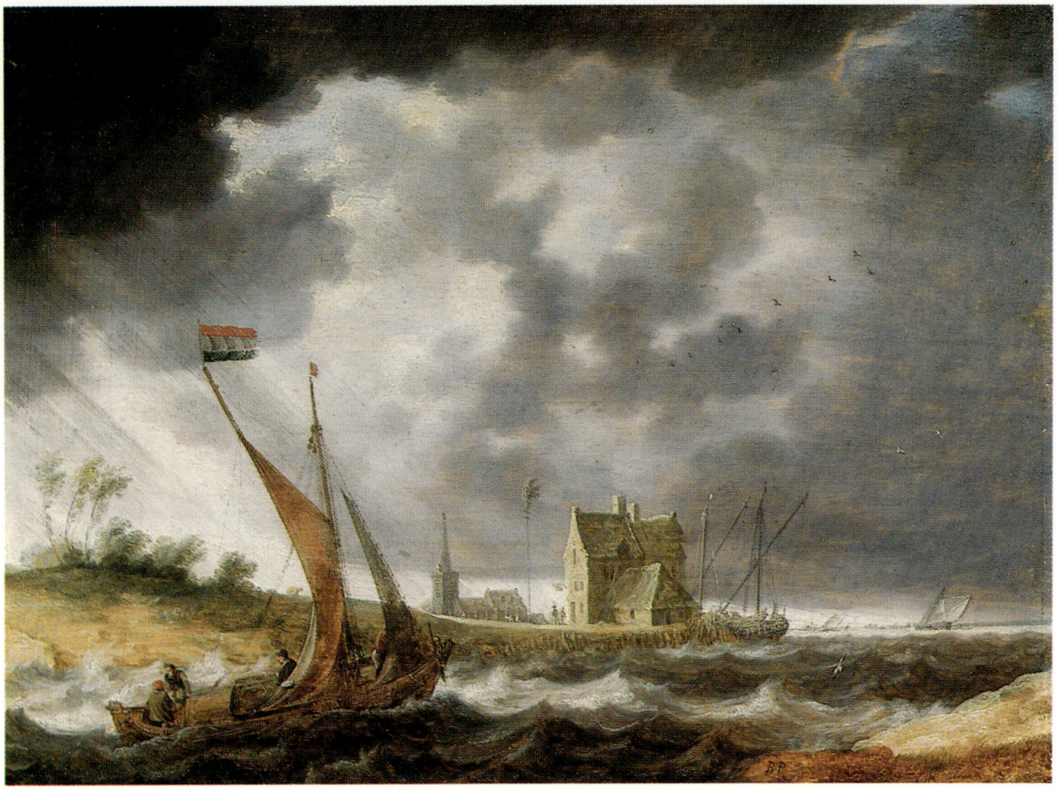

Bonaventura Peeters
1614 Antwerp - 1652 Hoboken near Antwerp

56 Coast with storm-tossed Sea

Oak. 25 × 35 cm
Acquired in 1945.
Inv. n° O 9678

Seascapes were a favourite theme with painters in the Netherlands of the 17th century. A master of the genre in the Flemish school, Bonaventura Peeters spent the greater part of his creative life in the little fishing village of Hoboken, near Antwerp, because his religious convictions brought him into conflict with the Jesuits and forced him to leave his native town. Beside dramatic scenes of men-of-war or merchant ships battling against a raging sea, in compositions of great power, this artist gives us seascapes from the vicinity of Hoboken, which he knew intimately. Characteristic of his work is the contrast effected between a gently billowing, or then a wind-thrashed sea or a landscape, and the over-arching sky, softened by light grey-white clouds or weighed down by their sombre mass. The masterly rendering of the atmosphere is obtained by an ingenious play of colours, runnning the gamut of the greys, and a control of light which adds dramatic tension to a natural scene. This *Coast with storm-tossed Sea* must rank among the most convincing of the artist's masterpieces, worthy to stand comparison with the seascapes of the greatest Dutch masters, Jan Porcellis (1584/1587-1632), Pieter Mulier (circa 1615-1670) or Simon de Vliegher (circa 1601-1693).

L.S.

Seventeenth century Dutch painting

Nicolaes Gillis

active from 1601 in Haarlem - died in Haarlem between 1622 and 1632

57 Still life on a table

1614
Wood. 74.5 × 110.5 cm
Acquired in 1931.
Inv. n° O 1478

This festive board displaying the gleaming colours of fruit, sweetmeats, cheese and wine appeals to the senses, the eye exciting the palate. Roses, more discrete, confide their fragrance to a subtler sense. Nicolaes Gillis, one of the earliest painters in Haarlem to specialize in still life, has concentrated on achieving an overall composition of great clarity, using the whole surface of his picture to create this harmonious ensemble of fresh colours. A pyramidal shape brings together the butter and the cheeses, while the porcelain dishes from distant China, the fragile goblets of Dutch or Venetian glass and other vessels are each set to be seen at its best while privileging none. A knife placed aslant in the centre and an apple peel overhanging the table edge reinforce the illusion of space. The same effect is made by the motif derived from Venetian Renaissance painting, the *cartellino* pinned up in the background, which bears the painter's signature and the date 1614. The rich variety of colours respects those proper to each object, the diversity of their beauties contributing to the festive atmosphere of the whole.

The still life paintings of Gillis, like those of his early 17th century contemporaries, can be read from a Christian view-point. The traditional bread and wine of the Eucharist are given the central position, while the butterfly, symbol of the human soul ever since antiquity, is there to remind us of our spiritual needs during our earthly sojourn. The various other foods will be seen as the gifts that God grants us here below.

H.S.

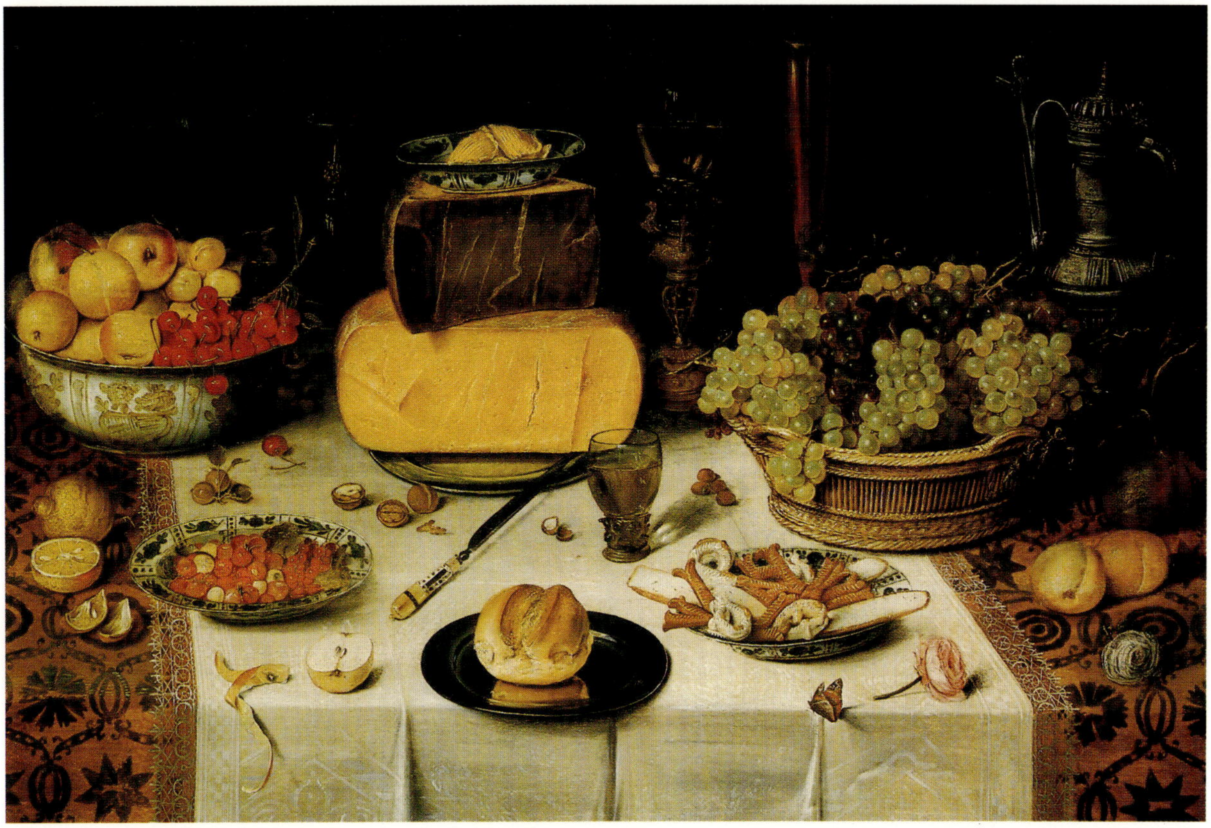

Esaias van de Velde

1587 Amsterdam - 1630 The Hague

58 Landscape with Ancient Temple

1624
Wood. 36.7 × 59.7 cm
Acquired from the Julius Singer collection in 1931.
Inv. nº O 1481

Italy, a country steeped in the traditions of antiquity, was a source of inspiration even for artists who never went there and could have only indirect knowledge of her beauties from engravings which celebrated her landscapes. Esaias van de Velde was one such, while remaining an admirer of nature in his own land. Under the influence of the Adam Elsheimer circle, the compositions he created reflect his own vision of an Italian landscape: a steeply sloping valley, its rocky crest surmounted by an ancient circular temple, identical in shape to the Temple of Vesta at Tivoli which was much favoured by artists active in Italy at the turn of the 16th century. Mountains of fissured rock are covered with luxuriant vegetation, and spring waters wind past boulders to reach a torrent cutting diagonally through the picture place, leading the eye downwards. Two paths lead up from either side of the stream obliquely towards distant horizons. The groups of figures set in this imaginary and yet entirely convincing milieu have a natural movement: the riders and travellers are depicted with an economy of means, and placed to enhance an impression of depth, that prove the hand of a master.

Esaias van de Velde painted this type of landscape many times during the 1620's when he moved to The Hague. They were more popular than those depicting the natural scene in Holland. Jan van Goyen was his pupil for a short time and was much influenced by him.

H.S.

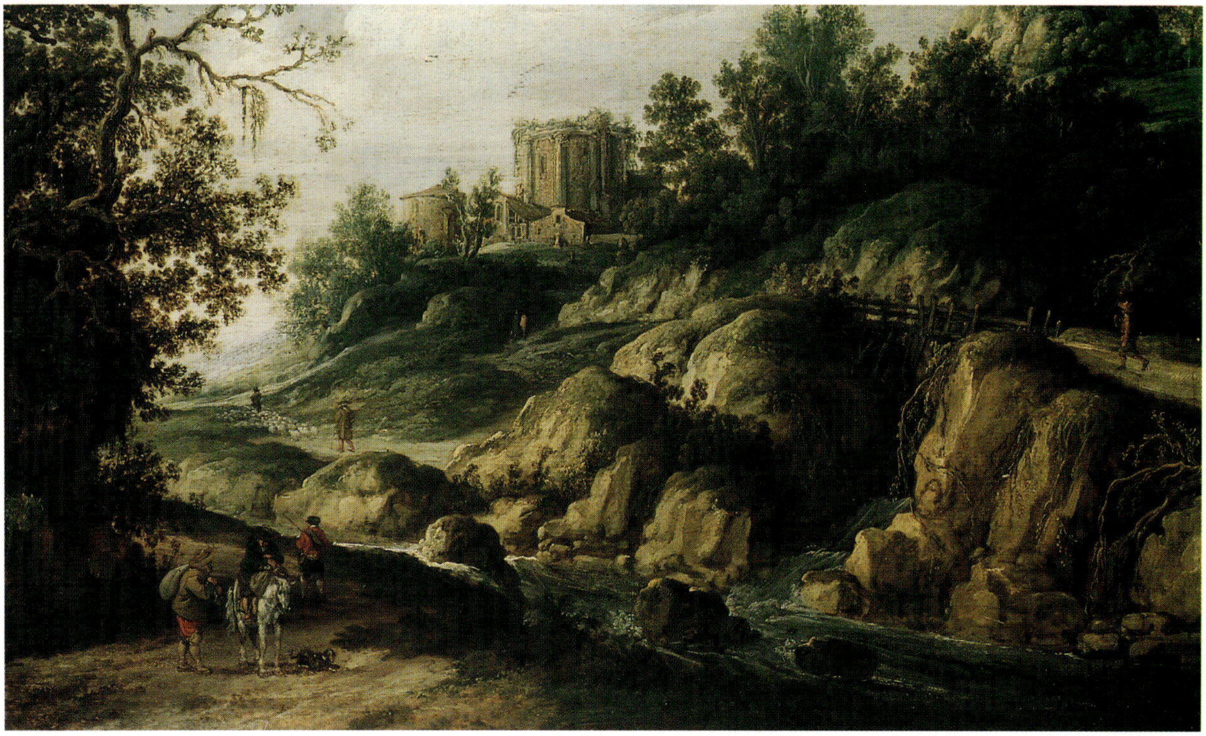

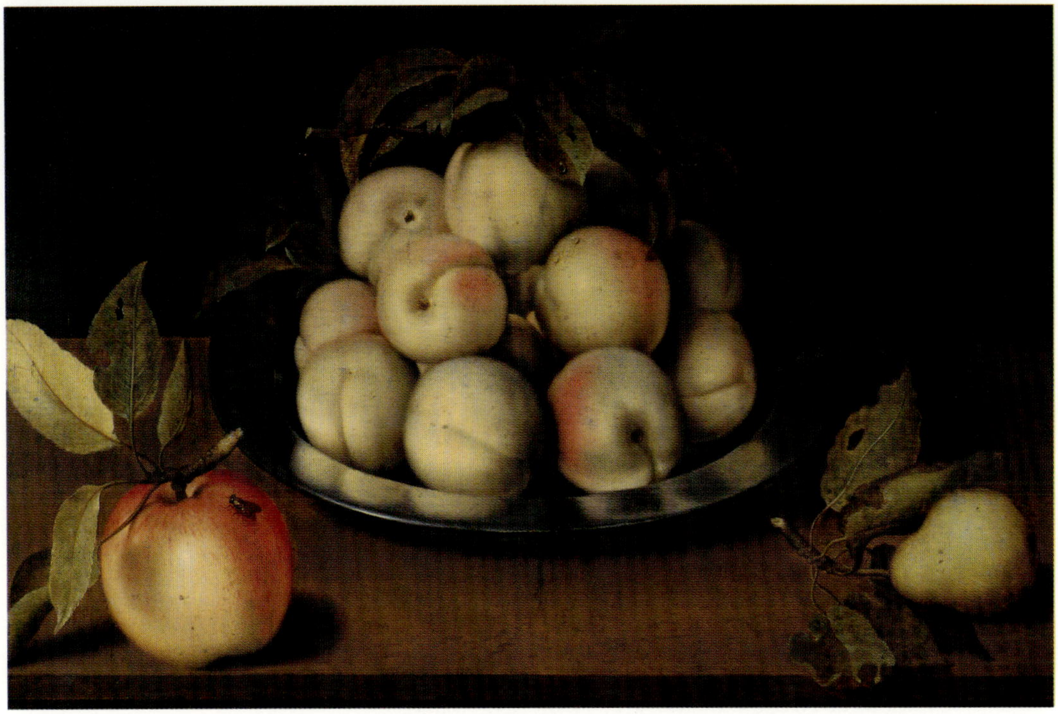

Ambrosius Boschaert the Elder
1573 Antwerp - 1621 The Hague

59 Still Life with Peaches

1620
Wood. 29 × 45 cm
Acquired in 1949.
Inv. nº O 2825

Ambrosius Boschaert is best known for his paintings of *Bouquets in a Vase*, which he composed symmetrically about a vertical axis using rare plants. Here the composition is also laid out symmetrically: in the centre is a pewter dish filled with peaches, with an apple on the left and a pear on the right. All the fruit is depicted with inimitable meticulousness. The harmony of their shapes and colours is achieved with brushwork so subtle as to evoke the finish of enamel. The strokes are invisible except where suggested by nature, as in the veins of the leaves, whose tone of colouring responds to variation from full daylight to half-shadow. Nothing has escaped the artist's eye or hand, not even the minute imperfections inflicted on the pear-tree leaves by the attacks of insects.

At this time works of art were expected to include some hidden symbolic meaning, which might be ambiguous, though often enough many were easily identified. This still life too is likely to have a hidden message. The apple and the pear were associated with original sin, while peaches evoked sensual pleasures. In shape they suggested a heart, and so might allude to the love of God. The fly on the apple, an obvious source of corruption, warns against a life spent in pleasure.

H.S.

Pieter de Molyn
1595 London - 1661 Haarlem

60 Village Lane

162 (8)?
Wood. 50.5 × 66 cm
Acquired from the Nostitz collection in Prague, in which it has been listed since 1765.
Inv. n° DO 4196

Dutch landscape painters endeavoured to depict a place as a man might come upon it in his travels, a project which demanded a purposeful conception and lay-out of space. Pieter de Molyn is one of the first to use the diagonal in order to achieve depth, in this case a farmtrack leading up from the ford as far as the horizon. The clumps of trees and village dwellings lining it on either side create alternating masses of light and shade. The cart appears at a break in the terrain like a wave which masks the distant view of the broad Dutch plain. High above, a luminous blue summer sky displays the majesty of its monumental clouds. The pair of travellers in the foreground sheltering in the shade from the sun's glare hardly disturb the overriding green and ochre tones that create the whole. The artist has given a masterly rendering of the loose grain of the sandy shore, the creased surface of the water, the wet earth in the muddy, high-banked track, the light of a warm summer's day. Thanks to Pieter de Molyn, his contemporaries learnt to appreciate the modest, discrete beauty of the Dutch landscape, so very different from the more famous attractions of Tuscany or Campania.

Pieter de Molyn belongs to the group of artists gathered in Haarlem early in the 17 century who opened up new possibilities for Dutch painting, and who include such names as Esaias van de Velde, Cornelis Vroom, Pieter Santvoort, Salomon van Ruysdael among others. Landscape painting in Haarlem became, thanks to Molyn, a highly individualized form of art.

H.S.

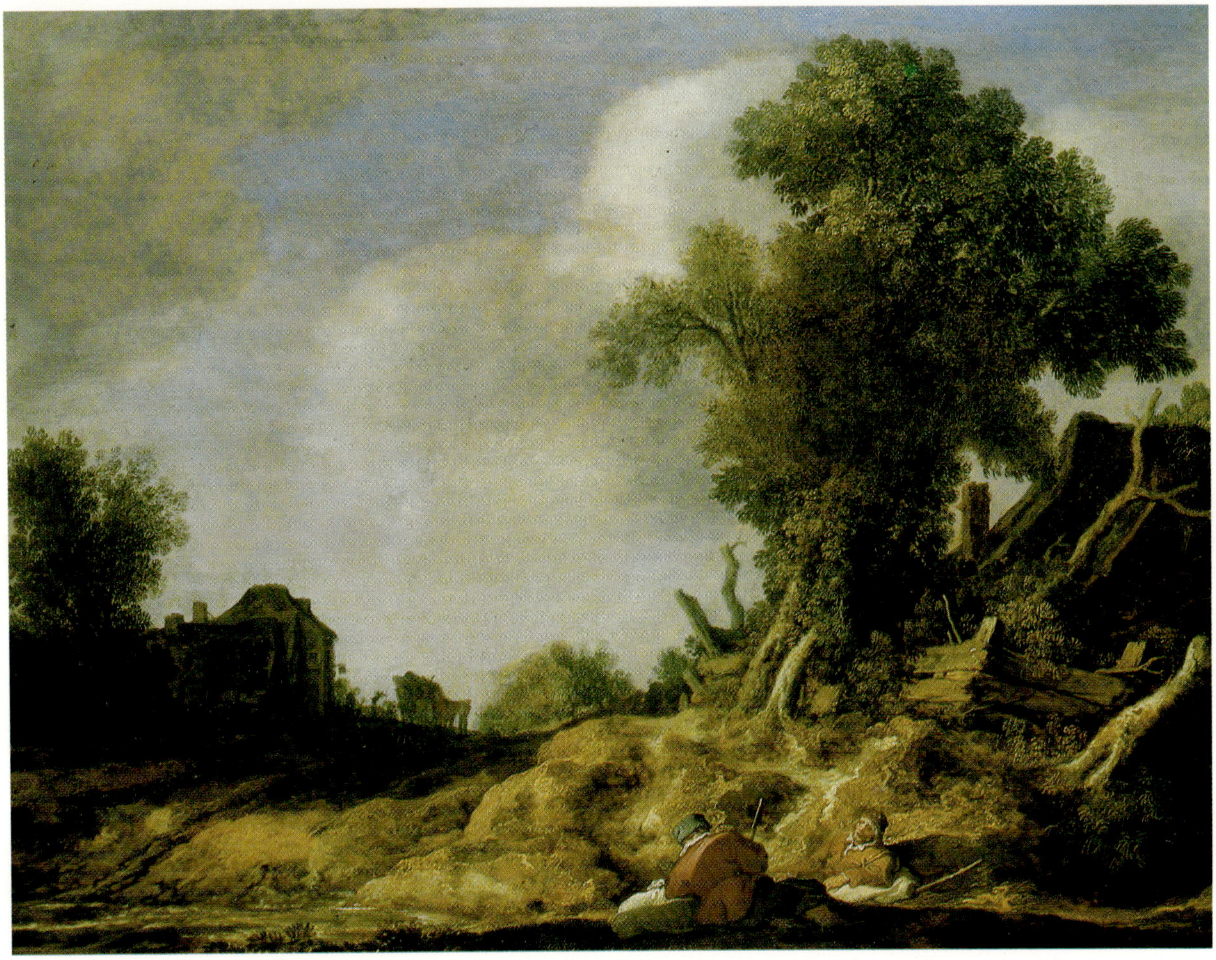

Rembrandt Harmenszoon (Harmensz) van Rijn
1606 Leyden - 1669 Amsterdam

61 # The Scholar in his Study

1634
Canvas. 114 × 135 cm
Acquired in 1945 from the Nostitz collection, where it was first recorded in 1765.
Inv. nº DO 4288

This canvas was painted in the year of the artist's marriage to Saskia van Uylenborch, for him an auspicious time when he was starting on a promising career in Amsterdam. He had made a reputation with pictures on historical subjects, as a portraitist and as painter of « tronjes », i.e. compositions with biblical or mythological characters depicted half-length.

In *The Scholar in his Study* Rembrandt is intent on bringing out the astonishing beauty of this majestic old man while rendering every feature with the keen eye of the portraitist. The face is familiar to us from others of Rembrandt's paintings dating from 1633-1635, where he is described as *The Oriental* or *The Jew*. In 1634 Rembrandt made a sketch of him in the album of the German merchant Burchard Grossmann, with the inscription: « The pious soul rates honour higher than gain », a maxim that sums up his attitude to life.

Here it is the compactness of the man turned towards us that dominates the composition. The objects depicted on the table are sufficient to suggest the interior of a study. The figure is seen slightly from below which gives it monumentality, as of a man looking upon us from his spiritual world. His face has an absent look, caught in a moment's distraction from his study. He is looking at us and yet is still completely absorbed by what he has been reading in the volume open before him. This is where Rembrandt would overstep the possibilities of painting, and depict the soul while representing the body. It was held against painting by art theorists of the time that it could not reflect changing states of soul as could poetry through the voice, the perfect medium of the spirit. Likewise it was thought that the flow of time which carries speech could not be apprehended by a painting. Now we know that Rembrandt was interested in these theories, and in this *Scholar in his Study* he proves that the expression in the character's face can make manifest changes of spirit that reflect events of past or future time.

What this canvas also demonstrates is Rembrandt's skill purely as painter. The balanced overall alternation of light and shade points up the artist's inimitable way with his material, especially in the perfect modelling of the face, the stiff leaves of parchment, the subdued glints of light and the shadows that deepen the folds in the velvet cloak. This is the only painting by Rembrandt in Czechoslovakia's possession.

H.S.

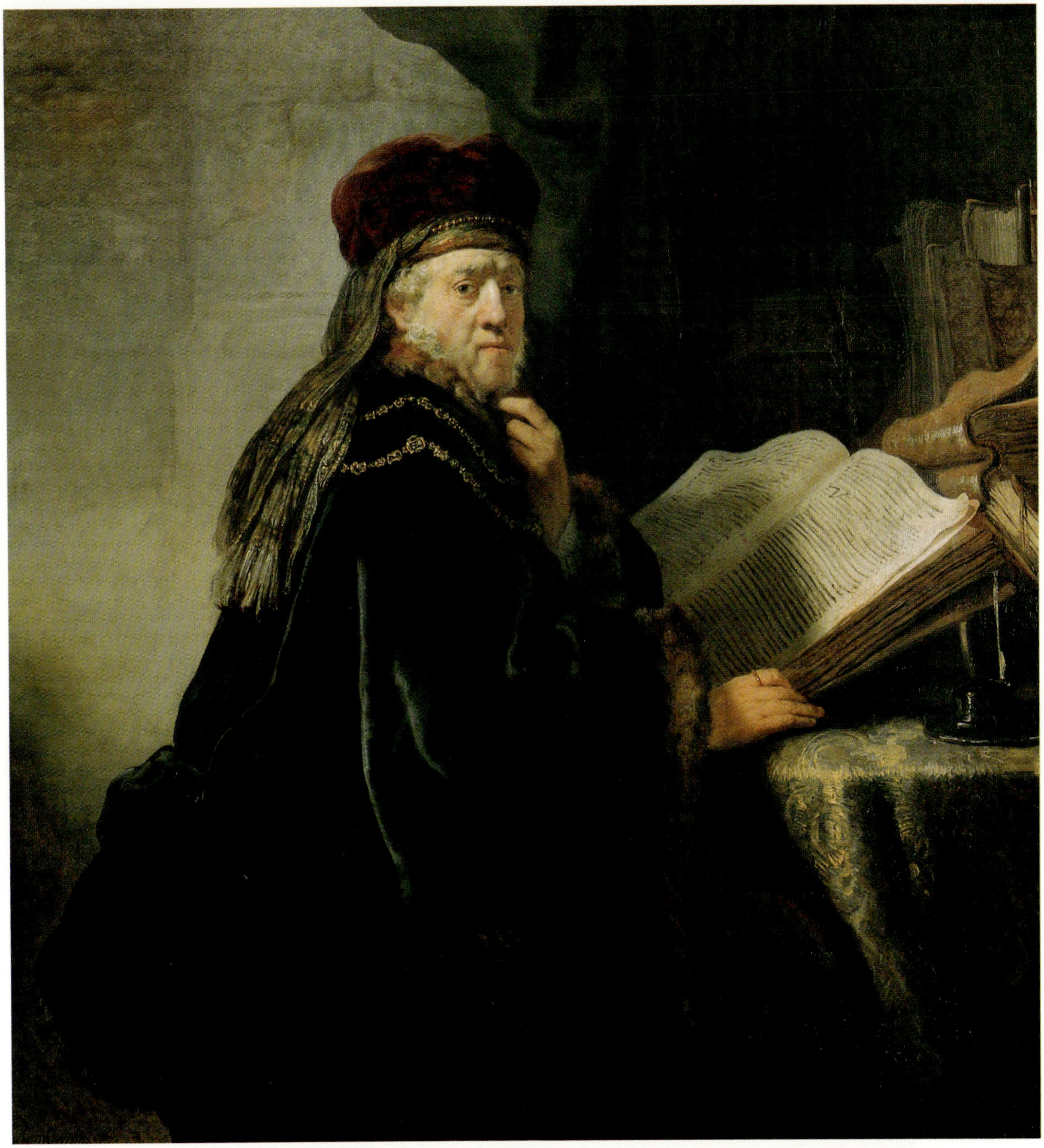

Jan van Goyen
1596 Leyden - 1656 The Hague

62 ## Farmhouse in the Dunes

1631
Wood. 27 × 46.8 cm
Acquired from the collection of Josef V. Novák in 1949.
Inv. nº O 2821

In the 1630's Dutch landscape painting takes on characteristic features of its own. The scene is often set on the coastline which, in the Low Countries, is bordered by sand dunes protecting the land against the ceaselessly invading sea. What attracted painters to these dunes was the sober charm emanating from their subtle ochre tones and humble vegetation, and the silvery light diffused from the sea up into the humidity of the upper air. Among the painters who devoted their art to this kind of landscape Jan van Goyen has pride of place for the hundreds of sketches he brought back from his walks, on which he based the compositions painted in his studio. Van Goyen studied painting in his native town and then, after some time spent in France, pursued his studies with Esaias van de Velde, who was then working in The Hague. In the 1620's his conception of landscape art was still very close to that of his master. Later he abandoned the principle of a landscape enclosed by a screen of trees and bringing together several narrative scenes, and began to aim for a greater overall unity of composition. Lowering the line of the horizon, he introduced the governing diagonal and restricted his palette to give predominance to subtle tones of ochre, grey-brown and grey-green. A simple, well-balanced whole was his aim, and this *Farmhouse in the Dunes* is a good example. The farmhouse is set in a wide-open undulating landscape which melts into the ochre hillocks of the dunes. The terrain is modelled by the light and shade, which are separated in the foreground by a path leading into the background. One senses the proximity of the sea behind those dunes. The distance, always fascinating in Dutch landscape painting, is suggested through gradations of lightbands drawing the eye upwards to the horizon. The travellers, briefly sketched by a master's hand, fuse into the almost monochrome environment to become an inseparable part of the whole.

H.S.

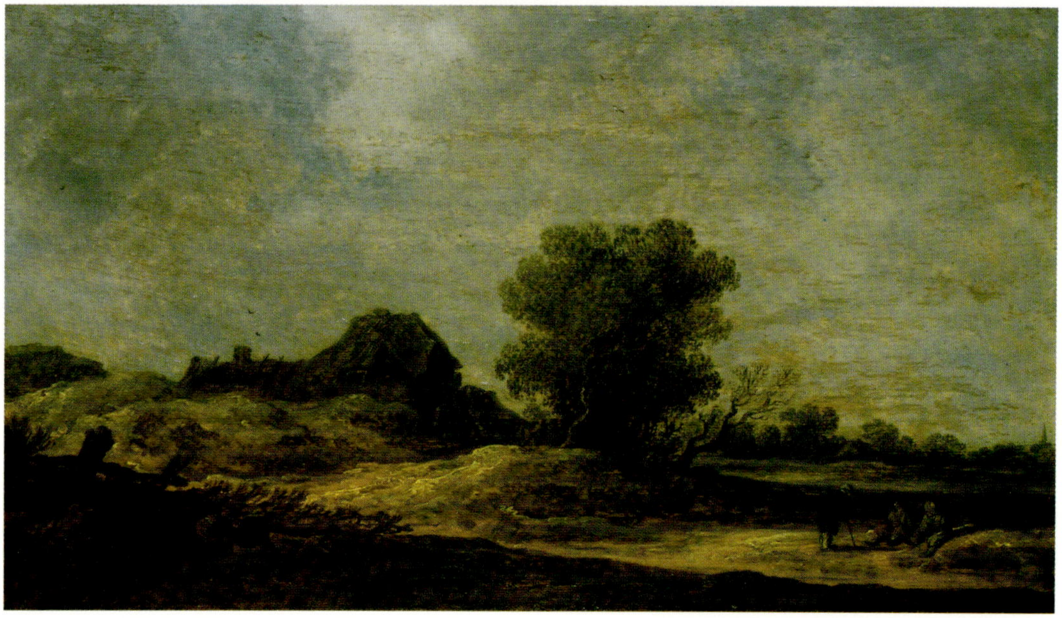

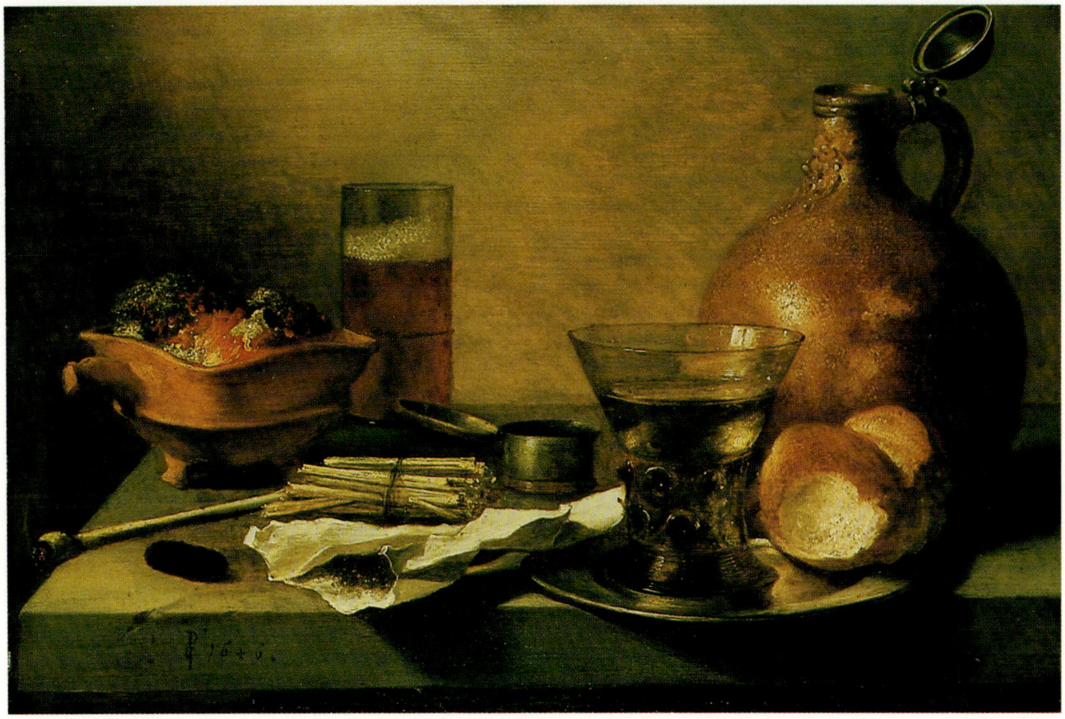

Pieter Claesz
1597/1598 Burgsteinfurt - 1667 Haarlem

63 Still Life with a Pitcher

1646
Wood. 39.8 × 60.8 cm
Acquired from the Van Diemen gallery in Berlin in 1924.
Inv. nº O 1409

The evolution of the still life picture, like that of landscape painting, tended towards the greatest possible unity of composition. The older artists, represented in the Prague collections by Nicolaes Gillis, sought to present in a single plane all the objects brought together on a table. The unifying element of the picture was the spotlessly clean table laid out for a feast. Then ideas changed, thanks to Pieter Claesz in particular and to his new approach, a change which is attested by *Still Life with a Pitcher,* and already evident in the choice of subject. What we see is the corner of a table with a half-finished glass of beer, a bowl of wine, a morsel of bread and an abandoned pipe - an everyday situation has been caught which could be the frame for an intimate moment, such as a conversation between friends.

The composition too is very different: a sophisticated network of diagonals brings together in the foreground the pipe with the smoker's accessories, the bowl of wine and the earthenware pitcher, and in a second plane an ale-warmer and the glass of beer. The pewter dish with the bit of bread occupies the far end of the table, giving a greater impression of depth to the picture. This principle was already known to the older still life artists, but in his application Claesz has linked the motif organically with the other objects shown. The range of colours has narrowed, giving predominance to the grey-browns and the ochres. The light makes for the unity of this composition by enhancing the objects' plasticity and their spatial relationships.

This work was executed in Haarlem in the period when Frans Hals was active there, experimenting with new techniques in which rapid brush strokes created an impasto that added relief to the picture surface. Claesz was sensitive to the inherent beauty of the coloured paste and loved to use its plastic quality in building up his highlights. It was a time when Haarlem became a centre of innovation and welcomed new esthetic conceptions.

H.S.

Frans Hals

1582/1583 baptized in Antwerp - 1666 Haarlem

64 Portrait of Jasper Schade

1645
Canvas. 80 × 67.5 cm
In the J. W. Wilson collection, Brussels, in 1873. Acquired in 1881 by Johann II of Lichtenstein in an auction in Brussels for an unusually high price for the time - 43.000 francs. In 1890 Johann II of Lichtenstein donated the canvas to the Picture Gallery of Society of Patriot Friends of the Arts, forerunner to the Prague National Gallery.
Inv. nº O 638

Frans Hals was born in the Catholic part of Flanders and spent his childhood in Haarlem, where he studied painting under Karl van Mander, painter and theoretician. Famous for his portraits, he was just as keen to devote his art to peasants, fringe members of society, drinkers, children. His group portraits are reckoned among the highest achievements of Dutch painting, where the artist not only gives us the appearance of his models but also catches their character traits, their temperament, their behaviour and social standing.

Jasper Schade (1623/1625 - 1692) was a member of the elite. Born into a well-to-do family, he came into a considerable fortune when still young. He owned residential property in Tull and Wael, was Dean of the chapter of Oudmünster in Utrecht, and deputy of the States General. At the time of this portrait he was only twenty-two, with a brilliant career ahead of him. Frans Hals seems to have divined the prestigious future awaiting the young man, and with characteristic irony, has hinted at it in the portrait. His composition gives vertical expression to the young knight's stance, full of assurance and energy; and being seen from below his self-important expression is accentuated. With his head slightly tilted back and a scarcely perceptible lift of the brows, the young man's eye reflects ennui and contempt, while that little smile bespeaks arrogance rather than amusement. The impertinent angle of the headgear adds an elegant touch to the costume, whose simplicity is but a feint belying a strict adherence to the canons of French taste. There is documentary evidence to prove that Jasper Schade's wardrobe was the object of lavish expenditure, exemplified here in the costly silk taffeta which is the occasion for Hals to display a vigorous yet nonchalent technique that was not to be fully appreciated until the days of the impressionists. Brilliant in its craftmanship, masterly in its grasp of the character's psychology, as revealed despite the young dandy's air of indifference, this must surely be one of the painter's masterpieces.

Yet this portrait's mastery of execution and incredible modernity, its freedom and concision, have led to doubts about its authenticity. However the restoration of the canvas in 1962 dispelled all suspicions, and when shown in the exhibitions of Frans Hals held in 1962 and 1990 the *Portrait of Jasper Schade* was hailed as one of the painter's most interesting works.

H.S.

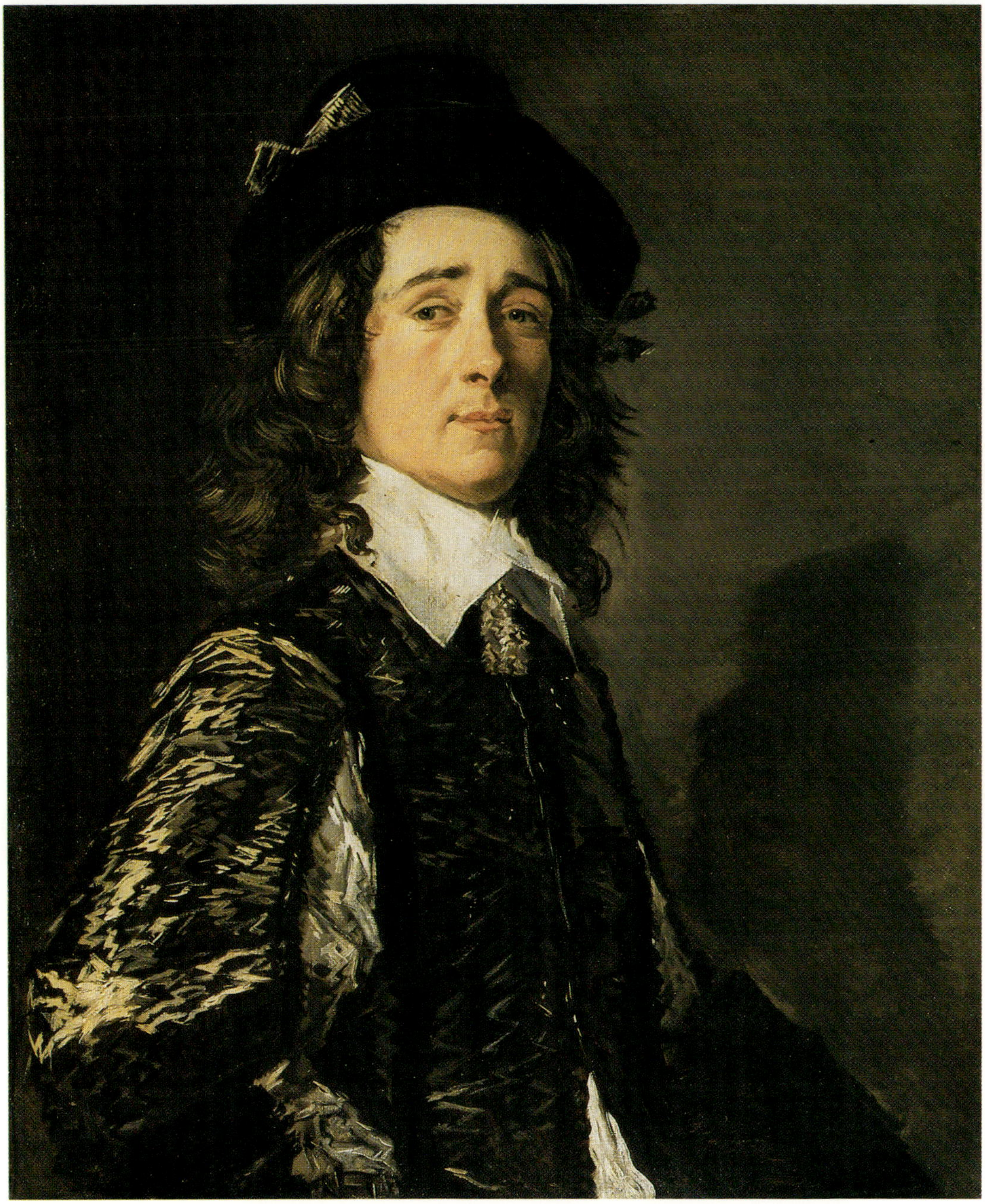

Leonard Bramer
1596 Delft - 1674 Delft

65 The Raising of Lazarus

circa 1640
Wood. 52.5 × 47.5 cm
Acquired from the Nostitz collection in 1945.
Inv. n° DO 4322

During his youth Leonard Bramer spent some time in France and Italy, and after his return home he acquired a great reputation for his paintings of biblical and mythological scenes. The experience in painting techniques he had gained in Italy enabled him to execute even frescos.

Today however his oil paintings, on canvas or oak, are the most highly prized. In the *Raising of Lazarus* Bramer depicts an episode from the Gospel of John (11. 1-43). Lazarus and his two sisters, Martha and Mary, all three beloved by Jesus, lived in Bethany, near Jerusalem. Lazarus fell sick and died. Summoned by the sisters, Jesus was led to the tomb of Lazarus, where he had lain already four days, and brought him back to life. Bramer succeeds in conveying the tense atmosphere of expectation attendant on the miracle by focussing attention on realistic details, and he gives a dramatic interpretation of the climax of the scene, when, according to the gospel, Christ cries out with a powerful voice: "Lazarus, come out!"

Christ's power and assurance, which his gesture and all his body make manifest, the mortal fatigue afflicting the face of Lazarus in the moment of his re-awakening, the figures lightly sketched as they approach the tomb, all these are in the manner characteristic of the artist. Although no more than suggested, the various reactions of those witnessing the scene are clearly distinguished.

There can be no doubt here of the influence of Rembrandt, who devoted many paintings and etchings to this theme. Both artists are intent on rendering the miraculous event in all its drama. But Bramer has a technique all his own. He works spontaneously, using rapid, energetic brushstrokes. He is a master of light effects, catching the glints reflected in the surface of fabrics and revels in contrasting light against dark. A sophisticated sense of colour inhabits this temperamental painter.

H.S.

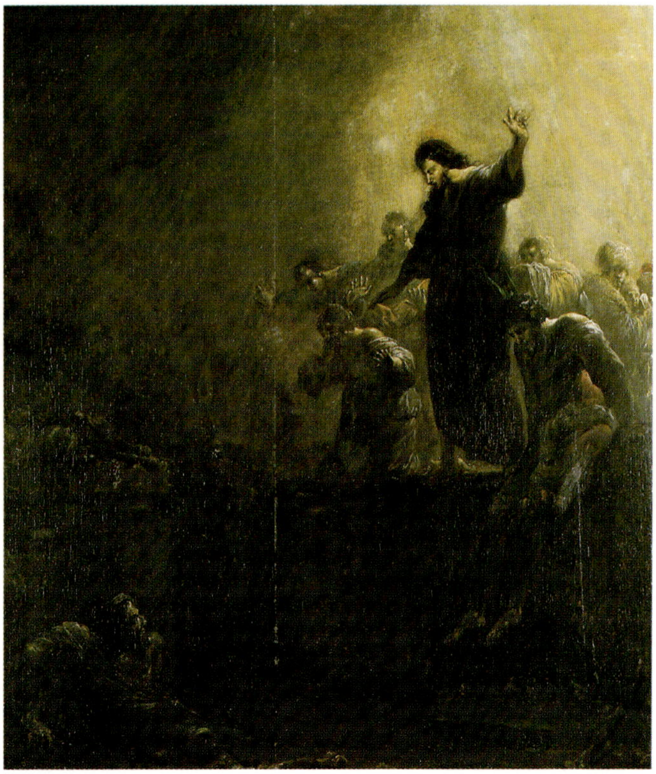

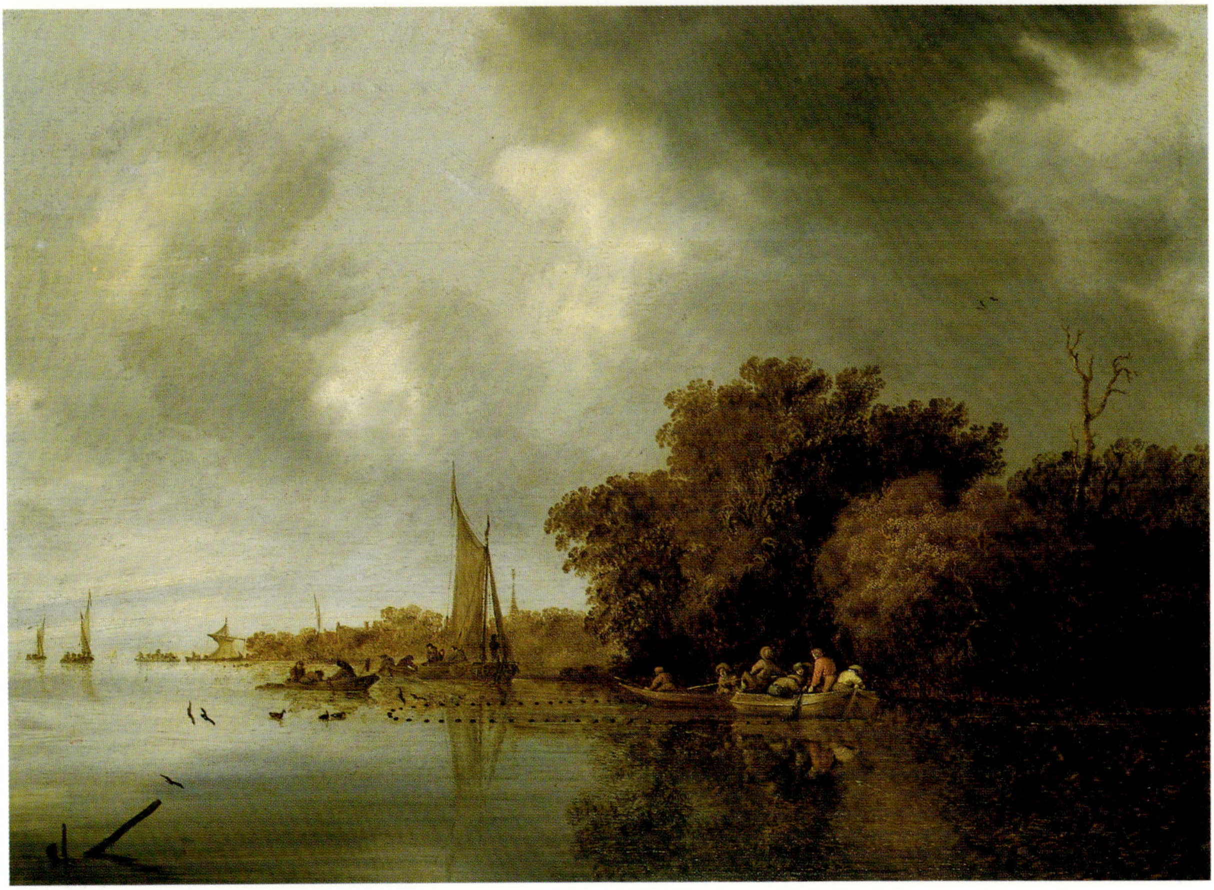

Salomon van Ruysdael
1600/1603 Naarden - 1670 Haarlem

66 ## The Fishermen

1642
Wood. 64 × 89 cm
Acquired in 1959.
Inv. n° O 7909

Haarlem was one of the most important centres of painting in Holland, especially landscape painting. Salomon van Ruysdael won himself very early on a solid reputation in the genre. He was a member of the Haarlem guild of painters from 1623, and master from 1648.

This picture typifies the way he conceived landscape art in the 1640's, when he was using colour to achieve the overall unity of his composition. Here, we are looking out from a boat afloat in mid-stream. Near-by farm buildings can be glimpsed between the trees lining the river-banks, which recede towards the distant horizon in a fore-shortened perspective. The minutely variegated plant life of the foreground is reflected in the surface of the water, giving a restrained palette of greens and ochres. The sparkling reflections of trees, boats and fishermen are rendered with consummate skill, and the broad, peaceful stream with its little river-craft conveys serenity and harmony.

Life on the waterways with their simple folk was a favourite theme with Dutch landscape artists at this time. Jan van Goyen's treatment of the subject has analogies with that of Ruysdael.

H.S.

Gerbrandt van den Eeckhout
1621 Amsterdam - 1674 Amsterdam

67 David and Bathsheba

1646
Canvas. 143 × 163 cm
Acquired in 1968.
Inv. nº O 11684

Eeckhout was one of Rembrandt's most gifted pupils. He attended the master's studio in Amsterdam from 1635 to 1640 and ranked high in his esteem. His talent is most fully revealed in his large canvasses with historical subjects.

David and Bathsheba is one of his earliest works. Affinities with those of Rembrandt are not far to seek, but in addition he has a sense of the spectacular in his scene-setting, an epic vein reminiscent of Pieter Lastman. This episode, taken from the Old Testament, occurs during the last years of King David's life, when his wife Bathsheba asks him, in the presence of the prophet Nathan, to bequeath the kingdom to her son Solomon (First Book of Kings, chap. 1, 1-34). The artist has imbued the royal apartments with a majesty not unlike that of Rembrandt's *Joseph interpreting Pharaoh's Dreams* (Greenville, private collection). Eeckhout has left us a sketch of his composition (Metropolitan Museum, New York) and a special study for the figure of the king (Kunsthalle, Hamburg). The large canvas reveals a masterly organization of the spatial relationships and a sure eye for each protagonist's frame of mind: Bathsheba humbly devoted, Nathan expectant, David listening attentively, while the young Abizah, engaged in preparing the king's bed, registers curiosity. The pathos of this decisive moment is counterbalanced by a detail intruding from everyday life: the trivial pastimes of the guards seen through an arcade.

Eeckhout was a master at handling colour. His combinations go beyond the conventions of the time and his palette is remarkably rich. He can give us the exact feel of luxury materials, no doubt taking over from his goldsmith father a taste for objects of value. The priceless receptacle on the table before the king is a fine example of goldsmith's art: it is the silver gilt ewer created by Adam van Vianen in 1614 and commissioned by the guild of goldsmiths. It became famous in its time and appears in the paintings of several Dutch painters of the 17th century.

H.S.

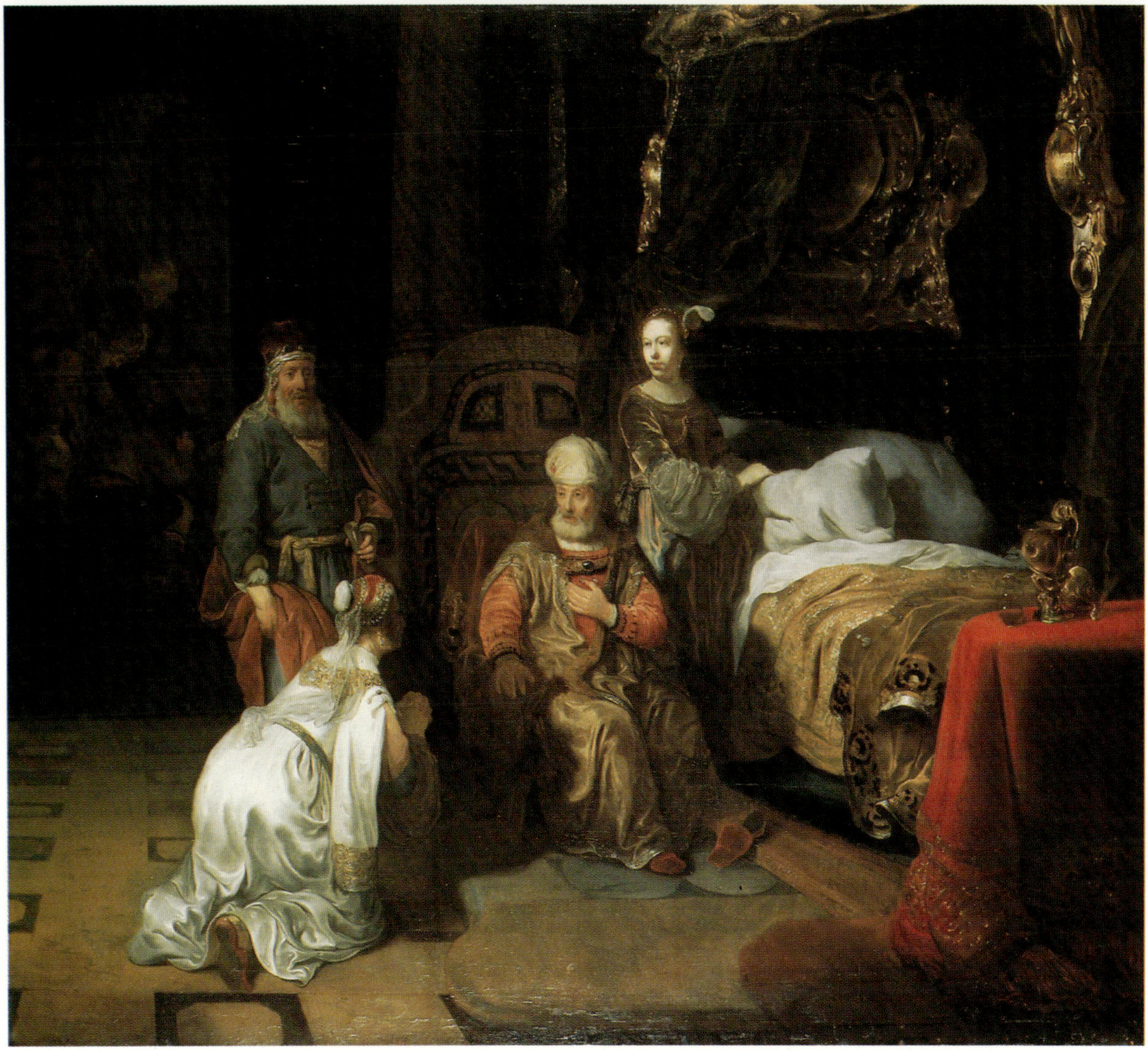

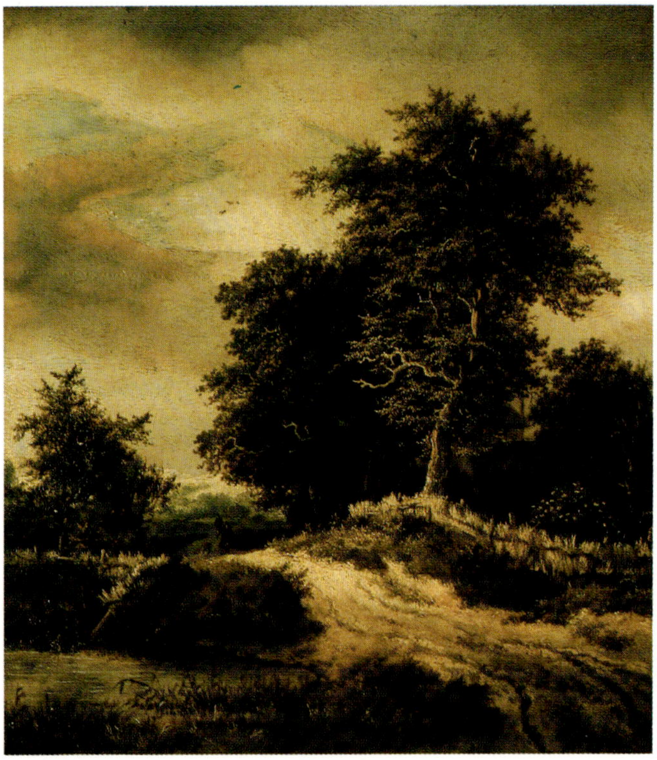

Jacob van Ruisdael
1628/1629 Haarlem - 1682 Amsterdam

68 ## The Lane

Wood. 30.8 × 28.7 cm
Acquired from an art dealer in Lucerne in 1923.
Inv. nº O 1377

Jacob van Ruisdael belongs to a new generation of landscape artists in Haarlem. He was the son of a picture framer and cabinetmaker, Isaak de Goyer. Isaak and his brother Salomon, the famous landscape painter, had adopted Ruysdael (Ruisdael) as patronymic from the castle of that name near Naarden, whence the family originated.

Following the example of Cornelis Vroom, who was a few years his senior, Jacob paid particular attention to trees, closely observing their growth and foliage, and the movement of their branches and leaves. Between 1640 and 1650 old oaks are the main subject of his pictures. Not that he was intent on reproducing them faithfully in their particularity. The sketches he made while on his walks were a point of departure from which to construct the very type of the old tree.

In this little composition he has brought together a group of old oaks and a lane running alongside a stretch of water. He devotes his skill to minutely distinguishing the various types of flora bordering the lane, using a rich scale of browns and greens. Within this limited register Jacob van Ruisdael successfully renders the detail of the rushes and waterside plants, and the thickly growing bushes under the oaks which shelter a farmhouse. Compared to these majestic trees, the figures just visible in their shade seem quite fragile, insignificant.

Ruisdael's sensitivity to nature and his admiration for her magnificence were a major source of inspiration for those 19th century artists who took up this genre.

H.S.

Gerard ter Borch
1617 Zwolle - 1681 Deventer

69 Portrait of Willem Marienburg the Younger

after 1661
Canvas. 81 × 65 cm
This canvas and its fellow, the *Portrait of Geertruide Marienburg,* were donated in 1890 by Johann II of Lichtenstein to the Picture Gallery of the Society of Patriot Friends of the Arts and later transferred to Prague National Gallery. Both portraits had been acquired for the Lichtenstein collection in 1869 from the Bols collection in Deventer.
Inv. n° O 640, O 639

Gerard ter Borch was a well-travelled, widely cultivated man, much admired in the first half of the 17th century for his "genre" pictures and his portraits, usually small in scale. He depicted his models full length but without ostentation. In 1648 he was invited to record for posterity the features of the political personalities who took part in the negotiations for the Münster peace treaty, which put an end to the Thirty Years' War (National Gallery, London).

Willem Marienburg (1634-1711) was a man of some importance. A well-to-do patrician of Deventer, he later became mayor of that town. Sober restraint is the hallmark of this portrait. The dark costume with its resplendent white collar, the tall headgear and the gloves, all combine to inspire respect for the man. The face has a lively, inquiring look and betokens the self-confidence that comes with self-knowledge. The moment has been caught and rendered with the precision of a miniature. The dark, sober costume becomes a pretext for the artist to make great play with delicate shades of dark grey contrasting with the shimmering reds of the velvet tablecloth.

It must be recorded however that for all its discretion this painting fell victim to changes in fashion at the time when Marienburg became mayor. The lofty hat and squared-off shoes were now out and were painted over in a later style. The companion *Portrait of Geertruide Marienburg* was similarly touched up, and for the same reasons.

H.S.

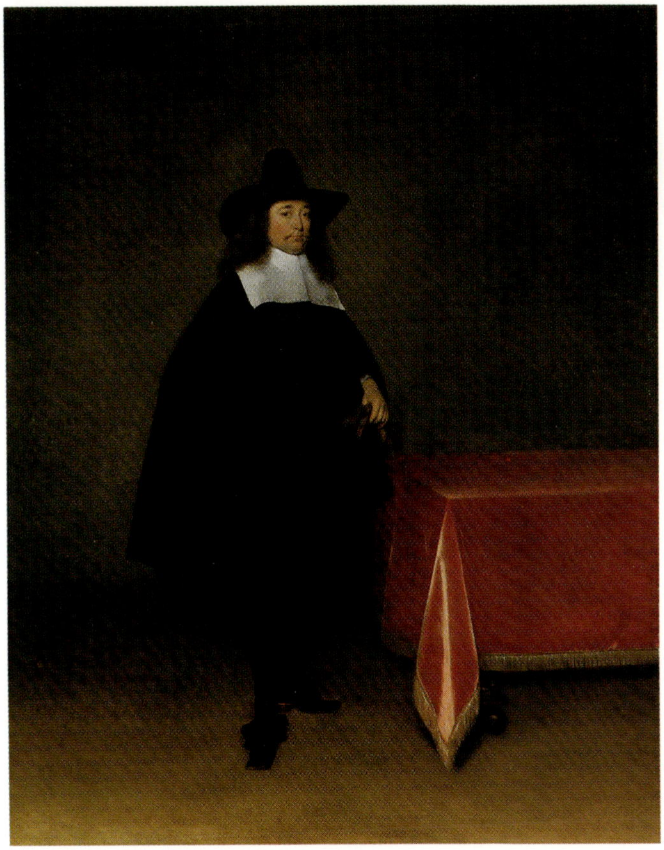

Jan Steen
1626 Leyden - 1679 Leyden

70 The Physician with his Patient

circa 1665
Wood. 49 × 46 cm
Acquired in 1945 from the Nostitz collection, where it was first recorded in 1765.
Inv. n° DO 4598

Jan Steen was one of those painters who was attracted by scenes of everyday life. His sense of humour turns his work into a mirror of human folly. He found inspiration in the theatre and literature of his time, and could therefore overlay his pictures with allusions and sly hints.

A physician calling on a female patient was a favourite subject for moralizing anecdotes so popular in the Low Countries in the 17th century. Both the physician's role and the woman's sickness were derided. Here the scene is enacted in a respectable burgher's interior. The lady is quite obviously suffering from that incurable sickness known as the malady of love. Her melancholy expression and gesturing hand make this clear, and the sly smile on the serving girl's lip shows that the "sickness" is no mystery to her. Besides, the small bottle in her hand proves that a test for pregnancy has been carried out. The physician, or rather charlatan, makes one think of some of Molière's characters or of the commedia dell'arte, so self-important as he draws up his prescription.

Steen is a first-class narrator. He has the sharp eye of a man of the theatre, together with the miniaturist's precise notation. He has furnished the interior of this burger's house with several details hinting at an immoral background to the episode. The lute for example, set against the back wall, suggests the female form, an association frequently exploited in the literature of the time. The clock marks the passage of time, but also of life, which may be either virtuous or depraved, Even the picture hanging above the door has hidden meaning. It shows the sea and some ships, symbols of love-relationships. The surface of the sea, now calm, now agitated, was compared to love, and the ship to the lover.

H.S.

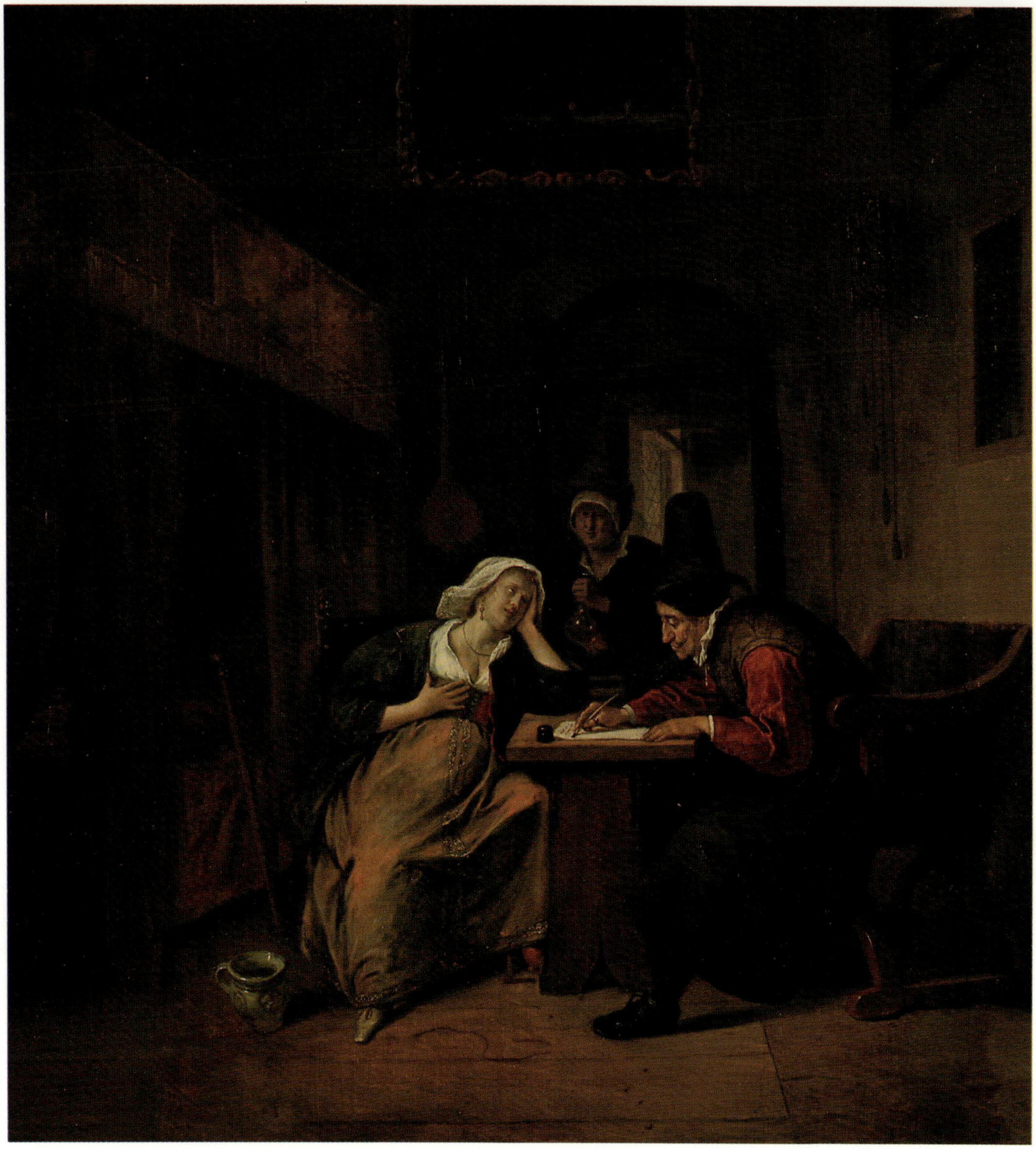

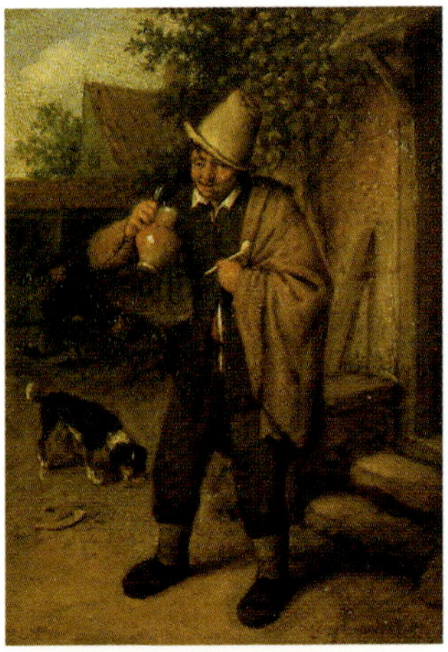

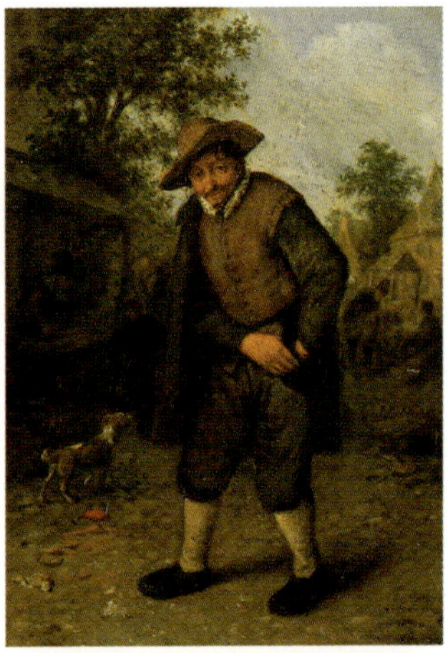

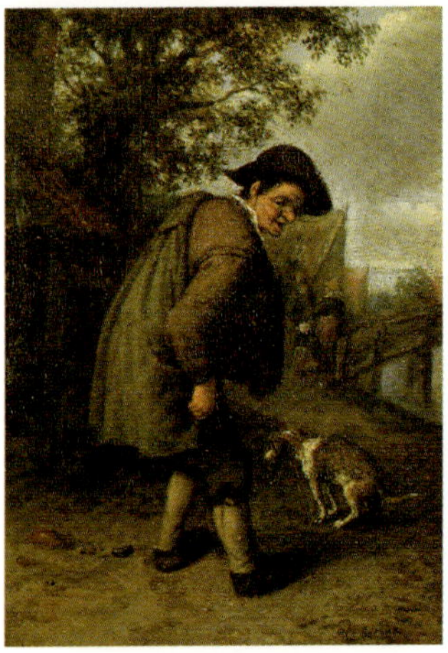

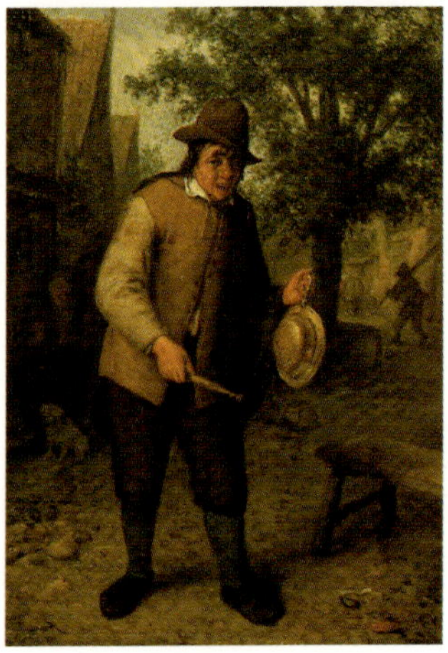

Adriaen van Ostade

1610 Haarlem - 1685 Haarlem

71 Hearing

Touch

Paper on wood. 15.2 × 11 cm

Smell

Taste

Paper on wood. 15.1 × 11 cm

At the end of the 18th century this series belonged to the collection of Moritz Fries in Vienna, then to those of the merchant D'Allard, the Dalstein chambers and Josef Hoser. Donated by Dr Hoser in 1843.
Inv. n° O 182, O 157, O 158, O 144

The Haarlem painters always gave their works the stamp of individuality, whether landscape, still life, or other genre. The subjects they treated were extremely diverse: the interior of taverns, barns or workshops, the rude world of peasants and low townspeople. Adriaen van Ostade ranks among those who took on these themes with most zest, often introducing a hidden meaning. We would be hard put to understand the artist's intention in each of these four pictures if the series they form had not been preserved almost complete (a fifth, *Sight,* is now lost). Traditionally the five senses were represented by mythological figures or by gallant couples of knights and ladies. Ostade is less high-flown and depicts them with that pithy humour the Haarlem painters made their own. The drinker with his jug, pipe in hand, personifies *Taste.* The street singer hitting a plate with a fork as though striking a gong represents *Hearing.* The unshaven peasant assessing the contents of his small purse depicts *Touch,* while the luckless individual gazing at his shoe, on which a dog has just relieved itself is an eloquent representation of *Smell.* The faithful friend of man is in fact an actor in all four scenes. The senses are personified by quite ordinary men, wearing earthy grey-brown clothes and that emblem of male pride, a hat. The background opens onto a glimpse of daily life in a small Dutch town, rendered with sharp definition. Ostade describes this milieu of simple folk with a critical yet kindly eye. Although *Sight* is missing we can imagine the series as a whole because he painted a similar one in his youth, *The Five Senses,* which belongs to the Ermitage Museum in Saint Petersburg.

H.S.

Frans van Mieris
1635 Leyden - 1681 Leyden

72 The Toilet

1662
Wood. 31 × 24.5 cm
Acquired in 1945
Inv. n° DO 4608

Precise execution and a refined style were qualities highly valued in the middle of the 17th century, especially in Leyden, where Gerard Dou was their principal exponent, successfully followed by van Mieris, one of his most talented pupils. His intimate paintings show scenes from the life of well-to-do patrician society, catching its elegance and its fine manners.

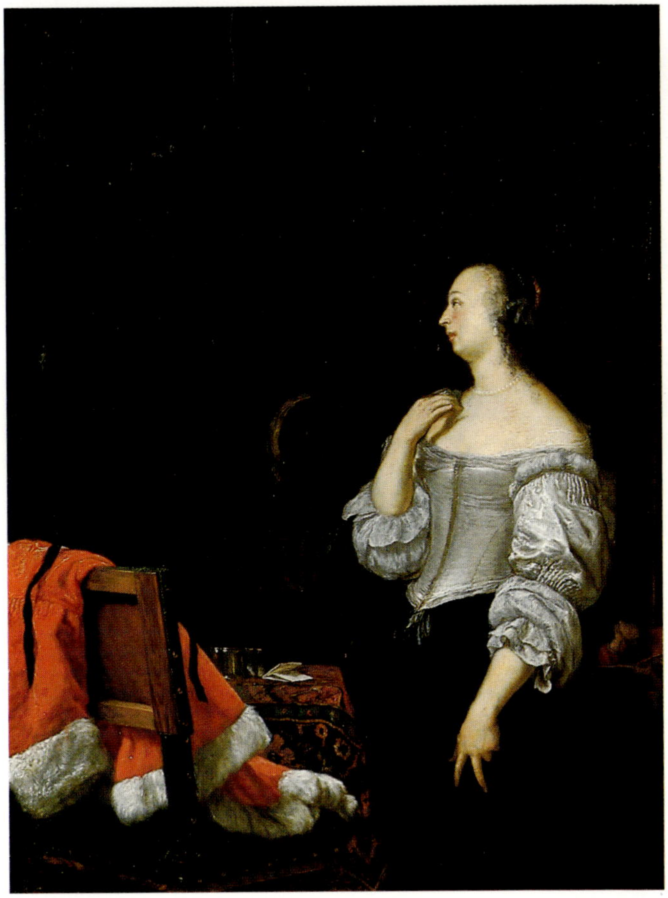

The Toilet is a remarkable example of the virtuosity that typifies the Leyden miniatures. A perfect enamel-like finish adds to the refinement of the colour composition. The foreground presents a chair with a lady's négligé carelessly thrown across it, and a table covered by an oriental carpet, both with a detail that invites prolonged contemplation. The background interior is no more than suggested where its architecture is lost in shadow. The painter is playing up the contrasts: the lady's fair complexion is enhanced by the dark skin of her maid, and the red of her négligé with the grey-white sleeves and the grey and black skirt of the girl.

The hidden symbolism of the scene proves how deliberately it was composed. The young woman contemplates her beauty in the mirror while choosing what jewels will best match her *toilette*. The letter lying on the table underneath the mirror hints at a love-affair. Mirror and jewels are both symbols of vanity, telling how ephemeral is life here below. The male figure in the background gives the message a further twist: the head resting on the arm as he reads gives him a melancholy attitude - the vanity of books?

This composition seems to have won great success from the outset, since van Mieris made several replicas of which the original is in Berlin (Staatliche Museen, Preussischer Kulturbesitz). The model for the young lady was the painter's wife, Cuner van den Coeck.

H.S.

German and Austrian painting from the fifteenth to the eighteenth centuries

Master of the votive panel of Saint Lambert
active in the first half of C 15

73 Panel of Zikmund Waloch, goldsmith

1434
Wood. 148 × 114 cm
Acquired in 1945.
Inv. n° DO 4597

This panel, commissioned in 1434 by Zikmund Waloch in honour of his deceased wife, is the only precisely dated work by an anonymous Austrian artist of the first half of the 15th century. His identity has not been satisfactorily determined: some specialists incline towards Hans von Tübingen, or the sculptor Hans von Judenburg; others prefer Master Hans or the master of the *Linz Crucifixion*. Where his studio may have been is equally uncertain: Vienna, Vienna New Town, Saint Lambert and Judenburg have all been suggested.

The panel represents the Virgin and Child in Majesty. The Jesus Child is blessing the donor Zikmund Waloch, goldsmith to Vienna New Town, and his spouse. The man holds up a scroll with an inscription derived from the Book of Psalms (51); a second inscription slipping from the woman's hands is dedicated to the Virgin. To complete the scene the two *orantes* are protected by their two advocates, Saint Barbe and Saint Judas Thaddeus, with their customary attributes, the tower with three windows, and the club, while two groups of angels look on. What makes the work remarkable is its plastic quality, the fullness of the figures being obtained through subtle shading and harmonious colours, and equally its static character, giving the overall composition a monumentality in which the only movement comes from the Child and prompts the Virgin's gesture catching the transparent fabric that keeps the little Jesus safe. In the architecture of the throne there is a noteworthy attempt at creating the illusion of space.

This Prague panel, exactly dated by the inscription on the frame, is a later work than the *Votive Painting of Saint-Lambert* (circa 1430, Joanneum, Graz) which is attributed to the same artist and gives him his customary appellation. Representing the Virgin of Mercy and a battle between Christians and Turks (opinions diverge as to the precise battle in question), its affinity with the Prague panel can be recognized in the face of the Virgin (which follows in the tradition of the early 15th century School of Cologne), in the composition of the colours, the motif of the angels in the upper left angle, and in the handling of the draperies falling in soft folds. These are works which break loose from the formal schemata of tradition.

The Prague panel, as well as other works by this artist, points to several distinct sources of inspiration, proving that its author was familiar with the artistic production of his time. His tradition is recognizably Austrian, but we can detect affinities with Italian art and with Bohemian painting of the fourteenth century.

J.Ch.

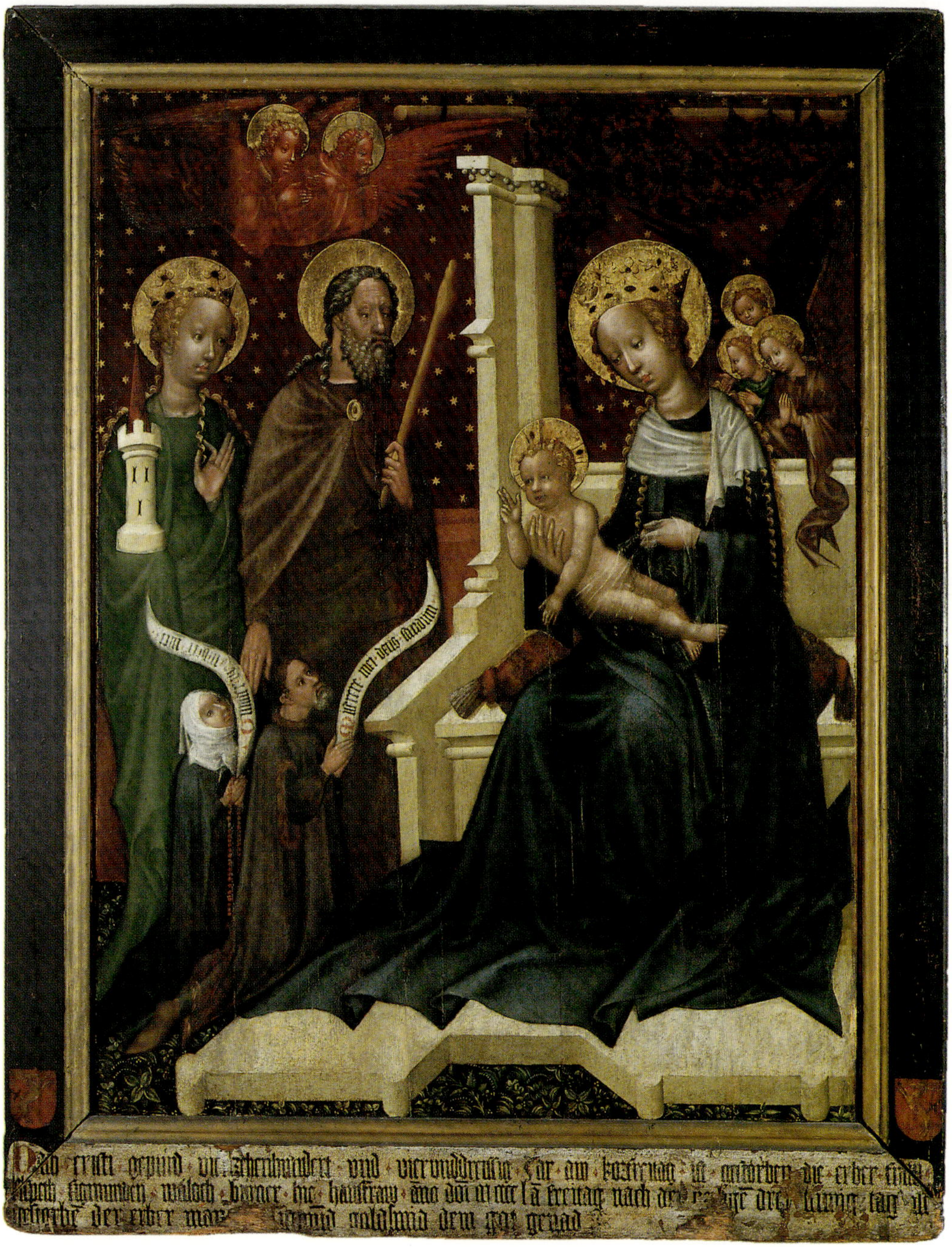

Hans Holbein the Elder
circa 1465 Augsburg - 1524 Isenheim, Alsace

74 Left Panel of the Hohenburg Altarpiece

1509
Wood. 135 × 79 cm
The altarpiece was probably intended for the monastery of Mont Sainte-Odile in Hohenburg.
Loaned by V. Vernier in 1801 to the Picture Gallery of the Society of Patriot Friends of the Arts.
Acquired by Count Sternberg-Manderscheid in an auction sale in 1826. Transmitted to the Friedrich Wallis collection in 1855.
Acquired in 1882.
Inv. n° O 40

This left-hand panel is painted on both surfaces and forms part of an ensemble of which the central panel is now lost. Its outer surface represents Saint Thomas and Saint Augustine (who has the signature "Hans" on the edge of his cloak); and the upper part of the inner surface shows Saint Sebastian, Saint Lucy and Saint Catherine with their attributees, while the lower part depicts the *Death of the Virgin*.

It is presumed that this altarpiece was originally intended for the monastery of Mont Sainte-Odile in Hohenburg, Alsace, where the artist had resided in 1509. Among the clues pointing to this hypothesis is the representation of Saint Odile, the foundress, in the lower part of the right panel, setting the soul of her father free from Purgatory; and the presence of the figure of Saint Augustine, since the monastery was intended for the Augustinian Order.

The panels have been executed according to the technique of *grisaille,* which indicates that Holbein the Elder was still under the influence of late Gothic sensitivity. Some Renaissance motifs were already making their appearance in late Gothic works but rather as decorative elements (for instance the arches enclosing the figures of the saints on the inner surface, or the frame surrounding the *Death of the Virgin*). These Renaissance ornaments may have been suggested to Holbein by title-pages of books.

The rigidity of the figures of the saints and the deep folds in their heavy cloaks, which are not always consistent with their body's shape, are very suggestive of sculpture, a feeling which is amplified by the choice of technique and the artist's own acute plastic sense.

In the *Death of the Virgin* the scene unfolds in a restricted space, overloaded with figures clearly Gothic in both type and gesture, which show Holbein still faithful to *late* Gothic forms. The influence of the painting of the Low Countries that he had come to know from his travels still marks his craftsmanship here. Not until the 1510's does inspiration from the art of Italy take hold in his painting, although he never went there. He remained profoundly faithful to the medieval tradition, which has left its mark on the whole of his work. There are interesting links between this work and some of his others, both earlier and later than the Hohenburg altarpiece, in which he has depicted the same characters, the same types of face or certain landscape motifs.

J.Ch.

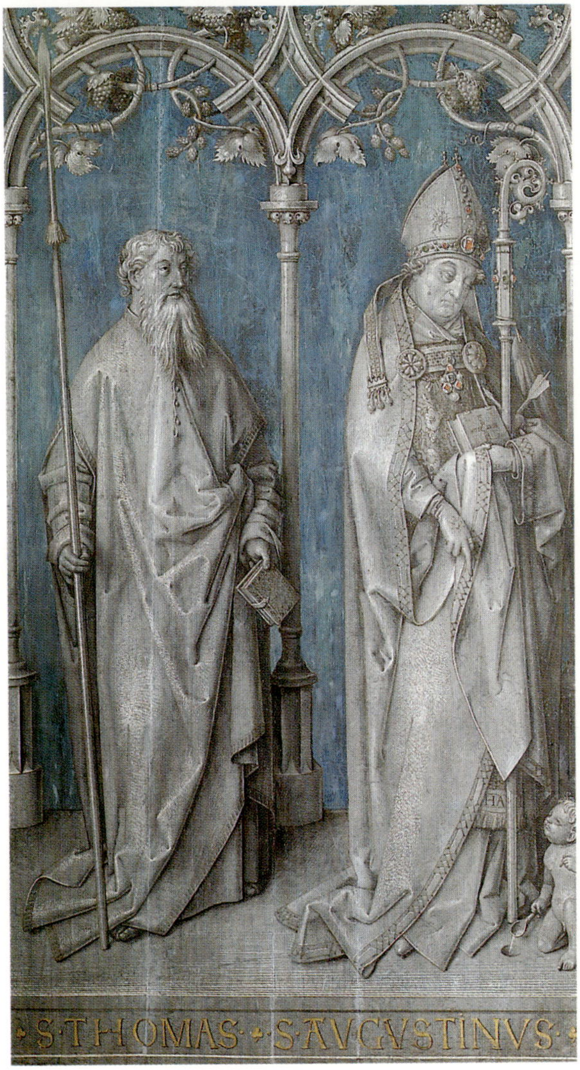
S·THOMAS· S·AVGVSTINVS·

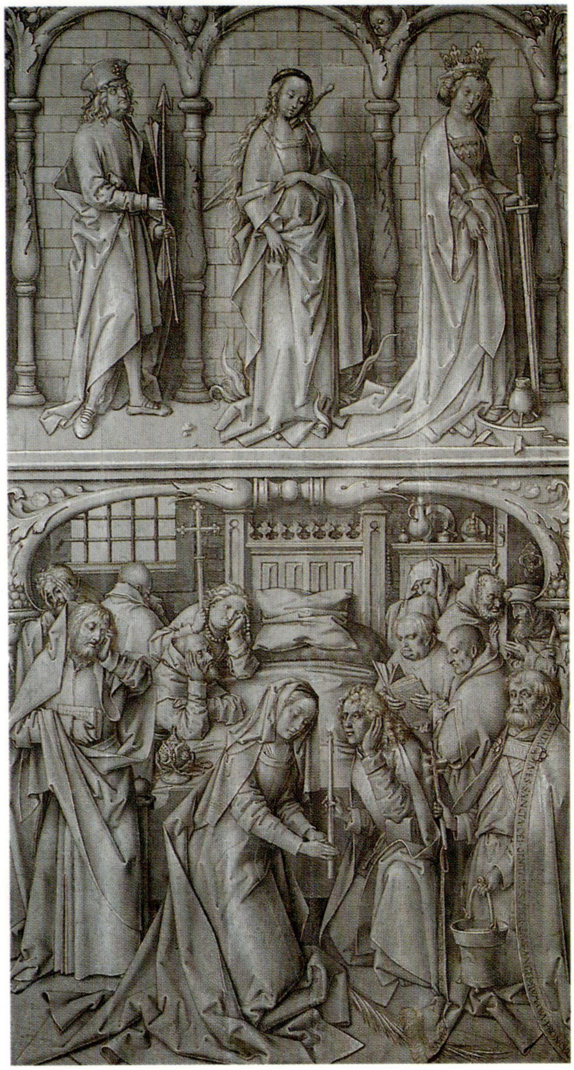

Bernhard Strigel
1460/1461 Memmingen - 1528 Memmingen

75 The Crucifixion

after 1515
Wood. 143 × 103 cm
Bought from the chapel of Zákupy castle in 1949.
Inv. nº DO 2102

Bernhard Strigel was one of a great family of painters, and his *Crucifixion* is one of his masterpieces. In this painting the Swabian tradition is confronted with those of other lands that this Swabian artist had visited - the Low Countries and the Danube valley.

This picture was no doubt originally the central section of an altar. Characteristic of Strigel's manner are the spatial construction of the composition, and the plasticity with which he endows the figures, the elements of landscape and architectural features; also the rich and radiant colouring and the individualization of the several figures. The latter display his talents as portraitist, much appreciated in his day. He was court painter to Emperor Maximilian I and also worked for aristocratic and patrician families. This *Crucifixion* is noteworthy for the thorough-going symmetry which governs its organization: the figures are grouped on either side of the Cross; the background landscape is laid out so that the architecture of the fortress counterbalances the piled-up rocks overhanging a vast stretch of water. The spatial depth of the picture rests on a deliberately elaborated basis, namely the acute angle at which the crosses of the two thieves are placed in relation to the central Cross (a feature with a long tradition in German and Netherlandish art), the distinct planes (one group around the Virgin, another of soldiers at the foot of the crosses, another group playing at dice, even the background landscape is peopled with various figures), and the gradation of the sky from dark blue to the light horizon.

Some of the pictorial elements indicate that Strigel painted this *Crucifixion* after his first journey into the Danube valley (1515), where he might have come into contact with the local painters of that time, as may be supposed from his conception of the landscape. Its idyllic character is troubled only by the sombre and dramatic sky, which is inspired by the gospel texts: St. Matthew (27; 45), St. Mark (15; 37), and St. Luke (23; 44).

It would seem that Strigel was influenced by the works that Cranach created in Vienna. A similar sky is to be seen in Cranach's *Crucifixion* of 1503 (Munich, Staatsgemäldesammlung) and in another work of his with the same title, painted around 1500 (Vienna, Kunsthistorisches Museum), where the crosses are placed in a similar way. But the affinity of composition is closest of all with Cranach's woodcut *Crucifixion* dating from 1502, where we see the body of the thief caught in the same moment of collapse, the same placing of the crosses, and a castle similarly dominating the background. What distinguishes the Prague *Crucifixion* from Strigel's other works of that time is its pronounced suppleness of execution, the stronger relief given to its forms and the greater depth of its landscape. It is thought that Strigel also found inspiration in the painting of the Netherlands, including that of Jan van Eyck, during his second visit to that land, shortly after 1507. The realist influence of Jan van Eyck is particularly noticeable in the suppleness which has modelled the body of the crucified Christ.

J.Ch.

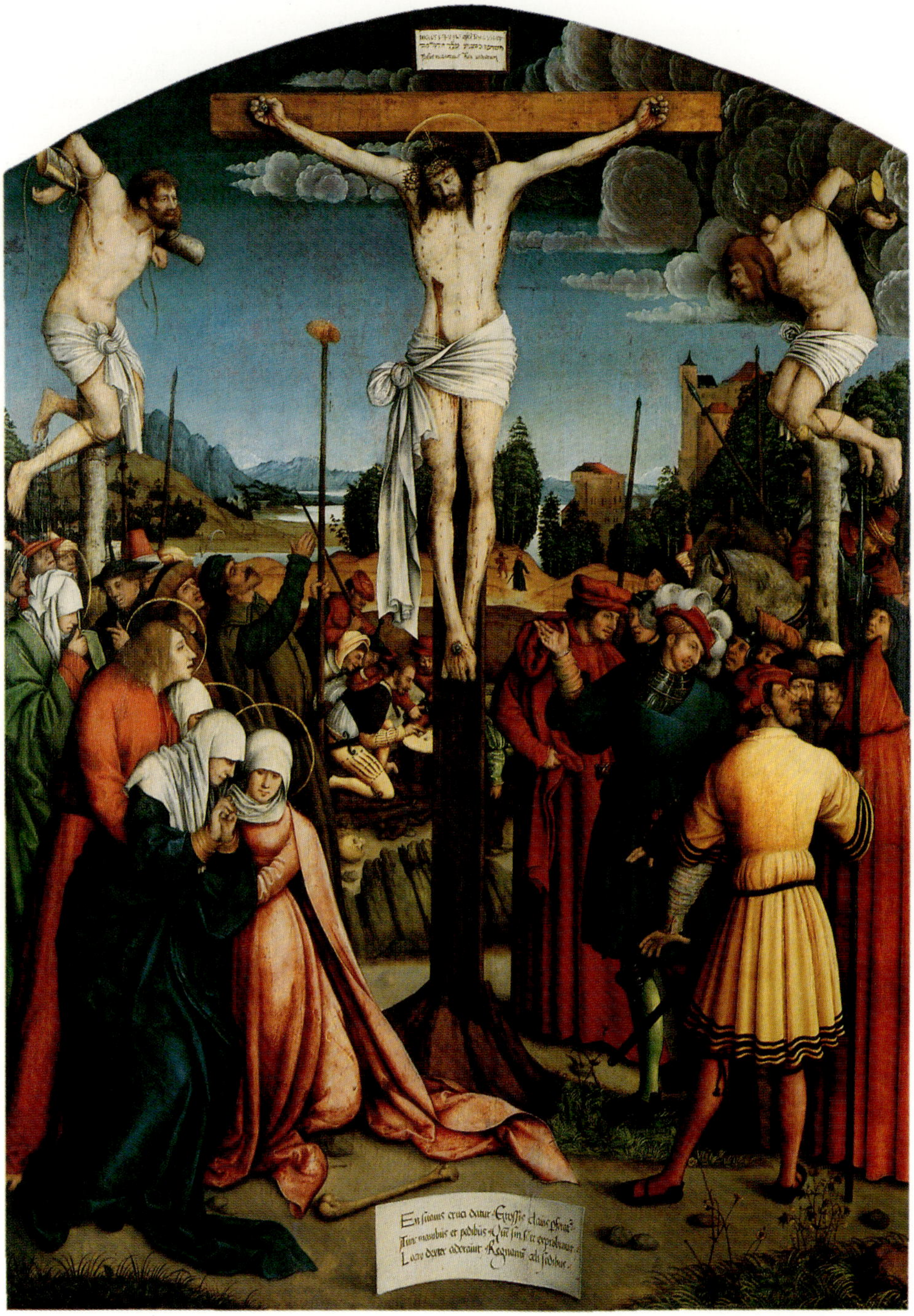

Albrecht Dürer
1471 Nuremberg - 1528 Nuremberg

76 The Feast of the Rosary

1506
Wood. 161.5 × 192 cm
This work was in the church of San Bartolomeo in Venice until 1606, when it was bought by Emperor Rudolph II. When part of Rudolph's collection was auctioned on May 15, 1782, it was acquired by F.L. Ehemant, and in the same year by F. Fillbaum. In 1793 the Abbot of the monastery of Strahov bought it from Fillbaum's heirs. It was acquired by the Czechoslovak State in 1934.
Inv. n° O 1552

"I have silenced all those painters who said I am a good engraver but a poor hand with the brush", was Dürer's proud claim in a letter addressed to his friend Willibald Pirckheimer in Nuremberg, from Venice, where he had just completed the *Feast of the Rosary.* This was his second sojourn in Italy and he was already well known, but it was this picture which was to win him well-deserved social and artistic prestige. It marks a turningpoint, not only in his own work but in the whole of north European Renaissance painting.

The painting was commissioned by German merchants for the church where they congregated, San Bartolomeo in Venice. Dürer first mentions it in January 1506 in one of his letters to Pirckheimer, which are the main source of our detailed knowledge of his activity in Venice. He completed the work in September of that year, in an atmosphere soured by the hostility of the Venetian painters, who saw him as a rival. Dürer was all the more appreciative of its success, especially with Giovanni Bellini, the doyen of Venetian Renaissance painting, whose judgement swayed the younger generation. Another source of satisfaction for him was a visit paid by the Doge, in fact the painting remained a focus of artistic interest in the town right down to 1606, when Emperor Rudolph II bought it for his collection. A lucky chance saved it from being included by the Swedish soldiery in the loot they carried off in 1648.

The subject of the picture is linked with the growth and spread of the cult of the Rosary, influenced mainly by the Dominican Order, in the second half of the 15th century. Here we see therefore, beside the Virgin and Child, Saint Dominic and several angels distributing crowns of roses to a congregation of believers symbolizing one of the fraternities of the Rosary currently being founded by the Dominicans.

The Pope and the Emperor, representing the spiritual and temporal powers, and also the figures kneeling around the throne, have been depicted with the precision of portraits, but except for a few the models are difficult to identify. The Virgin Mary and the Child are both gesturing towards Emperor Maximilian I and Pope Julian II. Some historians consider that the figure receiving his crown from the hands of the saint himself is Domenico Grimani patriarch of Aquileia, while the man in dark clothes on the right holding a set-square is Hieronimus of Augsburg, the architect of the "Fondaco dei Tedeschi", the house of the German merchants in Venice, which had recently been destroyed by fire. The painter's self-assurance has prompted him to include among the figures in the background his own self-portrait (on the right). The leaf in his hand carries his signature, details of his origin, the date of completion of the painting and the information that it took him five months. Doubtless this means only the execution and does not include the preparatory studies, of which several have survived.

In conformity with the content of the scene, its composition is strictly symmetrical. The Virgin and Child are in the centre, and the summit of the throne, which is on the central axis of the picture, coincides with the upper angle of an equilateral triangle of which Julian II and Maximilian I form the two sides.

This well-balanced harmony of line is reinforced by the placing of the figures on either side of the Virgin, while its apparent rigour is softened and enlivened by the variety of their stance and posture, and the joyful animation of the angels conferring the crowns adds an element of dynamism to the composition. The landscape in the background cannot be identified but looks back to the studies and drawings Dürer had made of the environs of Innsbruck and Trento during his first visit to Italy.

This is the earliest north European painting in which Renaissance ideas prevail, despite survivals from the past such as a strongly marked analytical tendency, a delight in detail, a somewhat loose rhythm and an accumulation of figures within the picture. Nevertheless several observations point to the influence of Venetian painting: the spatial composition is on a grander scale, there is a greater suppleness of line, a feeling for relationships of light, modulations of colour and plasticity of shape, and an enrichment of motifs derived from Venice.

Dürer has drawn on many sources for his *Feast of the Rosary.* The composition of the work has often suggested comparison with a woodcut on the same subject in a work by Jacob Sprenger dated 1477. Among the Venetian works showing some affinity we should note Giovanni Bellini's *Madonna with angels playing the violin, together with Saint Mark, Saint Augustine and the Doge,* dated 1488. The angel playing the lute is a motif probably also derived from a Bellini painting which was intended for the church of San Zaccaria in Venice. J.Ch.

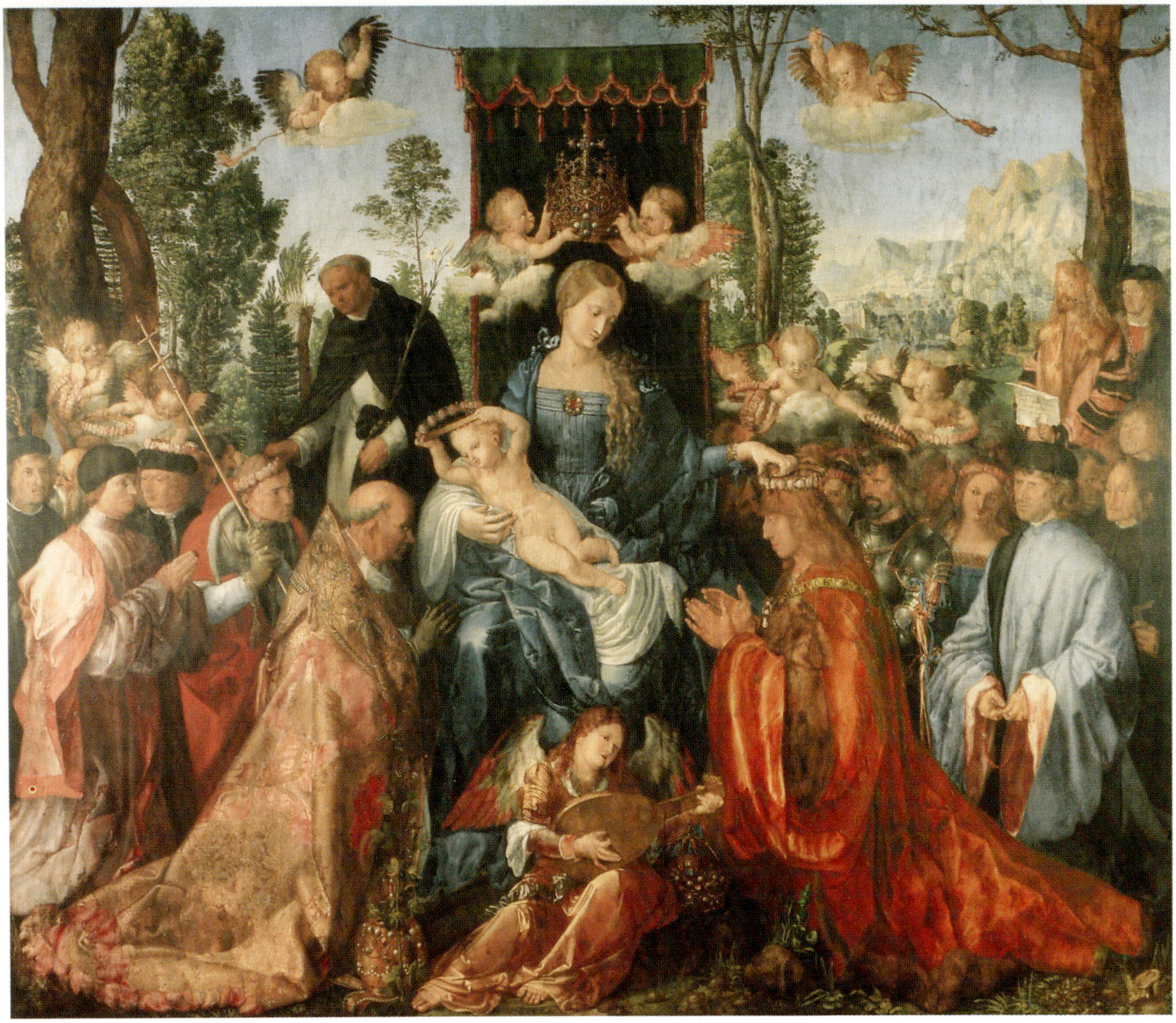

Albrecht Altdorfer
circa 1480 Regensburg - 1538 Regensburg

77 The Martyrdom of Saint Florian

circa 1516-1518
Wood. 81.5 × 66.5 cm
Loaned from the Lobkowicz collection in Mělník in 1940.
Inv. nº VO 1202

According to tradition Florian commanded the vice-regency of the Roman province of Noricum during the reign of the Emperor Diocletian. As a Christian he refused to worship the Roman gods and was therefore exiled and then, persisting in his faith, condemned to death by drowning in the river Enns, Lower Austria, in 304 A.D.

This panel, bearing the signature of Altdorfer, was part of a set of seven paintings, the others being preserved in the Uffizi in Florence, the Germanisches Nationalmuseum in Nuremberg and in a private collection. This cycle was from the first probably not intended for an altar as a whole, but its individual paintings are likely to have decorated a church.

In this work Altdorfer, principal exponent of the *Danube school,* gives expression to his passion for nature and displays his virtuosity in the handling of light effects. For this artist nature is no longer complementary to an event but a significant supporting element. He is rightly held to be the pioneer of north European landscape art, raising it to the level of an independent genre. His experiments with light effects on landscape and in architectural interiors anticipate the luminism which is such a feature of 17th century Dutch painting. The Prague panel presents a dramatic scene of martyrdom inside a Gothic church. Its dynamic quality is given not only by the composition of the movements and gestures of the individual figures but also by the light penetrating into the nave from several directions, which both enhances the spatial depth of the interior and accentuates the rich variety of the colours in the actors' costumes. Altdorfer's feeling for the architectonic construction of space is clearly visible in this picture and is characteristic of his work, linking him to his predecessor Michael Pacher. Another likely source is the copper engraving of the *Interior of a Church,* executed after a Bramante drawing by an anonymous master from the Mantegna circle. But these are not the only sources of Altdorfer's inspiration; he was an architect by profession and his experience as a builder shows through in his work as a painter.

In the narrative quality of the scene it presents, the dynamic thrust imparted by the vigorous activity of the figures, the wealth of colour in the costumes and the effects of light inside the building, this *Martyrdom of Saint Florian* has close affinities with the *Martyrdom of Saint Sebastian* from Altdorfer's large altar of Saint Sebastian (1509-1516), both being intended for the church in Saint Florian in Austria.

J.Ch.

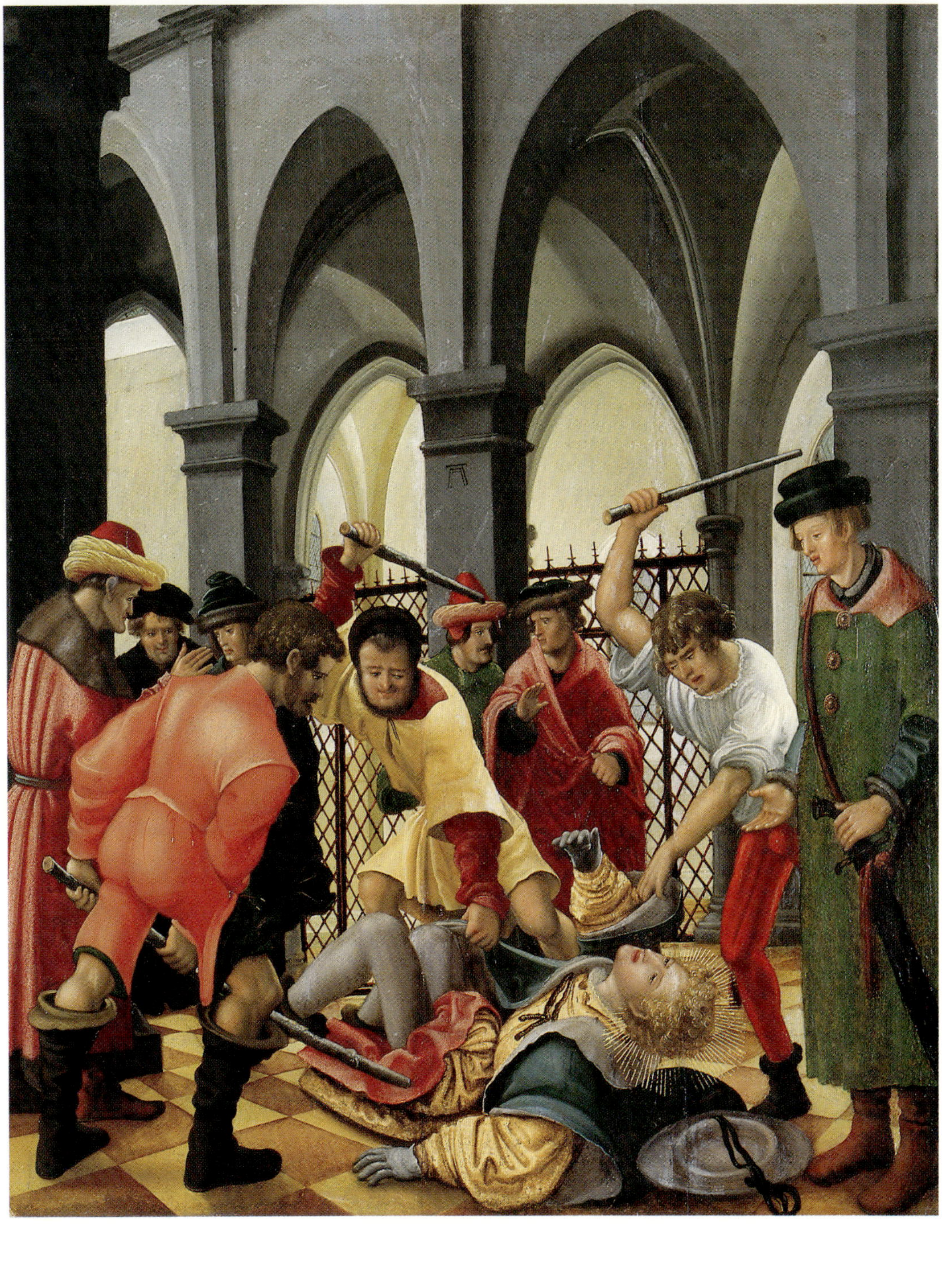

Lucas Cranach, the Elder
1472 Kronach - 1553 Weimar

78 Saint Christina

circa 1520-1522
Wood. 74 × 51 cm
Originally in the Saint Vitus Cathedral, Prague.
Bought in 1939.
Inv. n° O 8781

This panel representing Saint Christina is one of the surviving fragments of a very large marial altarpiece in Saint Vitus Cathedral, Prague. The altarpiece was largely destroyed during an attack launched by iconoclasts in December 1619 during the rule of Frederick of the Palatinale. One part, representing Saint Catherine, Saint Barbe and fragments of Saint Dorothea and Saint Margaret, is preserved in the Prague National Gallery; another part, a fragment of Saint Margaret, is in Aschaffenburg (Staatsgemäldegalerie), and one panel representing Saint Agnes of Rome, is in Karlsruhe (Kunsthalle).

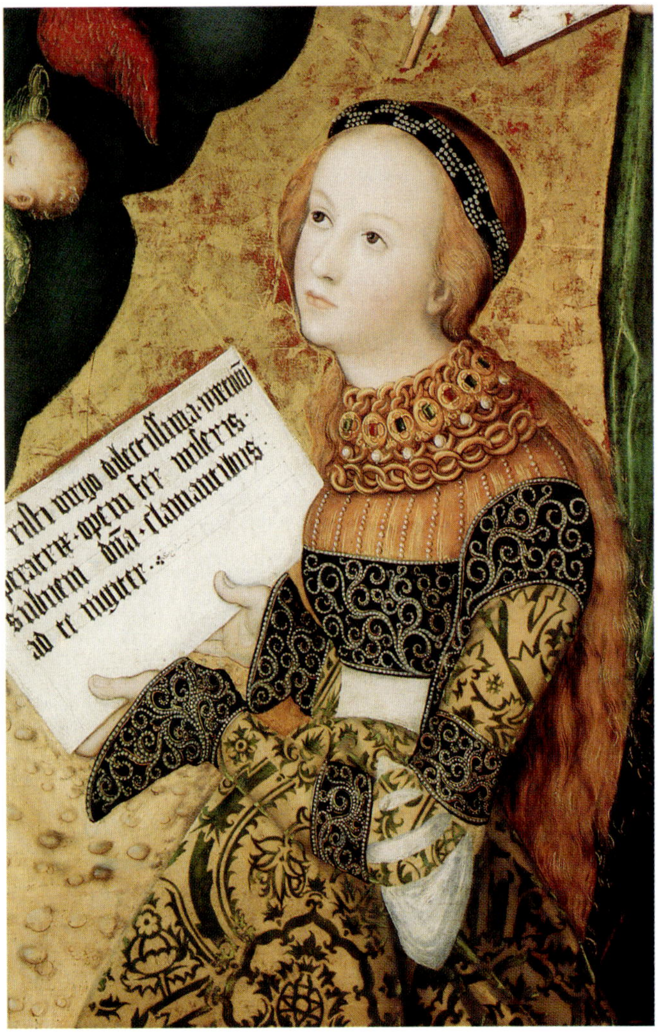

The central scene of this monumental winged altarpiece, which engaged Cranach's collaborators in much of its decoration, was probably the Glorification of the Virgin, surrounded by angels and saints; and when closed the wings of the altarpiece showed the Annunciation. Saint Christina, in a rich Renaissance robe, forms part of the right wing (with the fragment of an angel on the reverse), and like the saints of the remaining panels she is holding the Latin text of a prayer of which the first word conceals the name of the martyr (Cristi virgo dilectissima...)

Two suggestions have been put forward regarding the identity of the person who commissioned this altarpiece, which was unusually large among Cranach's works (its height is estimated at 2.5 metres). According to one it was King Louis Jagellon, acting on the advice of the bishop of Olomouc, Stanislav Thurzo, and wishing to mark the occasion of the coronation of his wife Marie, in 1522. In this view the altarpiece would have been placed in the axis of the cathedral choir and transferred later to the chapel of Saint Sigismond. The alternative hypothesis is that the work was commissioned by the Provost of the Saint Vitus Chapter and administrator of the archbishopric of Prague, Arnošt of Šlejnice. The Electors of Saxony could be the intermediaries since Cranach had worked for them and Arnošt was in close touch with the court of Saxony, where he could well have met Cranach and persuaded him to take on the project.

J.Ch.

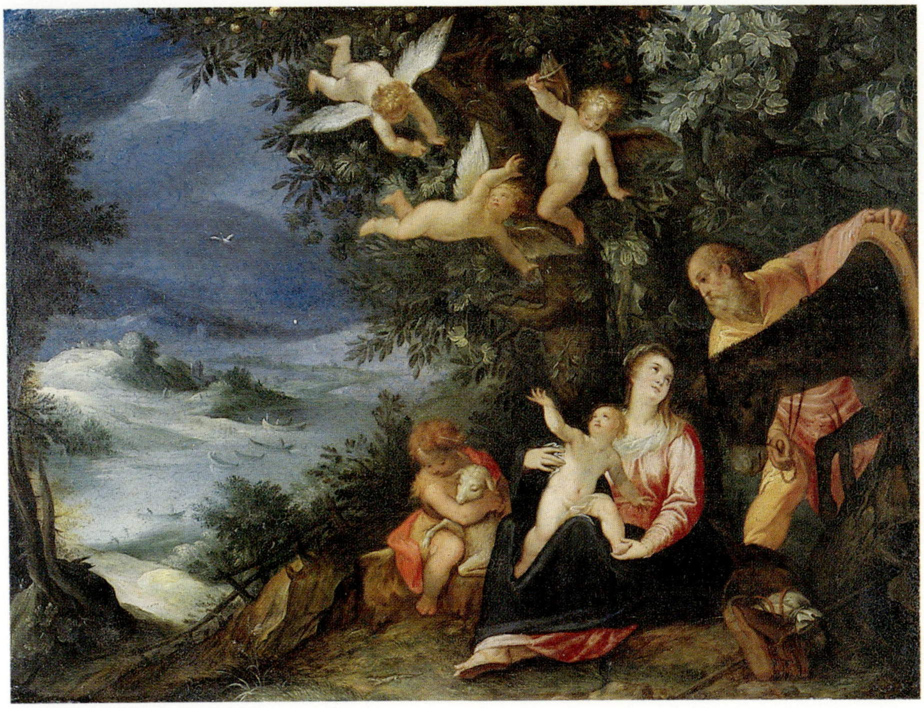

Hans Rottenhamer
1564 Munich - 1625 Augsburg

79 A Rest on the Flight into Egypt

after 1596
Copper. 26.5 × 35.5 cm
Around 1900 this work was in the collection of Hans Bernhard Greve in Berlin, in 1909 it was in the hands of the art dealer Rudolf Lepke in Berlin, then in the Hugo Weisgal collection in Prague. Donated by Hugo Weisgal in 1946.
Inv. nº O 2630

Like many other German painters Hans Rottenhammer chose to study painting in Italy, leaving his home town in 1589 for Treviso. Between 1590 and 1595 he was in Rome, where he collaborated with Paul Bril, a landscape artist of Flemish origin, and became a friend of Velvet Bruegel. Between 1595 and 1606 he was living in Venice, following the work of Tintoretto and Veronese with keen interest. He made himself a great reputation with his intimate paintings of biblical and mythological subjects executed with minute care on copper plates, and he attracted the attention of important collectors, such as cardinal Borromeo of Milan or the Gonzagas of Mantua. He also worked for Emperor Rudolph II.

The present work was probably painted during Rottenhammer's stay in Venice. Its small scale the group of figures placed in front of a wide-spreading tree. Here the influence of Veronese can be seen in the features of the Virgin, the Child and Joseph, while the whole effect shows how much Rottenhammer admired the colouring of Venetian artists. The left-hand part opens out on to a seashore with a billowing sea and distant ships, a seascape painted by Paul Bril.

As with the work of Albani (catalogue nº 21), the subject of this picture is derived from a text of the apocryphal gospel of Saint Matthew (chap. XX) relating the Holy Family's journey into Egypt and their resting under a fig-tree. Rottenhammer brings in the figure of John the Baptist as a reminder of his role as precursor of Christ. The little lizard in the foreground symbolizes death and resurrection.

H.S.

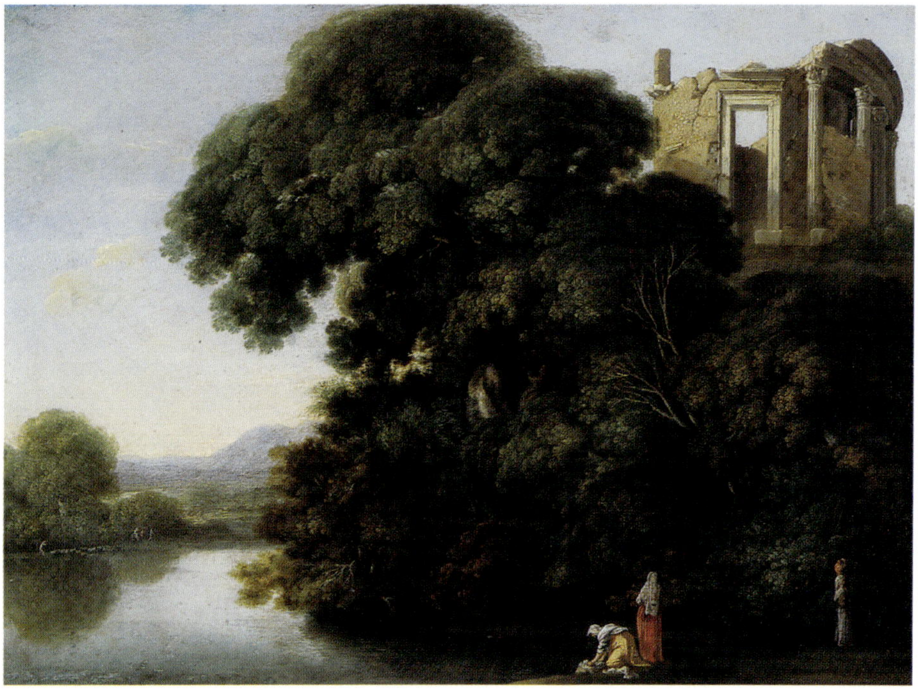

Adam Elsheimer — circle
1578 Frankfurt-on-Main - 1610 Rome

80 Landscape with Temple of Vesta at Tivoli

circa 1610
Copper. 23.5 × 33.5 cm
At the end of the 18th century this work was in the collection of Morits von Fries, who had bought it in Rome, and then in that of Dr Josef Hoser. Donated by Dr Hoser in 1843.
Inv. n° O 195

Until the late 1960's this painting was considered to be an authentic work by Adam Elsheimer, who played an important role in the evolution of European painting in the early 17th century. But from 1967, when Frankfurt put on an entire exhibition devoted to Elsheimer, the authorship of this *Landscape with Temple of Vesta* became open to doubt. However that may be, what we have here is a remarkable example of early 17th century landscape art, one which betrays the painter's intimate knowledge of Elsheimer's work.

This painting takes its motifs from the landscape in the vicinity of Tivoli (the ancient Tibur), dominated by the architecture of the circular temple of Vesta. Despite its small-scale format it magnifies nature - nature as found in Italy, near Rome - by means of its typically north-European approach. In the foreground the meticulous working of the details enables the varieties of flora to be differentiated. In the background, the misty distant shores, reflected in the water, are given more summary treatment. The artist's perfect mastery of contrasting light and shade models the architecture of the temple and the mass formed by the trees. The figures by the riverside become insignificant in comparison with surrounding nature, and the monumentality of the overall impression achieved is a declaration of the painter's admiration for nature in Italy and for the ancient world. The temple of Vesta on Mount Tibur was a motif much favoured by painters of the late 16th and early 17th centuries. The Prague collection gives us another example in the *Landscape with ancient temple* by Esaias van de Velde.

H.S.

Georg Flegel

1566 Olomouc - 1638 Frankfurt-on-Main

81 # Recess with fruit and flowers

Canvas. 92.5 × 62.5 cm
Donated by Dr Leopold Katz in 1927
Inv. n° O 1451

Like Adam Elsheimer, Georg Flegel figures among the significant personalities of German 17th century painting. He was probably the first painter of still life in Germany and contributed to the early spread of the genre in northern Europe. His approach was new in that he looked for novel methods, or reintroduced old ones that had long been forgotten.

This *Recess with fruit and flowers* is surprising for its inventiveness, an unusual quality in that period. It represents an exactly realistic recess containing Venetian and Rhenish glassware, various receptacles, sweetmeats, fruit and flowers. The challenge is to create a picture so convincingly real that it fuses into its surroundings. This is a tradition known to antiquity which the Italian Renaissance rediscovered. Pictures of this type are rare in Renaissance painting north of the Alps, and Flegel probably found inspiration in Italian marquetry with similar subjects. This would have given him the division of the recess into two compartments and the trompe-l'oeil painting of the ornamented frame. But Flegel's feeling for the uniqueness of each object, his ability to translate into paint the specific quality of each material - the transparency and fragility of glass, the rich glitter of gold or silver utensils, the darker tones of pewter, the beauty and variety of the fruit and flowers - all this belongs to the painterly practice of northern Europe.

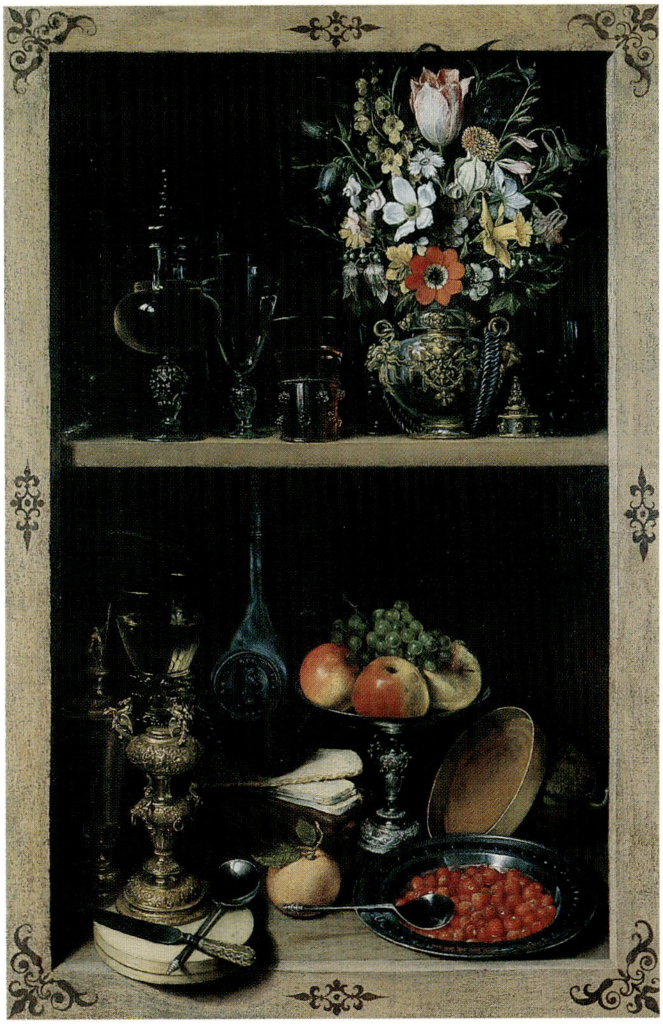

We should not exclude the possibility that Flegel's intention here was to depict a subject familiar to antiquity and called *xenion*. Pictures with this subject represented what the host was offering in honour of his guests, and they are described by Philostrates of Lemnos in his book *Eikones,* which came back into circulation in the 16th and 17th centuries, with the entire literary heritage of antiquity.

The picture was modified at some time in the past by being cut horizontally, the halves being then touched up to match one another. This fact came to light in the 1970's and the work was reconstituted in its original state.

H.S.

Johann Michael Rottmayr
1654 Laufen - 1730 Vienna

82 The Death of Seneca

before 1695
Oil on canvas. 127 × 181 cm
Acquired in 1950.
Inv. nº O 9664

This canvas displays the art of Rottmayr at its purest, during his most productive years, the 1690's. In Venice, he had been a pupil of Johann Karl Loth, called Carlotto. The influence of Loth is evident in the smooth aspect of the robust figures, executed in a gamut of warm browns or dull reds, their expressivity enhanced by the highlights which bring out the rounder shapes modelled by subtle grey shading. The facial types are also inspired by Loth: their exaggerated ruggedness is attenuated, and in the case of the men, there is a certain academicism, while the woman, devoid of expression, appear mask-like.

The painting was commissioned by Count Thun, who several times engaged Rottmayr's services. This work along with others by Rottmayr formed part of the Thun family collection, kept in their various castles, palaces or churches.

A passage in a letter from Maximilian Thun to Rottmayr, dated May 12, 1695, probably refers to this picture. In it the count is asking the painter how to deal with the mould that has appeared on one of his canvasses. We may deduce that the picture was completed before that date.

Seneca's suicide, freely accepted at the command of his pupil, the tyrant Nero (Tacitus, Annals, xv, 60-65), is a theme which was frequently represented by baroque painters. Seneca's serenity at the moment of death, likewise the moving suicide of the republican Cato of Utica, were evidently of striking interest to the aristocracy of the day.

The contrast in this scene between the dying man's composure and the wild grief of his friends and pupils as they record their master's last words undoubtedly had a fascination for painters. Rottmayr adds to the cruelty of the moment by including Nero and his wife, both looking on avidly, pitilessly.

P.P.

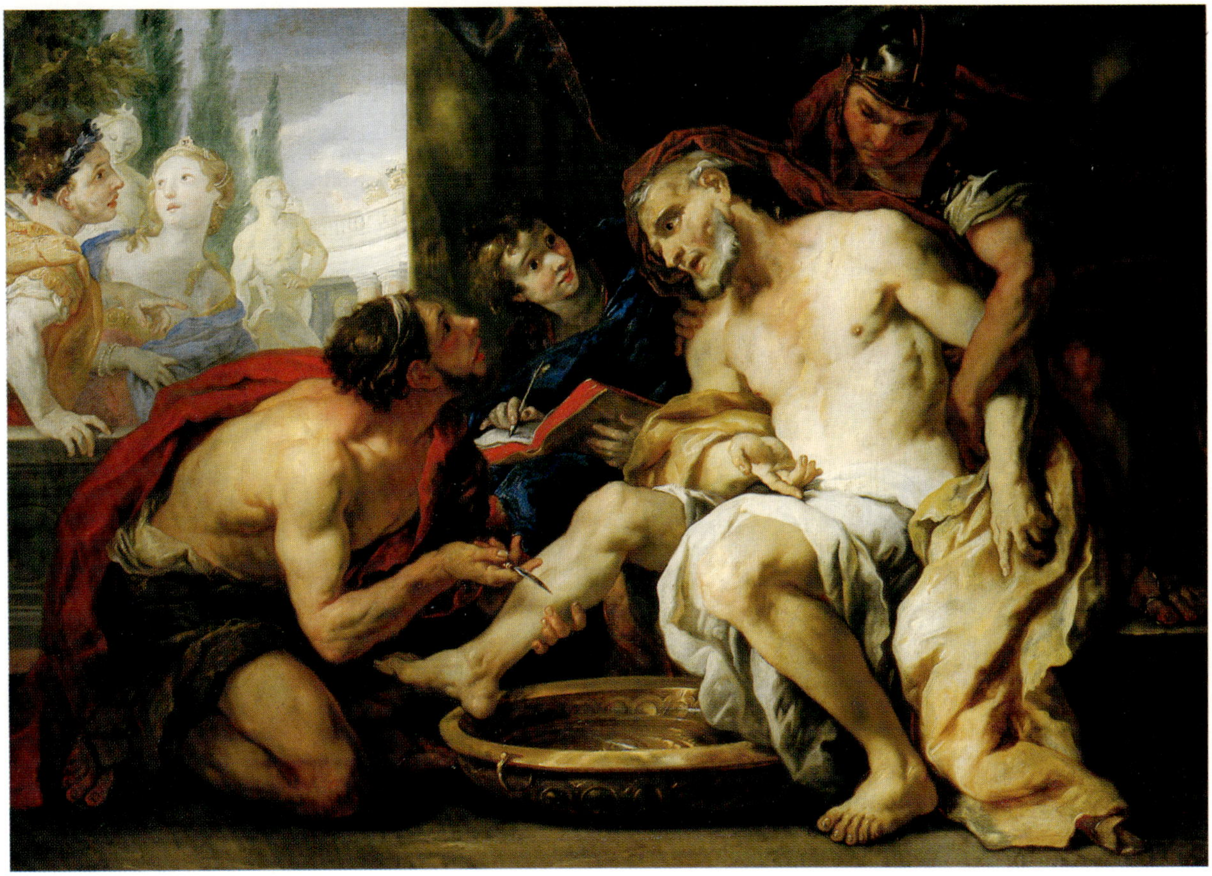

Martin Altomonte
1657 Naples - 1745 Vienna

83 Alexander the Great cutting the Gordian Knot

before 1709
Canvas. 86 × 86 cm
Acquired in 1922.
Inv. nº O 1329

Martin Altomonte's original name was Hohenberg. Born of German parents, he adapted so well to Italy that he Italianized his name. Among his most important works is a cycle of scenes from the legendary life of Alexander the Great, which he painted in collaboration with Johann Michael Rottmayr for the winter residence of the archbishop of Salzburg, Count Franz Anton Harrach. A contract was signed with Altomonte in 1709 for 3,700 florins, a very large sum for the period, in respect to ten ceilings to be executed and placed in stucco frames in the conference hall and the antechamber adjoining.

In reality the cycle is unfurled through several of the castle's rooms: in the knights' hall, the conference hall, the antechamber, the audience hall, the study, the cabinet and the bed-chamber. Several drawings have been preserved which indicate that Altomonte was to execute still other paintings, which were later entrusted to Rottmayr. The work for the bed-chamber was carried out by Rottmayr in 1710. He executed nine canvasses for the audience hall in 1711, and six others in 1714. The scene representing the generals paying hommage to Alexander was painted in collaboration with Altomonte.

During the Renaissance and Baroque periods Alexander the Great was the symbol of the heroic virtues, and near-divine qualities were attributed to him. It was even reported that he had met God in person, had later venerated him and sacrificed to him in the temple of Jerusalem. This scene is recorded in a drawing by Altomonte which is preserved in the Prague Museum of Applied Arts.

The Staatliche Graphische Sammlung in Munich preserves a drawing by Altomonte which is a first sketch of the idea for this painting and which antedates this unique study in oils for the Salzburg Alexander cycle. Here Altomonte expresses the firmness and vigour with which Alexander cuts the legendary knot which no one previously had succeeded in untying, hence the proverbial expression denoting resolute action. Altomonte's sketch for this scene is undoubtedly one of his best works.

P.P.

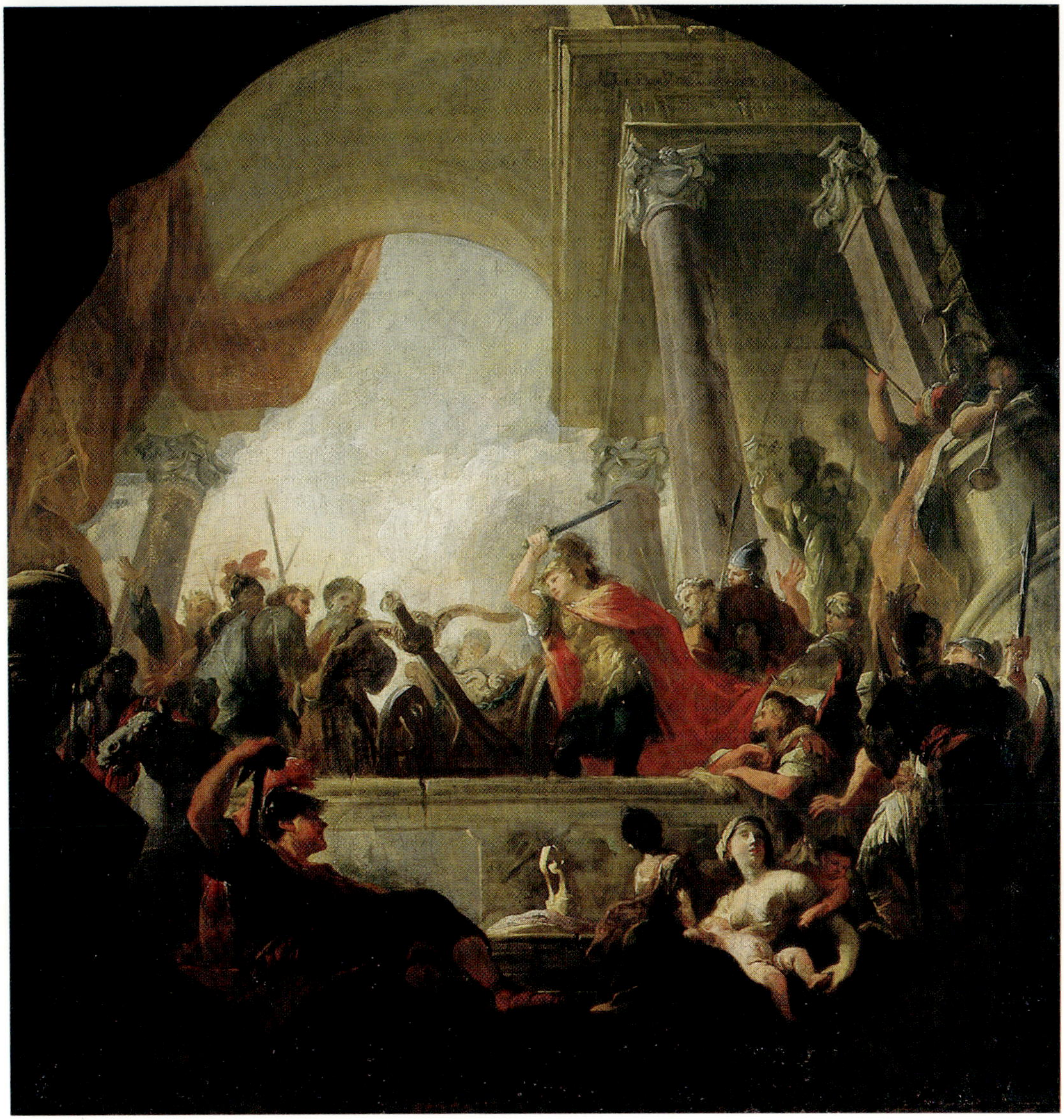

Johann Christian Brand

1722 Vienna - 1795 Vienna

84 # Landscape with Děvín Castle at the confluence of Morava and Danube

1752/1753
Oil on canvas. 78 × 127.5 cm
Passed through the collections of Miklós III Palffy, Count Kollonitz, Count M. Fries and F. Gabet in Vienna, then Dr J. Hoser in Prague. Donated by Dr J. Hoser in 1843
Inv. n° O 223

This canvas is important as it is the first expressly realistic painting is central Europe. It represents the Carpathian foothills overlooking the Danube at a point where the Palffy family had one of their domains. The painting was commissioned by Miklós III Palffy and is mentioned in the inventory of his possessions. It was subsequently to change hands several times.

The site to be represented in the painting was specified in the commission, only the angle of vision was left to the discretion of the artist. Brand was the son of a famous landscape painter whose later works are often taken to be by his own son. Brand himself tended towards realism. The colour and light effects of the bare mountain summit above the river are in marked contrast with those of the plain, which has more affinity with the landscapes of his early years. The impressive solidity of the mountain is set against the sailing pale grey clouds, whose shadows enhance the ochre-greens and the dull ochres of the plain. The few figures in the foreground are hardly more than decorative. Several sketches show that Brand had already in his youth studied the effect of such figures in a landscape.

This canvas marks a turning point in the evolution of the Austrian *veduta*. Brand is applying the new principles of the genre before they have been theoretically formulated, when the interpretation of the landscape is free, its originality given by the choice of viewpoint from which it is seen. The second half of the eighteenth century made this conception of landscape the object of theoretical reflexion.

P.P.

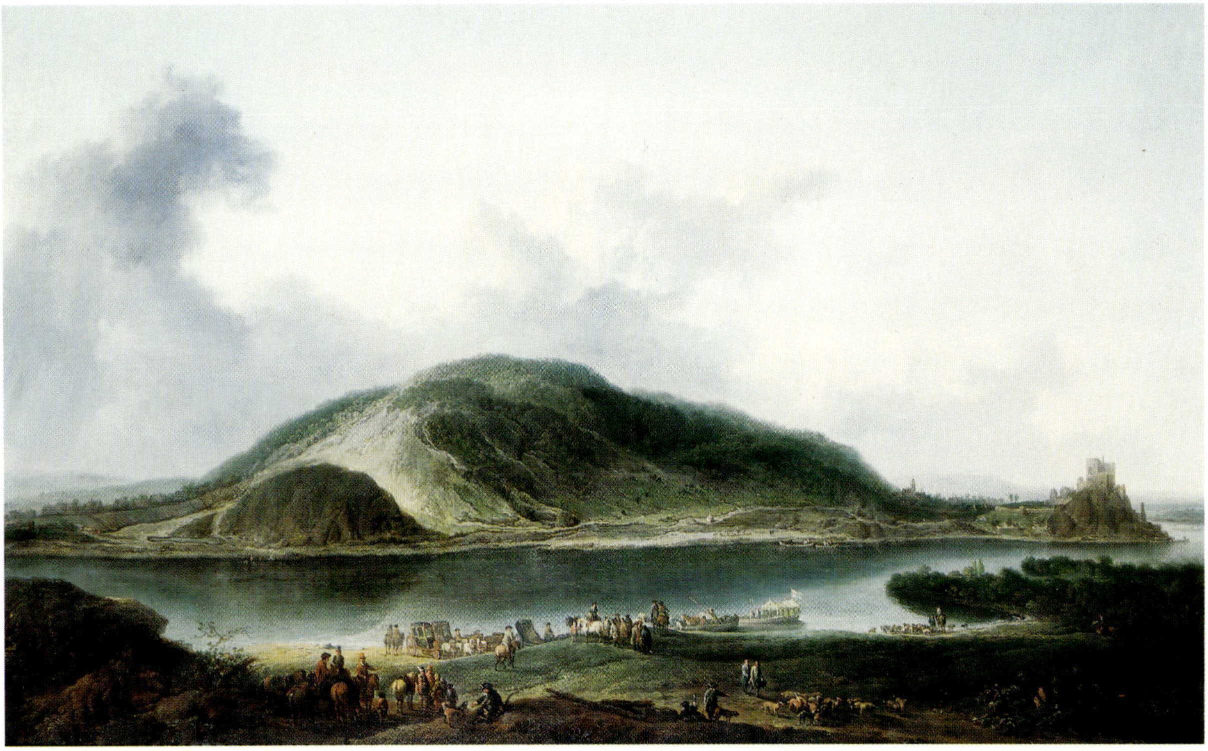

Index

National Gallery in Prague
European Old Masters
Šternberk Palace

Contributors:
Jan Chlíbec, Ladislav Daniel, Olga Kotková, Pavel Preiss,
Olga Pujmanová, Hana Seifertová, Lubomír Slavíček.

Translation:
Michael Hecht

Editor:
Gilles Fage, Růžena Semrádová

Lay-out:
Bruno Pfäffli

Photographic Credits:
National Gallery in Prague (Milan Posselt)

This book, edited by the Réunion des musées nationaux in Paris
and the National Gallery in Prague,
was printed in January 1993 on the presses of Mame.
The text was set by Optigraphic in Brussels
and the illustrations were engraved by Bussière Arts Graphiques in Paris.

Dépôt légal janvier 1993
GA 20 2674